# Healing-Centered Writing in the Secondary Classroom

This book offers an expansive vision of what writing can look like and feel like, both in classrooms and in our lives. In a time when automation of the writing process is being normalized at every stage and level, it challenges readers to remember why writing from our own bodies still matters.

The book presents the concept of a healing-centered framework for writing, which covers five tenets: 1) "Who Is 'I'?," which focuses on identity and authorship; 2) "The Body of Writing," on embodiment and form; 3) "Forgot, but Then Remembered," on memory and reclamation; 4) "Found Joy in Pieces," on fragmentation and collage; and 5) "Stones to the Pile," on civic engagement and purpose. Each tenet is designed to help teachers foster conditions for a healing-centered approach to writing—one with the capacity to be humanizing, affirming, empowering, liberatory, trauma-sensitive, restorative, and transformative for student writers and for their teachers.

This book is especially well-suited to high school and middle school teachers who assign and teach writing in any subject area.

**Ioanna Pettas Opidee, MA, MFA, PhD,** is a writer and educator with more than twenty years of experience teaching writing in a variety of settings, including high school and college classrooms, as well as community-based spaces.

# *Equity and Social Justice in Education Series*

Paul C. Gorski, Series Editor

Routledge's Equity and Social Justice in Education series is a publishing home for books that apply critical and transformative equity and social justice theories to the work of on-the-ground educators. Books in the series describe meaningful solutions to the racism, White supremacy, economic injustice, sexism, heterosexism, transphobia, ableism, neoliberalism, and other oppressive conditions that pervade schools and school districts.

**Teaching Indigenous Studies**
An Introduction for K-12 Educators
*Leilani Sabzalian, Meredith McCoy, and Helen Thomas*

**Peacebuilding Pedagogies**
Racial Justice, Dialogue, and Belonging in the Classroom
*Crystena Parker-Shandal*

**Cultivating Critical Advocacy**
A Framework for Educators of Multilingual Learners
*Rebecca E. Linares and Kate Seltzer*

**The DEI Practitioner's Handbook**
A Guide for School and District Leaders in Pursuit of Educational Justice
*Erica Buchanan-Rivera*

**Teaching Multilingual Learners in Rural Schools**
Four Movements for Educators
*Maria Coady*

**Healing-Centered Writing in the Secondary Classroom**
An Identity-Affirming and Restorative Approach
*Ioanna Pettas Opidee*

# Healing-Centered Writing in the Secondary Classroom

## An Identity-Affirming and Restorative Approach

Ioanna Pettas Opidee

Routledge
Taylor & Francis Group
NEW YORK AND LONDON

Designed cover image: Cover art © Cheryl Dyment, "Tour du Soleil," 2026.

First published 2027
by Routledge
605 Third Avenue, New York, NY 10158

and by Routledge
4 Park Square, Milton Park, Abingdon, Oxon, OX14 4RN

*Routledge is an imprint of the Taylor & Francis Group, an informa business*



ISBN: 978-1-041-27109-3 (pbk)
ISBN: 978-1-003-75272-1 (ebk)

DOI: 10.4324/9781003752721

Typeset in Palatino
by SPi Technologies India Pvt Ltd (Straive)

*Dedicated to all the writers and teachers*

# Contents

# Meet the Author

**Dr. Ioanna Pettas Opidee, MA, MFA, PhD,** is a writer and educator with more than twenty years of experience teaching at the high school and college levels. Currently an English teacher and literacy lab specialist in Weston, Connecticut, Ioanna holds a PhD in Educational Studies from Lesley University, an MFA in Creative Writing from Fairfield University, an MA in English from the University of Massachusetts Boston, and a BA in English from Boston College. Her novel, *Waking Slow* (2018), which the *Boston Globe* called an "arresting, timely" take on sexual assault, was named a finalist in the multicultural category of the Foreword Indies Book of the Year Awards in 2018.

Ioanna's scholarly work focuses on humanizing and healing-centered approaches to the teaching of writing, along with trauma and the body, as well as identity and belonging. In her writing and in her work as an expressive arts facilitator, her methods are rooted in contemplative inquiry and artistic exploration, emphasizing process and practice. With strong ties to her own Greek-American heritage, she is deeply interested in cultural hybridity and place-based learning. Her studies of embodiment have been enhanced through her completion of a yoga teacher/social-emotional learning facilitator training through Breathe for Change.

In addition to being honored twice with the David Trigoux Innovation Award by the Weston Education Foundation, Ioanna completed a Research Associate fellowship through the Lesley University Institute for Trauma Sensitivity and a Social-Emotional Learning Educator Fellowship through LiberatED. You can reach her at www.writetheway.org.

# Preface

*When I was younger, I loved to write …*

A sentence I've read countless times, so often followed by the phrase, "But then …"

Many children do love to write. *But then* they are asked to do it in a certain way. *Then* they are told that they are not doing it right. *Then* they are given a grade. *Then* they begin to believe that they are not good at writing; that they are not a writer, they can't write, they fall too low on the rubric. They don't like it anymore—at least not in school. And why would they? Writing now yields anxiety, confusion, and red slashes across the page as much as, if not more than, it leads to soul-awakening creativity, expression, and intellectual pursuit.

Does it matter? Not everyone needs to be a writer. It doesn't have to be everyone's "thing."

In fact, some people *never* love writing or even mildly *like* it. Many people *hate* it. For example: young children with dysgraphia or fine motor skill challenges who find writing to be the most demoralizing part of their day; neurodivergent teenagers who are beyond exhausted by demands to explain their thinking—to *elaborate*; English language learners whose essays return spattered with literal or metaphorical red ink, with low grade after low grade.

Writing matters because that simultaneous combination—of strictures and evaluation imposed upon a space and activity that can elicit extreme openness and vulnerable exploration—holds enormous potential for lasting harm, not only upon a person's psyche and social-emotional well-being but also on their identity development, self-concept, and sense of belonging. It can even, as I aim to demonstrate here, cause trauma.

Yet, despite its capacity for harm, writing can also bring freedom, opportunity, connection, and transformation: of expression, of self; of community even. I know because I have experienced these openings and transformations myself, and I know because I have witnessed their occurrence for countless students in my 20-plus years of teaching writing. True and radical transformations have occurred right before my eyes, sometimes within a matter of days or even moments. To me, the privilege to witness such a moment is the gift of being a teacher of writing.

Even today. A student walked into my classroom just to talk about a short story she is writing for a class. Not for me to tell her what to fix or how to write it. She didn't even ask me to read it. She wanted to discuss the *feel* of the story. After writing two separate versions, she couldn't find a bridge between them; she would get stuck feeling unsatisfied with one, only to leap over to the other and feel unsatisfied there too. So I asked her questions: about what the main character wants, about the meaning of her journey, about what sort of atmosphere she as the writer was trying to create, about what the relationship between these two versions really is. In a long pause between questions, her eyes squinted into a smile that stretched across her face. "I think I know what to do," she said. "Okay," I encouraged, nodding. "Anything I can help with?" "No, no, I'm good," she replied. "I'm good." And she practically ran out of the room to dive back into the writing.

After instances like these, I think about how lucky I am to do this work. No doubt, it is hard, hard work. We haul virtual mountains of essays home, written with wildly varying degrees of care, and we labor. But we also experience some of the most human moments possible. We witness people pursuing their curiosities, sharing their knowledge, finding their voices, mining their souls, uncovering their insights, exposing their wisdom and genius, stepping into themselves and their power. I love nothing more, in my professional life, than being able to stand back and watch the author emerge from the fog of many messages and dictums they've received about what it means to write well.

Over time, through writing honestly, people can learn to express themselves, *be* themselves more freely. I recall a student who wrote passionately in their sophomore year analyzing the repressive dangers of assimilation in a short story set in colonial Nigeria, who turned up in my class the following year with not only a new name and pronoun but a wider smile and a greater willingness to strike up conversation, speak up in class, make eye contact, be *seen*. Or a student who wrote about what it felt like to be biracial in a predominantly White school, who began wearing her hair in braids by the end of the year.

Writing may not be the cause of these transformations, but it can be a vehicle for them. Better yet, a channel *toward* them—one that needs to be kept open and, most importantly, protected.

But how? What are the forces that enable writing to remain a safe space of passage toward positive opportunity and, potentially, transformation? This question has been central to my entire career and has prompted me to craft the framework and model that I outline in the following chapters.

Yet the complexity of these questions has compounded tremendously since 2022, when OpenAI released ChatGPT and launched the sudden onslaught of artificial intelligence (AI)-related mayhem in the classroom. The widespread adoption of generative AI tools creates even more imperative around a set of correlating questions: how do we write, and teach writing, in a way that feels *human?* How do we write in a way that honors who we are as individuals as well as members of society and the human collective?

In a time where automation of the writing process is being normalized at virtually every stage and level, there is no choice but to explicitly address an even more fundamental question: Why does writing still matter?

What do we stand to lose if we relinquish some or even parts of the writing process to large language models that can quickly and easily do it all for us? How do we, as teachers of writing, reclaim, restore, and preserve the writing *experience*?

In this book, I attempt to engage with all of the questions above and raise new ones as well. Most importantly, I invite you, fellow educators, to consider your own answers and to do so with others in your communities as well.

Because none of us can do this work alone.

# Acknowledgements

First, I thank Paul Gorski for welcoming this project into his estimable series. I am beyond grateful for his generous reading of so many drafts. His guidance and insight made the writing—but, more importantly, the *thinking*—so much clearer and deeper. He is an editor who never forgets the greater purpose of the words we write: the better world we are collectively trying to build.

Many thanks as well to Megha Patel and the team at Routledge for supporting this project and bringing their editorial expertise to the endeavor.

Without my friend Elizabeth Bishop's unwavering support for me, and for Write the Way, I am not sure I would have been able to carry the work to this point. Her clarity of intention and artistry as a scholar, practitioner, and person in the world are an endless source of inspiration for me and for so many others.

I thank as well my advisors and teachers at Lesley University, where I completed the doctoral research and dissertation that informed this book: Grace Enriquez, Valerie Shinas, Lisa Donovan, Kaori Miyazawa, Kabba Colley, Michelle Vital, Jeff Perrin, and Victoria Gill.

I have had the good fortune to learn from many amazing teachers in my life. To name a few: Baron Wormser, Kim Kupperman, Da Chen, Lary Bloom, Rachel Basch, Eileen Donovan-Kranz, and Rita Green. I am enormously grateful for their influence.

Cinthia Gannett has been a mentor to me since I began teaching in her Core Writing program at Fairfield University in 2008. This work would not have been possible without her taking me so seriously as a teacher and scholar and opening me up to a world of possibility for imaginative scholarship.

I am grateful as well for the scholars, writers, and thinkers whose work I drew on throughout the course of my doctoral studies and in these pages. I am humbled and honored to join their conversations.

I feel immense gratitude for all my students, past and present, who have entrusted me with their writing and, through that, with a part of their hearts, minds, souls, and selves. I have learned so much from all of them.

I thank my colleagues, from and with whom I learn every day—in particular, the teachers and writers who graciously shared their stories and experiences with me during my research process, pseudonymously represented in these pages.

And, of course, for their support and encouragement, I thank my family: my parents, Joan and Periklis; my mother-in-law, Nancy; my sisters, Tina and Eleni; and my daughters, Joni and Mary, who always feel like the ultimate partners in all my work. Finally, I thank my husband, Eric, without whom none of this feels possible; who understands me and my work at the soul level that sustains it.

# 1

# Introduction

## Why Writing *Still* Matters

As a student, I often struggled with writing for school. I had my own vision for what I wanted to create, and it was hard to force that into a digestible format. From the other side of the desk, I now understand *why* my teachers needed me to follow certain directions—to learn particular skills and apply content in specific ways. But I longed for opportunities to write in exploratory ways about what I was learning, with a messiness and artfulness that didn't have to clean itself up or make perfect sense to the reader, my teacher. I would dispatch my off-assignment essays like secret missives, hoping my teachers would uncover the hidden messages within the subtext and help me decipher my own muddled purpose and meaning. A form of magical thinking.

And yet many teachers of mine did just that; they heard the hints of a deeper voice within my words and helped me to hear and nurture it, too. I remember the teacher who put stars in the margins of a sprawling conclusion I wrote on a research paper about Abraham Lincoln, where I granted myself the liberty of adding my own "two cents" about slavery and the war. I remember the one who submitted my poems to a contest I didn't win but who told me to keep writing anyway. I remember the one

DOI: 10.4324/9781003752721-1

who read my creative nonfiction piece about the harmful effects of "pro-ana" communities online that propagate eating disorders and who wrote at the bottom, "This could be your life's work."

I also remember the one (in graduate school) who told me I was a "real writer," even though I write "too much like a woman." (Not even veiled in a nudge to write more like Hemingway!) The second part rolled right off my back—I knew enough by then to recognize that his sexism was more about him than me. And I didn't really need to hear the first part. I have always seen myself as a writer, before I had anyone to validate me as such. Growing up, I was the third grader drafting a notebook-novel series with a flashlight under my bedcovers. The fifth-grader typewriting stories and slipping them under my sisters' bedroom doors or leaving them on the kitchen table for my parents to find. The middle-schooler writing poetry and song lyrics on stray scraps of paper. The teenager scribbling constantly in my journal, desperately trying to make sense of myself and the world.

As an adult, I was the novelist writing essayistic fiction to investigate deep and probing questions of identity, culture, violence, and trauma in order to uncover—or create—some sort of meaning that might help me to heal and coalesce into a self that could withstand the harsh climes of the external world. I was the new mother parked by the Connecticut shoreline in December, with the heat on full blast and my infant daughter sleeping behind me in her car seat as I wrote letters to her in a journal that she may never read, letters expressing the ache of my unbridled love for her and the near-debilitating fear it instilled in me.

Writing, for me, is a mode of emotional, intellectual, and spiritual survival as much as it is a way of connecting and communicating with others. At times, writing has been a source of joy, a mechanism for making sense of and attending to my relationships: with myself, with others, with society, and with the rest of the natural world. The process of writing itself has shaped me and my thinking in ways that I—like most writers who have tried—can't fully capture in words.

Joan Didion (1976) famously claimed, "I write entirely to find out what I am thinking, what I am looking at, what I see and what it means. What I want and what I fear." Early in her essay, "Why I Write"—a title she admits to stealing from George Orwell—she describes herself as a writer because she is "a person whose most absorbed and passionate hours are spent arranging words on pieces of paper." She ends the essay with, seemingly, no more definitive reason: "Let me tell you one thing about why writers write: had I known the answer to any of these questions I would never have needed to write a novel." She understood why it mattered to grapple with the inquiry—why do I write?—even as she ultimately acceded to the question's need to remain open. Writing itself is a process of engaging with questions.

There is something vital in this never-ending search for answers. In *Letters to a Young Poet*, Rainer Maria Rilke (2016) advises his mentee, "There is only one thing you should do. Go into yourself. Find out the reason that commands you to write; see whether it has spread its roots into the very depths of your heart" (p. 16). Addressing his creative writing students at Howard University, Ta-Nehisi Coates (2024) writes in *The Message*, "There has to be something in you, something that hungers for clarity" (p. 19). Both of these writers capture the spirit of pursuit, the excavation for wisdom and truth, that can propel an intensive writing process.

I know that, for many students and even teachers, the act of writing may never attain such urgent status. It's not that thing for everyone. Still, writing is always a personal act, even as it is (outside of journaling) inherently social and most often meant for an audience. In this sense, it is a vulnerable act in which we offer a window into our minds, sometimes into our hearts and souls, if only in tiny glimpses. For this reason, writing as a process and product should be handled with care.

In this book, I make a call to help preserve what matters most about writing—its capacity to liberate, transform, and heal communities, societies, and individuals—in a way that feels sustainable for those of us guiding young people toward that inheritance. The pages that follow are based on my research but, more fundamentally, by my practice as a teacher and my experience as a writer.

## The Hard and Important Work of Writing

While I am someone who has felt in my bones the admonishment of Adrienne Rich (1993)—"You must write, and read, as if your life depended on it"—my relationship with writing has always required its own maintenance, vigilance, nurturing, recentering, and recommitments. There are times when writing comes easily, but more frequently, writing feels very very hard. I regularly quote to my students Thomas Mann, who said, "A writer is someone for whom writing is more difficult than it is for other people," and maybe that's because we who consider ourselves writers know how much writing—as a process *and* product—is capable of and how hard it is to achieve those greatest possibilities.

In her classic essay, "Poetry Is Not A Luxury," Audre Lorde (2007) writes, "The quality of light by which we scrutinize our lives has direct bearing upon the product which we live, and upon the changes which we hope to bring about through those lives." Coates (2024) cites Lorde's words in that same address to his students at Howard, encouraging them to reject oppressive standards:

> We require another standard—one that sees the sharpening of our writing as the sharpening of our quality of light. And with that light we are charged with examining the stories we have been told, and how they undergird the politics we have accepted, and then telling new stories ourselves.
>
> (p. 19)

His words are a reminder that we do not just write for ourselves; we write for and to become a self who takes their place in the world and proceeds—with other selves—to shape that world with a vision that can either accept what it sees without question or problematize the status quo and dream up new possibilities.

As a teacher of writing for more than 20 years, I have been a deep witness to the ways in which writing can be liberatory, healing, and transformative for people, whether they consider themselves writers or enjoy writing at all. Writing a never-before noticed, known, or confronted truth can change the way the writer sees, feels, and acts within the world, creating more space and easeful movement in their lives, relationships, and even bodies.

Often, these transformations come in the form of admitting to oneself a long-buried truth about one's life or identity—"I was born a boy but always knew I was a girl;" "As a Chinese American, I feel caught between two cultures, like I'm being asked to choose." Such discoveries may appear to the writer as a surprise in response to a seemingly unrelated prompt, whereas other epiphanies may emerge out of desperation or a rare feeling of emotional safety. Sometimes, these shifts happen after learning and writing about an aspect of history, society, politics, or nature—the Tulsa Race Massacre, the Holocaust, the cataclysmic status of our warming planet—and never quite seeing or acting within the world in quite the same way.

These transformative experiences flood my days and memories too plentifully to fully capture. I witness them as remarkable phenomena that come and go so frequently yet so invisibly as to remain barely detectable. Sometimes it feels as if I am glancing around an empty classroom after seeing a meteor shower, and saying to no one, "Did you see that?" I would guess that many teachers of writing have had similar encounters. But in the course of our days filled with frantic lesson planning, observations, cafeteria duty, parent phone calls, team meetings, and grading, in addition to the main job of teaching, these instances are easy to miss; they are swept into the frenetic whirlwind of each day as we are frenzied by the stress of kicking our legs and arms to stay afloat within it.

## The Social Importance of Writing

As a human being, I value writing as a vital form of meaning-making and expression. I agree with Robin Wall Kimmerer (2022), who wrote:

> Other beings have gifts with attributes that humans lack. They can fly, see at night, rip open trees with their claws, make maple sap. What can humans do? We may not have wings or leaves, but we do have words. Language is our gift and our responsibility.
>
> (p. 264)

While writing is not our only use of that gift of language, it is an important one—not just for writers but for the readers who receive their words. Reading and writing are reciprocal processes that tie us with others beyond the constraints of time and space. Written communication is one of the few ways we can close that metaphysical gap and enjoy our connectedness.

As a member of society, I believe in the power and history of written words sparking change. Inspired by an assignment created by the late essayist Ned Stuckey-French (2011), I have spent full class periods with students poring over one elaborate sentence from Dr. Martin Luther King, Jr.'s "Letter from Birmingham Jail," in which he opens with "But when you have seen vicious mobs lynch your mothers and fathers at will and drown your sisters and brothers at whim" and ends with "then you will understand why we find it difficult to wait," with an elaborate list of "whens" in between. I have watched as the metaphorical light bulbs flick on in students' brains, not just because the human impact of racism and segregation has become more real to especially my White students, not just because they better understand the evergreen nature of King's arguments about the dangers of White moderation, but also because they begin to see, on a whole new level, how King's way with words, his command of language and rhetorical flourish, spoke truth in a manner that people could truly hear.

King's words convey, too, a sense of his *soul*. Ursula Le Guin (n.d.) writes:

> A writer is a person who cares what words mean, what they say, how they say it. Writers know words are their way towards truth and freedom, and so they use them with care, with thought, with fear, with delight. By using words well they strengthen their souls … And their words make the souls of their readers stronger, brighter, deeper. (n.p.)

King's words strengthened his soul, along with the souls of all of us who have the privilege to be part of his secondary audience. Like Coates (2024), writing about the true cost of book bans, I am concerned "about the [souls of] writers to come—the boundaries of their imagination, the angle of their thinking, the depth of their questions" (p. 110). The stakes, indeed, are high for those of us in a position to nurture the souls of those very writers to come: our students.

## My Journey with Writing in School

My commitment to the need for care (and access to creative and intellectual freedom) in educational spaces is rooted at least partly in my own struggles with schooling. As a highly creative, introverted, and sensitive young person whose ways of knowing were greatly informed by emotion and intuition, I didn't always feel like school was "for me," though I never quite understood why. I loved to learn. I read voraciously, wrote prolifically, and craved ideas.

Yet I felt both stifled and overwhelmed by the classroom environment and became largely disengaged from school at an early age. In the fourth grade, my teachers could not get me to do my homework; looking back, I think I was oblivious to the fact that it had even been assigned. While highly intelligent and hardworking in their own right, my parents were not overly academic. My father, an immigrant from Greece, grew up in an island village and attended schools with vastly different norms than mine, while my mother came from circumstances that led her to take a non-traditional path for high school, with college out of reach.

There have been times when I wondered why my parents didn't push me more, and what I would be if they had. But then I remember the value of wandering—how everything important I've ever learned has essentially come from that. From wandering through the winding stony paths of my grandparents' island village in summers when I was eight. From wandering through the recesses of my imagination and curiosities while writing novels in my notebooks about figure skating champions and San Francisco earthquake survivors. From wandering through the city streets of Boston as a college student trying to make sense of my life and identity. From wandering through different career paths as a part-time journalist/waitress/editor/adjunct professor.

School, though. During high school and college, depression, anxiety, an eating disorder, and an overall sense of unbelonging led me toward total avoidance beyond the frequent trips to the nurse for a nap which dominated my elementary school days. My own relationship with schooling has sensitized me to the experiences of students for whom school is a struggle for a variety of reasons that are difficult for many people to see and understand.

When I began teaching high school after almost a decade of teaching college part-time, the return was enormously difficult for me. I had to practice deep breathing exercises in the hallway when walking from class to class, just to get through the day without completely coming apart. Not unlike many new teachers, I worked until the early morning hours grading papers and preparing for classes. On top of that, the pressure I felt to perform in front of a class five times a day, along with the helplessness I felt in the face of struggling students, emotionally drained me to a point of pure exhaustion, and I became riddled with self-doubt.

Just like when I was a student myself, it's possible that no one would have guessed I was floundering; I was handling the challenges with apparent grace, adapting to a new environment with enthusiasm and dedication, and I developed remarkably strong relationships with my students and colleagues. I found meaning in the work; I saw myself as someone who could help foster for others what my younger self had so badly needed: a safe space to be, discover, nurture, and wholeheartedly embrace who I was and wanted to be.

While I felt eager to manifest the possibilities of my role, it became difficult for me to do so in a way that was anything short of total consumption. Keeping up with the functions of the job was one thing; doing so effectively while feeling like I was adequately attending to the needs of the human beings in front of me was another. My sensitization to students' pain and discomfort was overwhelming. The bells kept ringing no matter what, hustling the day along, and I'd find myself thinking, like Auden, *Stop the clocks, this is a crisis!*

I got to know my students largely through their writing. Coming from the college writing classroom, where I had almost total freedom to teach writing in whatever ways I saw fit, I frequently asked my students to reflect not just on their writing process but also on open-ended questions that invited them to bring their own interests and experiences to bear. Reading their reflective writing closely made me a better teacher, but it also made my job harder. I learned not just how hard writing was for many of them, not just how much some dreaded and hated it, but also how much else my students were carrying around all day. Patterns began to emerge: how many young people in my care felt they didn't belong, that they weren't smart enough, good enough, popular enough, rich enough, "normal" enough. Yes, as teachers, we know these insecurities are fairly typical in adolescence, but reading about it, we *feel* it. And we may feel that we need to *do* something about it. I know I did. To paraphrase Maya Angelou, when you know better, you have to *do* better.

In regard to writing, it was hard to miss how many of them believed that they would never be good writers. How many used to love writing but now hated it. How many seemed ashamed of their perceived inability to write well.

Ironically, I could see how, through writing about their struggles, their confidence and clarity of thinking and expression were building, even if they couldn't yet see the positive developments themselves.

## The Issue at Stake

While writing can be a source of affirmation, empowerment, liberation, healing, and joy, it can also be a source of dread, oppression, and identity-based harm. Because at least some degree of writing is almost always required in a school setting at any level, it is important not just to *know* this but to better understand *why*.

Although personal preference and disposition may come into play, the people who experience the most harm from traditional literacy instructional practices in the United States tend to be students who are already marginalized in schools: students of color, students who are economically disadvantaged, students who are learning English, students with disabilities, students who are neurodivergent.

An identity-affirming and restorative approach demands that we center the needs of the people who are most at risk for being disenfranchised, because in community, every person matters. And in classrooms and even more so in schools—large-scale communities that operate on systems—addressing every individual's needs cannot be left to a game of Whac-A-Mole. The systems need to be explicitly designed to work for *everyone*.

Writing's potential for identity-based harm on *anyone* is greater than we may take for granted. Writing is fundamentally linked to the self because it is always a product of our own authorial choices and therefore a reflection of some refraction of our voice. That means the self is in a place of acute vulnerability to harm when we write. Even if the comment is not as extreme as *This is terrible!*, it's not hard for a writer to make the leap from "Your writing is too simple" to "*You* are too simple." "I can't understand your writing" to "I can't understand *you*." When we're assessing someone's writing, we're assessing their thoughts, their ideas, their means of expression, their uses of language, their points of reference, their *voices*.

This capacity for negative impact is caused in large part by the fact that writing—particularly the kind done for school—is also an inherently social act in that it is typically intended for an audience. That audience is us. We, their teachers, are compelled and most often required to rank and sort students according to perceived "ability" and skill-level, as measured against the "standards" to which we are beholden and by which we are required to assign numeric grades against a 100-point scale.

Statistically speaking, most teachers in the United States are White, cis-female, middle class, English-speaking (National Center for Education Statistics [NCES], 2023), and (at least ostensibly) neurotypical (Mueller, 2021). That means many of us cannot fully understand the needs of our students with marginalized identities. And almost all of us, as teachers, were educated and trained within a system historically designed to meet the needs of a White, male, able-bodied, cis-hetero, English-speaking, neurotypical student. No matter who we are, we all have implicit biases—beliefs, senses, attitudes, and experiences that shape our perspectives and reactions—that we will bring into the light, disrupt, and surpass only, if ever, with deliberate effort and a willingness to confront ourselves critically.

Many of us have tried—again borrowing the language of Maya Angelou—to know better so that we can do better. Nonetheless, students and teachers still find ourselves enmeshed within dehumanizing processes, systems, and policies we have inherited that perpetuate negative and harmful experiences with writing.

And it doesn't feel good for any of us—or at least for many of us.

As someone who has always had a pervasive love of reading, writing, and learning but was deeply school-avoidant throughout much of high school and college, I have viscerally understood the need for change. My own experiences and feelings resound with those of Leigh Patel (2015), who writes, "Having been an educator in secondary and tertiary institutional settings, I have often felt that my love of learning and knowledge as uncontainable has led me to be in a constant state of heartbreak." She acknowledges that "learning and human growth" *do* happen frequently in school settings but usually "as the result of individuals who have committed themselves to swimming upstream," who have "created spaces beyond hegemonic policies and practices" (p. 4).

This book endeavors to help make that upstream journey less harmful on the bodies and psyches of those swimming it and to maybe counter the force of the stream itself.

## What Do We Mean by "Writing"?

The objective to "enlarge our sense of what it means to write, and to write well" has been etched into almost every syllabus I've ever written, and my students never fail to surprise me with what they can produce. That's why I deliberately use the pronoun "our" in that statement. It's just as much a process of discovery for me, as their teacher.

I have had the great fortune, too, of working with amazing teachers who are open to the many possibilities of what it means to write, who realize that writing doesn't always mean thesis statements and five-paragraph structures. It doesn't even always mean words on the page. Some of the best "writing" does not take the form of an essay, poem, or short story; it might become a video or a painting with a reflection or something truly outside the traditional lines, like a boardgame. These products still need to be "written": fashioned for an audience, with a purpose and often an argument, with choices made for style and clarity.

In cases like this, is the word "writing" still accurate or necessary? The word "composition" has been favored over "writing" in higher education for the very reason that it nods toward a more encompassing definition, one that incorporates the concepts of "multimodalities" and "multiliteracies" (Cope & Kalantzis, 2016). But "writing," to me, is bigger than that. Writing is not just what happens in school and certainly not just what academia says it is.

I use the word "writing" in the same spirit that Paulo Freire and Donaldo Macedo (1987) do when they write about "reading the word and the world." I mean *writing* the word and the world, like I imagine Amy Stornaiuolo and Erin Hope Whitney (2018) do when they write about "writing as worldmaking." I mean writing not just as producing a product—a poem, an essay, a story—but also as an opportunity to make choices, find movement, interact, connect, take action, and create change.

While these wide-ranging definitions of "writing" may have struck many teachers and students as a bit too far out in the past, the impacts of generative artificial intelligence (AI) have destabilized the entire landscape of writing in schools. Now—as I will argue in the following chapters—is a great time for reimagining.

## Who and What This Book Is For

The healing-centered approach to writing that I present within these pages is intended to help improve and restore people's relationships with writing, which were troubled well before AI's interferences. I outlined the framework in this book with the intention of helping us teachers to not just avoid harmful practices, but also establish safe and equitable conditions for writing that hold the capacity to support healing.

Most prominently, though, the book is meant to support teachers in this difficult work because that support is the piece we are most often missing. I know because I have been in those professional learning sessions countless times, hearing about well-intended strategies and "new" approaches we need to adopt, where I have left wondering, *Why isn't it enough?* The late nights of writing feedback on student papers, the hours of lesson planning, the weeks of researching for a new assignment or text adoption, the time spent after school conferencing with students, the meetings with colleagues to share strategies or discuss solutions to pressing issues, the emotional toll it takes to care so much and try so hard. *Why is it never enough?*

And it's not just all the *doing* but the constant *learning* we are *always* engaged in, mostly through first-hand experience and practice every day. Even now, after finishing my doctoral research with an institutional review board–approved study and a committee of scholars guiding me, I know that my most in-depth, high-quality research has always dwelt in the iterative and recursive process of testing out new strategies in the classroom, seeing how they work, analyzing and reflecting on the results, and making adjustments, only to start the process all over again.

In the 2021 Oscar-winning film *Coda*, there is a scene when a large group of Gloucester, Massachusetts fishermen gather at a town meeting to fight the new requirement that they pay for costly federal inspectors to board their boats and monitor them on their fishing expeditions. One of the fishermen in attendance tells the representative from the National Oceanic and Atmospheric Administration that his data is wrong, to which the "expert" asks, "Oh, you've tested?" The fisherman then replies: "Yeah. I see what's coming in my nets!"

As teachers, we see what's coming up in our nets. We are constantly researching—gathering data in the form of student writing and countless observations of our students in real time. What we don't always have are the space, opportunity, and support to process the input we take in, make sense of the patterns, and find our own solutions to the issues we identify—solutions that align with what we value, and where we want to take our teaching, instead of the newest initiative that is sure to come and go.

> What do we need to unharness our own potential, to liberate our best teaching selves, without sacrificing our own humanity, balance, and well-being?

I wrote this book not to superimpose external solutions but instead to extend a framework that can help us tap into the answers we already hold within ourselves, our students, and our communities. The text is a vulnerable offering, from someone whose writing and teaching have been honed by years of approaching both practices with a seriousness of intent that reaches Adrienne Rich levels—as if our lives depended on it.

## Structure of the Book

The center of this book is the healing-centered framework that I outline in Chapters 3–5. This framework seeks to clarify *what* a healing-centered approach to writing is, *why* it is important, and *how* it can be enacted.

In the following chapter, Chapter 2, I provide an overview of healing-centered education and what it is in relation to other important approaches, such as social-emotional learning and trauma-informed education.

Chapter 3 defines seven characteristics of a healing-centered approach to writing: (1) humanizing, (2) affirming, (3) empowering, (4) liberatory, (5) trauma-sensitive, (6) restorative, and (7) transformative.

Chapter 4 examines four values and priorities: (1) psychic and affective safety, (2) belonging, (3) belief in the writer's abilities and possibilities, and (4) positive experience.

Chapter 5 describes six processes and practices: (1) "grace and space," (2) body awareness, (3) contemplative inquiry, (4) arts-based engagement, (5) positive identity engagement, and (6) communal experience.

In Chapters 6–9, I share four fictional case studies. In each one, I apply the framework to the stories of a teacher–student pair to help illuminate some of the common challenges that arise for and between teachers and students and highlight ways in which the framework can provide a healing-centered way through them.

In Chapter 10, I examine some of the challenges that make it difficult for teachers to embody a healing-centered approach to writing. Acknowledging the barriers is a crucial step toward making any shifts or changes because it's hard to contend with what we cannot see.

In Chapters 11 and 12, I describe the origins of my own healing-centered ethic within my experience as a teacher and writer, and I tell the story of the research project that shaped the framework. I include this personal experience to provide both a deep sense of how the ideas in this book were shaped and formulated, and living proof of how this ethic and these approaches have come to be embodied within my life and practice.

In Chapter 13, I devote space to examining the "pivot point" of generative AI and its relation to healing-centered writing.

Finally, in Chapter 14, I present a model called Write the Way, including reflection questions designed to help guide and foster a healing-centered approach for teachers and students alike.

A healing-centered approach is by no means the only way to frame the good work we are already doing, and want to do more of, in our classrooms. It is simply *one* way. I present it to you not as someone with all the answers but as someone who is continually posing and grappling with the questions.

## References

Coates, T. (2024). *The message*. One World.

Cope, B., & Kalantzis, M. (2016). The things you do to know: An introduction to the pedagogy of multiliteracies. In B. Cope & M. Kalantzis (Eds.), *A pedagogy of multiliteracies: Learning by design* (pp. 1–36). Palgrave Macmillan. https://doi.org/10.1057/9781137539724

Didion, J. (1976, December 5). Why I write. *The New York Times*. https://www.nytimes.com/1976/12/05/archives/why-i-write-why-i-write.html

Freire, P., & Macedo, D. (1987). *Literacy: Reading the word and the world*. Routledge.

Kimmerer, R. W. (2022). *Braiding sweetgrass for young adults: Indigenous wisdom, scientific knowledge, and the teachings of plants*. Zest.

Le Guin, U. K. (n.d.). A few words to a young writer. Ursula K. Le Guin. https://www.ursulakleguin.com/a-few-words-to-a-young-writer

Lorde, A. (2007). *Sister outsider: Essays and speeches*. Crossing Press.

Mueller, C. O. (2021). "I didn't know people with disabilities could grow up to be adults": Disability history, curriculum, and identity in special education. *Teacher Education and Special Education*, *44*(3), 189–205. https://doi.org/10.1177/0888406421996069

National Center for Education Statistics (NCES). (2023). Characteristics of public school teachers. *Condition of Education*. U.S. Department of Education, Institute of Education Sciences. Retrieved May 26, 2026, from https://nces.ed.gov/programs/coe/indicator/clr

Patel, L. (2015). *Decolonizing educational research: From ownership to answerability* (1st ed.). Routledge.

Rich, A. (1993). *What is found there: Notebooks on poetry and politics*. W.W. Norton.

Rilke, R. (2016). *Letters to a young poet*. Penguin Classics.

Stornaiuolo, A., & Whitney, E. H. (2018). Writing as worldmaking. *Language Arts*, *95*(4), 205–217. http://www.jstor.org/stable/44809960

Stuckey-French, N. (2011). *The American essay in the American century*. University of Missouri Press.

# 2

# What is "Healing-Centered" Writing?

Healing-centered pedagogy came to my attention on a hunt for answers.

When I began my doctoral program in July of 2022, I was trying to understand—beyond my own instincts—why and how writing can be experienced in these radically different ways: as oppressive and painful or as liberating and transformative. I wanted both a theory and practical answers embedded within it.

Simultaneously, I had stepped into a new role as an English teacher in my high school's alternative program for school-avoidant students. It was my first year teaching in the program and just the second year of the program's existence. Much was still left to be determined and understood, individually and collectively, in terms of *what* the program was, *why* it was needed, and *how* it should operate. In meetings with my administrators and fellow teachers, we deliberated tirelessly, sometimes through shared tears, to determine the best ways to support our students. I felt an acute need for clarity and common ground. We were trying to get through the day, but we were also trying to do things *right*. Our students were people for whom school had not felt safe and fruitful for quite some time, and it was more than our job to help change that; it was our moral responsibility.

DOI: 10.4324/9781003752721-2

While working on my doctoral coursework during early mornings and late nights, I pored over the literature with a genuine sense of inquiry, seeking urgent guidance and understanding. Everything I knew, thought, believed, and had learned about writing and writing instruction was being put to the test as I strove to discern and serve the needs of student writers who were contending with trauma within, beyond, and in many cases caused by their schooling experiences.

Many of my students struggled to write a full sentence in response to a question and not for lack of skills or ideas but for a number of reasons too complex for conjecture or brief explanation. The more research I did on trauma, the more I came to understand how the seemingly unavoidable aspects of education—with its focus on standardization and linear, quantified markers of success—were not serving these students, who were exhibiting the magnified effects of dehumanizing systems that affect all members of the educational community. At the same time, I came across research highlighting the dangers of centering trauma, which can lead to further marginalization and deficit notions. My studies eventually led me toward healing-centered pedagogy, which acknowledges the ubiquity of trauma but centers the healing instead.

## Defining "Healing-Centered"

In this book, I advocate for and outline a healing-centered approach to writing with an understanding that terms like this shift, evolve, and even grow stale or distorted over time. New applications of language emerge accordingly, to address the fact that old habits and patterns can creep insidiously into fresh pathways just as they do in our relationships, just like the concept of "the family dance" so widely referenced in psychotherapy. Language evolves while we do and so that we can.

Sean Ginwright (2022) coined the term "healing-centered engagement" as a more "holistic" way to foster well-being, as a necessary evolution from the term "trauma-informed," which tends to emphasize individual experience without full consideration of collective impacts such as systemic racism, poverty, and cultural erasure, which includes moves like whitewashing history or banning the use of heritage languages.

The term "healing-centered" in education emerges from the imperative realization that, in the words of English Language Arts (ELA) scholar Sakeena Everett (2021), "people are more than the traumas they experience." Healing-centered pedagogy is informed by an understanding of trauma but notably does not *center* trauma. Instead, it centers and makes space for healing. It doesn't pathologize the individual; on the contrary, it "builds an awareness of injustices," which allows people to see how their trauma is not rooted in personal failure or hardship but may be induced by systemic factors beyond the individual's control, by policies and practices that are morally and ethically wrong and in need of change. At the same time, healing-centered education "restores cultural identities" by fostering an authentic sense of belonging and inherently inviting people to bring their full selves into their learning (p. 10).

And that's not just for students. Healing-centered education also seeks to "support adults in their healing as they work with youth" (Everett, 2021, p. 10). In this way, healing-centered pedagogy is intrinsically linked with Freire's (2000) notion of a liberatory education as mutually humanizing for teacher and student. It also resonates with bell hooks' (1994) concept of "engaged pedagogy," which explicitly emphasizes the link between teacher and student well-being.

hooks (1994) writes, "Any classroom that employs a holistic model of learning will also be a place where teachers grow, and are empowered by the process" (p. 15). The significance of this recognition cannot be overstated. Despite increasing awareness, the importance of teacher thriving, empowerment, and humanity is still grossly underestimated and—even more so—under-addressed.

The healing-centered approach to writing in this book seeks to help fill in that chasm of missing attention.

## What Healing-Centered Writing Is (and Is *Not*)

The power of writing to promote healing is something many of us who write and teach know well. It has also been backed by science, and advocated for by many scholars and practitioners, including clinicians such as James Pennebaker and Joshua Smyth (2016), who suggest so specific a method as writing about one's trauma for 20 minutes a day, at least four days in a row. Denise Sloan and Brian Marx's (2019) *Written Exposure Therapy for PTSD* method provides a scripted protocol for mental health professionals to administer in five fifty-minute sessions during which clients write narratives about their traumatic experiences.

Despite some overlap, healing-centered writing is not the same as a writing-as-healing or writing-*for*-healing model. The clinical approaches noted above offer scientific evidence of writing's effectiveness as a healing modality, but the research on how these benefits might safely transfer into a non-therapeutic setting (such as a classroom) is not conclusive.

In terms of academics, many scholars have argued that students writing expressively about challenging experiences, emotions, or trauma not only can be healing and therapeutic but also can help them develop skills that transfer to a variety of academic and professional contexts (Liu, 2019). Anecdotally, I have found this to be true, and I'm sure many other teachers would agree. As a high school English teacher, I find the college essay-writing process—which commonly provokes students to write about challenging or traumatic experiences—is where the most transformative writing happens. The "best"—the most moving and authentic—college essays demand that the writer not only write about the trauma but process it in such a way that they uncover new meaning and significance; they see themselves on the other side of suffering and confusion, with deeper awareness, even if the trauma is not all the way "healed."

Yet many conversations about the positive effects of "personal, expressive" writing underemphasize the impact of identity and culture to the point of omission. Without an intersectional perspective, students with vulnerable identities are at further risk of harm. Encouraging (or, worse yet, requiring) students to write about traumatic experiences without adequate training and supports in place can be retraumatizing (a topic further examined in Chapters 3 and 4). Students with marginalized identities will likely not feel safe writing about trauma or challenging experiences in an environment they do not trust to respond with care and integrity rather than judgments and repercussions (Dutro, 2019).

## The Social (Justice) Nature of Healing-Centered Education

Just as healing-centered writing is not necessarily about writing-to-heal (even if healing might happen within it), it is also not focused on individual healing, devoid of social context. The focus of healing-centered education is inherently collective. That doesn't mean it bypasses the person. It means that, when considering an individual, a healing-centered educator will resist the question, "What is wrong with this student?" and will instead ask, "What is wrong with the system/culture/society that has allowed this student to experience harm?" And more importantly: "How can I provide a space where any and all of my students—no matter their race, gender, ethnicity, economic status, ability, or trauma history—can potentially heal from their woundings and thrive?"

And that is where a justice orientation comes in. Because without a clear understanding of what prevents such thriving from being the default case, we will perpetuate the same systems and practices that continue to harm the same populations of students. It is the very same reason why social-emotional learning interventions and strategies fail when they are applied without a critical lens, when they are applied without any serious understanding of how a student's behavior—or an adult's reaction to it—might be rooted in the expectation that they conform to a dominant norm (Lin et al., 2023; Simmons, 2021). In other words, in bias and biased actions.

In his book *The Four Pivots: Reimagining Justice, Reimagining Ourselves*, Ginwright (2022) explains that healing involves "more than repairing the deep wounds of racism, healing the scars of sexism, or easing the pains of poverty." Ginwright defines healing as "the capacity to restore our humanity and care for ourselves and others" and calls it "the only pathway to real justice because it requires that we take an honest look at what harmed us and pushes us to restore our humanity and finally to move us confidently into a possible future" (p. 3). Healing-centered writing, in this sense, is not a navel-gazing, personal-wellness endeavor devoid of social context and rigorous inquiry; in fact, it is the very opposite. It is serious work that requires critical thinking, vulnerability, and an enormous capacity for reflection.

Consider: how can each of these modes—critical thinking, vulnerability, and reflection—be fostered through writing? How have they historically been so for *you?*

## Healing-Centered as Restorative

To heal, from the old English word *haelen,* means to move toward wholeness, to bring the fragments together, to repair or restore. It signifies the process of becoming sound or healthy again—emphasis on the word *process*. To center healing, then, means *not* to fix or reach a state of completion but to be guided by an intention to move in the direction of wholeness. Intention is not everything, but it matters. In fact, a definition of the word "intention," little known beyond the medical community, is the *healing process of a wound*. Sit with that for a moment. An intention itself is a healing process.

In this way, a healing-centered approach is inherently restorative. Angel Acosta (2023) defines healing-centered pedagogy as "an emergent field of study" that is "rooted in the re-emergence of indigenous scholarship," exploring "the effects of racism and trauma, and the deconstruction of colonization" while interweaving innovative methods with "the restoration of formerly practiced ways of knowing, learning, and being." Given the collective nature of trauma and the need for collective healing, positioning healing-centered education in the context of a worldview that honors Indigenous perspectives is vital.

In recent years, the incorporation of restorative practices has become more than an educational trend; in states like my own in Connecticut, it has become a legal mandate. And yet I have found that, too often, practices such as "restorative circles"—where an object is passed around and frequently referred to as a "talking stick"—are presented as novel strategies without any recognition of their deep roots in Indigenous traditions. The neglect of cultural context and implications is not harmless, no less so than their absence in approaches to social-emotional learning or trauma-sensitive pedagogy.

While there is a very real risk of appropriation in applying Indigenous knowledge and traditions without substantial understanding, the risk is even greater when applied without naming them. Indigenous worldviews are applicable and beneficial to anyone; they are forms of knowing and living history to be honored and studied by all. According to Wahinkpe Topa (Four Arrows) and Darcia Narvaez (2022), "All people are indigenous to Earth and have the right and the responsibility to practice and teach the Indigenous worldview precepts" (pp. 4–5). Their text—*Restoring the Kinship Worldview*—is dedicated to "the future of the earth and all our relations" (p. ix) and underscores the interrelatedness among humans and all of the natural world.

When I look back on my growing up in schools, it is no surprise to me that my most influential educator was my high school English teacher who would regularly remind us that "everything interrelates." Even at the time, I found it to be a radical notion. Could she be right? I remember it prompting a plethora of "six degrees of Kevin Bacon" challenges, a play on the idea that any two people on Earth can be connected through acquaintances by six degrees of separation from one another. I remember, too, that it felt true in a way that didn't need to be perfectly literal. It spoke to a craving within me, to feel connected and bound to the world around me, even if from a distance.

The fracturing of connectedness is what Canadian physician, trauma scholar, and Holocaust survivor Gabor Maté (2022) calls "the essence of trauma" (p. 24). By this logic, trauma happens when people are fractured from themselves, from their families, from their communities, or from the earth. The fracturing can be the cause of that trauma—think family separations, a child outcast by his peers because of perceived "differences," or even a friend kicked out of the friend group. The fracturing can also be the effect of trauma. Consider a sexual assault survivor who suddenly pulls away from their family or friends. Or a student who has dealt with racism all their lives and struggles to connect with their White peers and teachers.

The word "restorative" can be confusing for people in some of these cases because they may ask: what exactly is being *restored*? If someone has never truly felt connected to their peers or community, for example, is it really a *restoration*? If there was never a sense of collective community or belonging in a school, how can we restore it?

An Indigenous worldview suggests *yes*, because it calls us to consider that we are already always connected; the pain of feeling fractured from one another and from the world around us comes from having forgotten, neglected, or abused this connectedness.

And it's not just, or even most prominently, individuals who forget, neglect, or abuse our inherent connectedness. It's entire institutions, which collectively shape culture and society—the entire environment in which we exist. And they have done so for so long that they have shaped our view of what's "normal." Restoration, in this sense, calls us to extend beyond the limits of our own finite existence, to aim toward restoring a connectedness we may never have seen in our lifetimes, to recognize a fragmentation we may have had no part in creating and yet have inherited.

Healing, by definition, is an antidote to fragmentation—a movement toward wholeness, "a direction, not a destination," according to Maté, with "no road maps" (pp. 261, 374). It is not only an uncertain or unseen path but also not typically a clean or easy process. Fariha Róisín (2022), in her book *Who Is Wellness For?*, describes healing as an "excruciating" and "messy business" (p. 1) that takes "immense courage" and "immense endurance" (p. 91). All the more reason why humility is required when we center healing. We do not have all, or maybe even *any*, of the answers. We, as teachers, cannot claim to know exactly what our students need, what will "heal" them and our communities. We can instead aim to build and maintain a conducive space for our students to move in the direction of their own healing while we support and guide them as best we can.

## Healing From and Within Human Society

As human beings, we are connected not just to each other but to the larger social world that we have together created. We are connected not only with one another but to the rest of the natural world as well. We, and this social world that we have created, become further fragmented and potentially traumatized when we—as individuals but also collectively and through our institutions—forget that we are also part of this natural world.

Maté (2022) writes, "To meet modern society's criteria for normality is, in many ways, to conform to requirements that are profoundly *abnormal* in regard to our Nature-given needs" (p. 8). He argues that "the entire context of social structures, belief systems, assumptions, and values" that "surround … and pervade every aspect of our lives" form a toxic social culture that creates and blocks the healing of trauma while perpetuating a false perception that this toxicity is normal or even natural (p. 3). The pervasiveness of this toxicity means that the need for healing is ubiquitous and must be viewed not just in terms of healing from individual harm and trauma but in terms of the collective as well.

While claiming and attending to our humanity is crucial to a healing-centered approach, we must simultaneously reckon with the harm we cause—to ourselves, to each other, and to all of the natural world—in being human. Ecological disasters and impending doom. Pandemic and plague, amid inequitable access to a beleaguered healthcare industry. Genocide and war. Mass incarceration, including of youth, fueled by the hyper-policing of students in schools. Extreme poverty and hunger, in a world with enough food and resources for everyone if not for the greed of those with the most, if not for the apathy, hopelessness, or nihilism of those, like many of us, with more than enough. Hate and discrimination, terrorizing and targeting those already marginalized by racism, sexism, homophobia, transphobia, ableism, antisemitism, Islamophobia, and countless other forms of oppression. Ubiquitous mental illness and trauma, at the individual and collective levels. Political polarization ever deepening the divides within and across our communities, neighborhoods, and families. Segregated lives, dominated by technology and consumerism, isolating us even further from each other and from the rest of nature.

In order to cope with all of this, we become fragmented—in our hearts, in our minds, in our spirits, in our communities, and in our connections with one another and the earth. Wounds form and calcify. And we find ourselves, individually and collectively, in need of healing.

For Róisín (2022), "Healing has been about integrating the fragments of mind, body, and spirit that were shattered by trauma" but also seeing "a parallel between the earth and humans." She adds:

> If I could heal myself—and what I mean by this is largely about acceptance, it's healing to accept a failing body and tell that body *I love you, unconditionally*—maybe we would have more proof for a way to collectively heal the Earth, too. Because the earth, like our own bodies, needs so much love, nurturance, and gentleness from us.
>
> (p. 153)

Indeed, "all our relations" are in need of attention in a healing-centered approach, which is why the healing-centered framework presented in this book is focused, most of all, on relationships: students' and teachers' relationships with each other, as well as each of their relationships with themselves, with writing, with the people in their lives, with culture and society, and with all of the natural world.

We need each other to heal. We also largely *want* to be in community with one another. We write in order to express, share, learn, connect, and understand. All of these actions come with complex difficulties and vulnerabilities, especially given the fraught and fragmented nature of our society. But they also come with great opportunity for liberatory and transformative experience.

Many of us as teachers are already engaged in that positive struggle to move, amidst the many challenges, in such a direction, to engage with the intentions that are the healing process of a wound.

A healing-centered approach helps keep us on our path.

## References

Acosta, A. (2023). *Healing-centered education: A primer course*. Dr. Angel Acosta. https://www.drangelacosta.com/healing-centered-education-a-primer-november-2023

Dutro, E. (2019). *The vulnerable heart of literacy: Centering trauma as powerful pedagogy*. Teachers College Press.

Everett, S. (2021). Editor's introduction. In S. Everett (Ed.), *Special issues, Volume 1: Trauma-informed teaching: Cultivating healing-centered ELA classrooms* (pp. 9–12). NCTE eBooks.

Freire, P. (2000). *Pedagogy of the oppressed* (30th anniversary ed.). Continuum.

Ginwright, S. (2022). *The four pivots: Reimagining justice, reimagining ourselves*. North Atlantic.

hooks, b. (1994). *Teaching to transgress*. Routledge.

Lin, M., Olsen, S., Simmons, D. N., Miller, M., & Tominey, S. L. (2023). "Not try to save them or ask them to breathe through their oppression": Educator perceptions and the need for a human-centered, liberatory approach to social and emotional learning. *Frontiers in Education*, *7*. https://doi.org/10.3389/feduc.2022.1044730

Liu, Z. R. (2019). Humanizing the practice of witnessing trauma narratives. *Journal of Adolescent & Adult Literacy*, *63*(3), 347–350.

Maté, G. (2022). *The myth of normal: trauma, illness & healing in a toxic culture*. Avery.

Pennebaker, J. W., & Smyth, J. M. (2016). *Opening up by writing it down: How expressive writing improves health and eases emotional pain* (3rd ed.). The Guilford Press.

Róisín, F. (2022). *Who is wellness for?: An examination of wellness culture and who it leaves behind*. Harper Wave.

Simmons, D. (2021). Why SEL alone isn't enough: Done poorly, SEL faces the risk of becoming "white supremacy with a hug". *Educational Leadership*, *78*(6), 30–34.

Sloan, D. M., & Marx, B. P. (2019). *Written exposure therapy for PTSD: A brief treatment approach for mental health professionals*. American Psychological Association. https://doi.org/10.1037/0000139-000

Topa, W., & Narvaez, D. (2022). *Restoring the kinship worldview: Indigenous voices introduce 28 precepts for rebalancing life on planet Earth*. North Atlantic Books.

# 3

# Embodying *What*

## Characteristics of a Healing-Centered Approach

To embody something means to take on its characteristics.

So when we're talking about embodying a healing-centered approach to writing, what do we mean? What exactly are we trying to *embody*?

In this chapter, I outline seven characteristics: (1) humanizing, (2) affirming, (3) empowering, (4) liberatory, (5) trauma-sensitive, (6) restorative, and (7) transformative.

While not exhaustive or exclusive, these words have helped me to crystalize my intentions as a teacher. They are guiding lights, explicitly reminding me of what I want my teaching practice to feel like—for me and for my students. These characteristics explicitly describe how I want to show up for all of us in the classroom. I offer this list to you along with these questions to consider as you read:

- Which resonate most?
- Which feel most aligned with your own practice?
- Which feel furthest away—and why?
- What might be getting in the way?
- Finally, what's missing from the list, for you?

DOI: 10.4324/9781003752721-3

## Humanizing

No way around it, we are already human. So what does it mean for a writing approach to be "humanizing"?

A humanizing experience, as I define it here, is one that counters and repairs the effects of dehumanization that surround and fill our lives. It emphasizes the shared humanities—rather than the prescriptive social roles—of individuals in community with one another. It honors who we are, our intrinsic selves, and gives us room to *be*—and to *become*.

In a classroom, humanizing experiences make room for and nurture the full selves, histories, identities, and communities of every human being involved in the educational enterprise. No small feat, considering the many pressures students and teachers face to *prove* their learning through numbers and performance on standardized assessments.

The act of writing offers a distinct opportunity for humanization because it demands that we use our *voices*; it requires us to consider what we know, think, feel, or believe and to make decisions about what, among those categories, we wish to share with other human beings.

Despite its keen opportunity for humanization, though, writing is often experienced in schools as just the opposite: a dehumanizing experience where we are compelled to equate "good writing" with adherence to rigid, conscripted norms that we have internalized as standard. Hierarchical rubrics reinforce this idea that we are doing things wrong or right. It's no wonder why the emergence of artificial intelligence (AI)-generated content feels like such a crisis. We have been teaching students to write like robots—to write as if, to apply bell hooks' (1994) comments about teaching, their writing "does not emerge from bodies" (p. 139)—so, now, we and they may be wondering: what's the point, when the robots can just do it for students, and we as teachers can barely tell the difference?

Overly standardized forms of writing, at least on the surface, appear to demand that writers keep whole facets of themselves entirely out of the process as well as the product. While not as ubiquitous anymore, requirements that ban the pronoun "I" and insist on an "objective," impersonal tone literally ask the writer to put themselves on hold and disassociate themselves from their inquiry. Surely, it is important to learn how to aim toward objectivity, to suspend a focus on the self in order to fully immerse oneself in a subject beyond. But how many of us teachers learned to equate good writing with this neutralized tone? How many of us learned to jump through awkward linguistic hoops to avoid uttering the word "I" on the page? And how does that conditioning affect our teaching now?

No matter what type of written product I may be asking my students to write, I *try* to give them space to ask themselves: what do I know about this topic? What do I think or believe about it? How does it connect to my life? To my culture? To my experiences? To my interests? To my observations about the world around me? I try to do this so often that it becomes a habit of mind, so that any time they are faced with a writing assignment, they are prone to ask themselves: where am *I* in this writing? When I'm using "I" here, who do I mean? If I'm not using "I," who is the "I" behind this writing anyway? Which aspects of myself can or do I want to bring forth in the process of writing—and maybe even in the final product?

## Mutual Humanization

There were many mornings, pre-Covid, when I would walk through the doors of my school in a fog, barely recalling how I got there. As I made my way down the long, bright-white hallway toward my classroom's wing of the building, the first line of a cumulative poem would reverberate in my consciousness:

> *Sometimes I wake up not a person but …*

And I'd add a new line each day: *not a person but a barren forest; a roving baseline; a fork with a bent handle; a train on broken tracks.*

Total disembodiment. I literally did not feel human, and this line sprouted up reflexively each morning as a reminder from some place deep within my intuition.

Looking back now, I see that I'd allowed myself to be consumed by my role as teacher. I worked all day, then went home and worked some more, grading papers, planning lessons, and generally striving to be perfect. I would catch myself running through scenarios from the classroom in my head while cooking dinner or playing with my children. Despite my life at home, once I entered my workplace, I could barely remember who I was anymore. I could not access my personhood.

Years later, the television show *Severance*—where corporate employees lose all memory of their identities and lives beyond the office—would resonate a little too strongly. A key difference is that my job as a teacher was not—as it was for the characters in the show—to stare at a computer screen and drag random numbers that feel "wrong" from one side of it to the other. My job was to engage in the deeply human work of teaching—of tending to the minds and souls of young people. And I gave it my all. Practically all of me.

During Covid, being home, I felt like my humanity had a chance to thaw out. It wasn't a clean or easy process; there was, for everyone and for some more than others, so much fear and loss. It was that very fear and loss, in fact, that brought me back to life and made me realize that I had been living half-alive, because I felt like I needed to, in order to be a good teacher. My perfectionism, a harmful symptom of my hyper-conscientiousness, had flattened my sense of self.

Out of what felt like emotional necessity, I started making collage poetry on the same dining room table where I taught my classes online. I reacquainted with my artistic self, my writerly self, my politically conscious self, and saw a clear line between those aspects of myself and my teaching, aided by the clear line of sight between my collages at one end of the table and my laptop at the other.

When I returned to school, I could no longer leave myself behind. I still worked hard, bringing papers home to grade when necessary, but the nature of the boundary had shifted. I began showing up with and as myself, for my students and for me. Outside of school, I attended more fully to my own writing practice and saw this not as cheating on my work as a teacher but as a way of nurturing it. The old "put your own mask on first" idea. Or, as Paulo Freire (2000) might put it, attending to the mutual humanization between myself and my students.

This mutuality eschews a false humanization that is more about granting a guise of humanity to those deemed beneath us in a power structure (Camangian & Cariaga, 2022). Instead, teachers and students must be, as Freire (2000) phrased it, "partners … in their relations" (p. 75). This isn't always an easy shift because it requires true power-sharing, balanced delicately with the need to remain in charge as the ultimately responsible party in a setting with countless variables to contend with.

Humanization of this sort is not hyperfocused on individual well-being and personal liberation; it is fundamentally concerned with the individual's relationship to social structures (Prilleltensky, 2008). It is a process of deliberate resistance to the conditions within society that allow us to lose touch with our—and each other's—inherent humanity. In this sense, humanization becomes a process of healing both society and the selves and communities within it.

Humans need each other, you might say, to remind each other of our common humanity. And because, as Freire (2000) puts it, "no one can be authentically human while he prevents others from being so" (pp. 85–86), those with differential power relationships (such as teachers and students) must work together toward a shared goal of humanization within a truly liberatory pedagogy.

Suppressing or repressing the humanity of others depletes and restricts the oppressor's humanity as well. This concept explains why many of us may feel pained ourselves when assigning and assessing writing against inflexible, conformist standards, or overemphasizing standardized tests in part because they affect our own teaching evaluations.

For teachers of writing, mutual humanization involves remembering that we are working with humans and seeking to hear our students' human voices. It also means remembering to listen for and attend to our own authentic voices as well.

## Humanization in an AI Era

Finding humanizing approaches to writing became all the more urgent in November of 2022, when OpenAI launched ChatGPT. From the start, polarizing opinions proliferated in education—some saw AI as the death knell of writing in schools. *The Atlantic* (2022) published an essay titled, "The End of High School English" nine days after ChatGPT's release. Others saw it as an opportunity for innovation as well as greater accessibility for students who struggle with writing.

In my experience, arguments about AI as a promoter of equity are sometimes wielded in conversations and professional development spaces as a mic drop or stonewall defense against those who resist or try to cautiously slow its widespread adoption. Yet I challenge this notion of AI being a mechanism of equity. I see it as a misconception or at the very least a partial conception. For one, the most advanced and sophisticated AI tools are behind paywalls, which perpetuates economic inequities in terms of access (D'Agostino, 2023). But more concerning to me is what we lose of the human voice. Large language models are trained on data sets dominated by standardized American English. An already harmful over-standardization and homogenization of writerly voice and expressed identity, in this sense, stand to worsen (Enriquez et al., 2024).

To embody a humanizing ethic, we need to be alert to this co-optation; we need to resist it and apply a critical lens, to ask ourselves: who, really, is being served by these promises of greater productivity and efficiency, of equity through mechanization? Is it the humans in our care—including ourselves? Unfortunately, teachers find themselves without the time, support, or resources to grapple with the larger existential questions while balancing the pressure to maintain academic integrity and keep pace with a changing technological landscape.

Nonetheless, we can consider a few core questions: (1) How might we be perpetuating an expectation of polished perfection in the finished product—the kind that generative AI aims to produce? (2) How can we try to make our assignments feel more personally meaningful, for us and for our students, so students may be less likely to want an external tool to do it for them? (3) How can we be more clear and explicit about if, when, how, and *why* our students can use AI tools in discrete and deliberate ways? Doing so can promote integrity, transparency, and—ultimately—a humanizing experience in the process.

## Affirming

A humanizing approach is fundamentally affirming. It affirms our shared humanity.

To be affirming means to say: I see you. I hear you. I honor your presence.

In my definition, an experience is affirming if it validates and reveres a person's or group's inherent right to be who they are. In a classroom, the environment is affirming when each student's—and teacher's—unique identity is honored and welcomed.

So, what does it mean to affirm a student writer, specifically? What can we do, as teachers, to actively see and hear our students in their writing—and to let them know that we do? How can we signal to them that we *want* to?

Partly it can come through the assignments we offer and in the responses we make to their writing.

Consider the times when you have felt affirmed as a writer. What did it feel like in your body? How did it impact your practice?

When I was interviewing teachers during my dissertation research, almost every single person told a story of feeling *seen* or *affirmed* by a teacher from their past. Lucy, a high school English teacher, talked about the time, in the fourth grade, when she wrote a poem about a leprechaun, and how much it meant when her teacher placed it on display in the classroom. She never forgot that poem. Now, in addition to teaching writing, she is writing a novel of her own.

Sammy, a Science teacher, talked about being published in her high school literary magazine when she was away at boarding school in the ninth grade—how it gave her a feeling of belonging in a place where she felt like an outsider. Now, she writes as a respite from the pressures of teaching and as a way to connect with other writers and readers online.

> When and how do you affirm your own students? What is the impact? How do you know?

## Affirmation from Within

If anyone told me I was a good writer, growing up, I would squirm. Even today, I have a hard time not just taking compliments but being told that I'm doing a good job. There's one part of me that has a hard time believing it, and then there is the part that is all too ready to believe. The latter is the one I fear more. What happens if I believe that I'm a good writer, a good teacher, a good anything? Will I take it for granted? Will I rest on my laurels, become complacent, stop growing?

And what happens if I don't believe it? Then I might be in constant fear of being exposed, of letting someone down, of disappointing people's expectations of me, of having to confront my own imperfection.

Affirmation is a powerful force, which is why—when doled out in the form of praise—it should be wielded with intentionality and authenticity. The type of affirmation I'm describing here goes deeper than surface-level praise—which certainly can be helpful but is not, in my view, as sustaining as a deeper affirmation of the self. Such affirmation can occur in an environment where people feel welcome to share, express, and learn about who they are, without judgment—positive *or* negative.

In contrast is the unaffirming environment where students don't see themselves reflected in the texts they read, where they feel compelled to stifle their authentic voices, cultures, or language practices in order to conform to implicit or explicit expectations. Perpetuating this lack of affirmation are repressive curricula that deny, ignore, stifle, or make assumptions about students' identities (Jones, 2022). Counteracting the violence of this repression are humanizing pedagogies that allow students to draw on their own experiences and identities as contexts for analysis and exploration (Camangian & Cariaga, 2022).

But inviting students to write about themselves is not enough. It requires truly putting them in the driver's seat, ensuring that they are treated as experts of their own experience, with the space and authority to represent and explore their often multilingual, multiethnic, or multiracial backgrounds and identities in the way they see fit (Kim, 2021; Muhammad, 2020). Not in the ways we dictate.

## To Feel Affirmed Means to Know You Matter

Students arrive in our classrooms with complex personal, familial, social, and cultural identities—some of which we can't necessarily see and some of which they won't always bring forth or make apparent to us. Nor should they have to, for them to feel affirmed. To feel that they matter.

"Writing is a way of mattering," one of my research participants, Miriam, eloquently said to me. "And so many people feel they do not matter." After decades of writing and teaching writers, she said her main goal is to help her students hear and respect their own voices, "to help them believe they have a right (maybe even a duty) to tell their stories," because someone out there may need to read it. Keeping this mentality central to her teaching makes Miriam an inherently affirming audience; she *wants* to hear her students' stories, and she lets them know that.

Still, many people struggle to feel this sense of affirmation; even Miriam—author of multiple published books and a creative writing teacher for decades—said she often feels the need to defend her choice to make art, to herself and others. For most novelists, writing is not a viable way to pay the bills. Without an editor or teacher actively seeking or assigning work, justifying the time and effort spent on writing can feel hard in a culture that does not affirm such work. It stands to reason that a middle or high school student might struggle to find a deeper sense of meaning and purpose in writing beyond fulfilling an assignment and receiving a grade.

And yet, for Miriam, the experience of writing is its own source of affirmation. "Writing's energizing," she told me, "because I went to that place, that imaginative place, and it doesn't really matter what comes of it, because for two hours, I was there." Her deep understanding of the magic that can happen in the process of writing, cultivated through practice, directly enables her to pass this wisdom along to her students.

To my mind, the type of intrinsic affirmation that Miriam describes—an affirmation that derives organically from the process and practice of writing itself—may be the most meaningful, rewarding, sustaining, and healing kind of all. The more we can offer opportunities for students to practice writing without the carrot and stick of a grade, with their own motivations and interests at the helm, the more we can help them feel that the writing is their *own*—and the more affirming their experience with writing may be.

## Empowering

> How do we empower student writers? What does it suggest when we think that we are able to?

While "empowerment" is generally viewed as a positive teaching outcome, the word can also reinforce a power hierarchy, suggesting that someone with power is equipped with the ability to bestow power upon another who is lacking it. In cases like these, "power" is bestowed in a form or to a degree that the power-holder decides.

The kind of empowerment I'm referring to here is one that cultivates an inner sense of agency and authorship. In this view, students are invited, welcomed, and supported to recognize their own authority and self-determination. They are invited to drive their own learning experiences, make their own choices, and pursue their own interests and questions. Such empowerment requires a teaching stance that poses questions and draws students inward, to attune to their own inner knowing, their own inner curiosities and compulsions, if only to challenge and enrich their inner experience with something beyond themselves.

Writing can serve as a unique vehicle of empowerment because it asks for the writer to acquaint themselves with and utilize their own *voice*. Writing demands that the writer make choices, an aspect of authorship (and authority) that can be feared, resisted, and quelled or revealed, fostered, and embraced—in other words, *empowered*.

For teachers, empowering students might mean inviting, guiding, and entrusting them to make decisions about the forms in which they choose to express themselves while suspending rigid expectations for what writing should look like or how it will be assessed. Such practices help students find agency within themselves instead of feeling that they need to reach for it externally, from someone with the power to withhold it.

## What Can "Whole-Self Engagement" Look Like?

Because the most authentic empowerment comes from within, the whole self is ideally invited into the process, so that the *author* has the *authority* to *choose* which parts or aspects of themselves to bring to bear.

Does that mean we stand in front of a classroom and say, "Put your whole self in," like we're playing the hokey-pokey? Maybe. Sort of.

But such a leap takes scaffolding—by which I mean, intentional, repeated offerings of opportunity, always invitational.

Here's an example of a writing exercise I try with any group of writers, no matter their age. I ask them to make two columns.

On the left, they list different aspects of their identities. I model it and say something like, "I might write: teacher, writer, mother, wife, daughter, sister, Greek American, vegetarian, person whose favorite season is summer." I encourage them to brainstorm as many of these descriptors for themselves as possible. Then I ask them to read the list to themselves and circle or star the one, two, or three that stand out; that maybe seem to leap off the page.

After that, in the right-hand column, I ask them to list topics they know or care a lot about. Again, I offer examples—this time less related to myself. Things like: "Basketball, World War II, hip-hop music, dogs." When a few minutes have passed, I say, "Now, again, reread your list and see which topics stand out. Circle or star them."

Sometimes I ask if anyone wants to share their list out loud before the next prompt; other times, I ask them to dive right in and do a freewrite, choosing something they circled from the left and the right and combining them in any way that feels right. Again, I give an example from my own lists: "I might write about climate change from the role of being a mother."

There are so many ways to vary this exercise. They could add a column of potential audiences, so that someone writing about "soccer" from the position of "son" might write to one of their parents or a coach. Or someone might choose to write as a Black teenager about racism to their White peers. A queer student might write about gender to their heteronormative teacher. A Jewish student might write about World War II to their grandparents or to their non-Jewish Social Studies teacher.

It's a simple exercise, but the whole point is to encourage the writer to notice what compels them, to notice which aspects of themselves are calling to be heard from, calling to speak. Repeated opportunities give students the grace and space (see Chapter 5) to test out the risks and see how they feel, see if they might take their inquiry further the next time.

Exercises like these also give students practice with and build their interoceptive awareness as they are prompted to notice what they feel pulled toward (see "Body Awareness," Chapter 5). Ideally, such practice becomes a habit of mind to check in with the self and its many dimensions to ask: "What does the Vietnamese American part of me think, feel, or know about this topic? How about the grandson in me? How about the devoted fan of *Star Wars*?"

## Mutual Empowerment in the Classroom

It is notoriously tempting for many White educators to see ourselves as savior figures, à la Hillary Swank's character in *Freedom Writers* or Michelle Pfeiffer's in *Dangerous Minds*, the latter being one whose title I feel uncomfortable even typing. So many of us want so badly to "help," or at least see ourselves as being *helpers*, for people whose identities face, and have for centuries faced, countless layers of systemic injustice.

But we need to be alert to, resist, and challenge these superficial tropes of empowerment, which too often focus on individual boot-strapping, or on opening the gates of opportunity to those deemed worthy, rather than guiding our students to see how many more paths they might discover for themselves, how many more skills and capabilities and possibilities they may draw out that are already within them.

One way to do this—a *necessary* way to do this—is to cultivate empowerment in ourselves by being vulnerable, taking risks, and tapping into our own creativities and unique talents (hooks, 1994; Muhammad, 2020). In this sense, mutual empowerment can be seen not only as an opportunity but as a responsibility, for any teacher hoping to help their students gain more autonomy, self-determination, and agency. And that empowerment asks us to be *in it* with our students: to share vulnerable aspects of our identities, to talk about the challenges we face, and to take risks ourselves, aligning our practices with what we believe and value, so we can experience our own journey of growth alongside our students.

We can ask ourselves: what and where am I holding back from my students, and why? What would it mean to share and reveal more of myself and my own struggles? How might I put myself in a place of discomfort and challenge, so I can better relate to my students and their experiences? What do I really care about and value, and how are my practices matching up with that?

### The Role of Critical Awareness

Empowerment, to some degree, requires recognition of *dis*empowerment. Because of this, students need to see their teachers exposing and explicitly naming real-life, contemporary examples of systemic injustice, drawing connections between the historic or fictional ones they may encounter in their studies.

Students also need the encouragement to explore and identify examples of injustice they find themselves, whether in their own lives, their communities, or the larger world around them. From that place of criticality, students are well positioned to imagine better possibilities, too (Muhammad, 2020; Prilleltensky, 2008). Writing—under the right conditions—can be a space for such imagining.

But all of that requires taking students and their perspectives seriously. Personally, I'll never forget my high school English teacher, Mrs. Green, who greeted our whole class as "scholars" every day. And I know from staying in touch with enough people from those days that I am not alone. So many of us—teachers now ourselves—vividly remember her words, her tone, and how it made us feel.

When we support students with the tools they need and provide a conducive space, we can help them feel empowered to not only examine but shape their worlds through their words and write their way toward a better future.

## Liberatory

An empowering approach to writing has the capacity to be liberatory.

My use of the word *liberatory*, as opposed to *liberating*, is greatly influenced by authors such as Freire and bell hooks who were formative in my learning to teach and think about teaching. It is also an acknowledgement that "liberation" is not finite; furthermore, the term is a political one, woven throughout histories that are not mine to appropriate. When Freire writes about liberation in the context of the colonized populations of Brazil and Chile; when Frederick Douglass writes about education as emancipation; when Primo Levi writes about being liberated from Auschwitz; I have nowhere near the right credence or experience to relate.

At the same time, I recognize the eternal wisdom in Maya Angelou's (2025) words: "The truth is, no one of us can be free until everybody is free," and so I am concerned—as a teacher, writer, and human being—with freedom. It is my business to be concerned.

No doubt, the banking model Freire (2000) exposed—with teacher as sole proprietor of knowledge, and student as empty vessel to be filled with information—doesn't dominate in the way that it used to in education, at least not on the surface, but traces and strands of it remain. Think rigid declarations about what constitutes "quality" writing and what doesn't. Specific directives about what to "fix" or "correct," instead of posing a question to a student about what else they might try.

Here's the thing. Seemingly small repressions, for some of us—for example, those of us who are White, able-bodied, cisgender, or middle class—can be easy to shrug off. Even in the process of writing this book, I can hear the faint voice of an imagined student whispering:

> So what? So they make me write and defend thesis statements in this rigid, normative way, using performative academic language, that perpetuates a hegemonic standard of intellectual dominance … I can write in my journal at home. Let's not overthink this.

But if we do think about these issues enough, we can see how the practices and standards whose primacy we help maintain reach their tentacles into the deepest roots of every other injustice and repression that rots the center that binds us all.

It's easy for those of us with some degree of default social capital we didn't earn to find the dominant norms of society to be annoying, an inconvenience, something to navigate around. This is partly because their dominance seems to benefit us; it maintains a status quo that is for some of us altogether manageable if irritating. But these norms are slowly and quietly harming everyone. "No one of us can be free until everybody is free."

This small inflection between the word "liberating" and "liberatory" acknowledges that no single practice, approach, or stance we take in the classroom can be inherently "liberating." We don't have that power to singlehandedly free anyone, and there is so much danger in thinking that we do. Thinking we do would imply that we have the power to withhold this liberation as much as we might hypothetically release it.

That said, it's worth examining and being honest with ourselves about what power we *do* have, to ensure that we are wielding that power in a way that supports liberatory experience for others, namely our students.

What I mean by "liberatory" in the context of writing in a classroom is the capacity for writers to find movement beyond constriction. Liberatory experiences are ones that help people or groups find a sense of movement or release from personal, academic, or social conventions, constraints, and pressures. Liberatory writing experiences foster and stem from creativity, self-expression, and inquiry; from the criticality to say, "Is this true?" "Does this have to be done this way?" "How else might we see this?"

## Reimagining the Writing Teachers' Role

In a classroom setting, a liberatory approach—such as those described by hooks and Freire—frees students and teachers from the rigidity of their roles in the classroom.

Miriam, who teaches creative writing to graduate students, talked about her role as being more of a witness and a guide.

Although many students come into her workshops wanting to write a story "good" enough to be published, she envisions her job as being more about helping writers excavate the story they most need to tell, to help them find a way to birth these stories into the world. In effect, this stance has been liberatory for those of her students who have discovered something much more powerful than being published or writing a perfectly crafted story (whatever that means).

A notable example she shared with me occurred during the height of the pandemic, when she was working with a young woman who held a great deal of trauma and was trying to write about her experiences but struggling to do so cohesively. Finally, she scrawled a five-page snippet, just getting her thoughts and feelings on the page. When reading her student's words, Miriam felt a visceral sense of their weight. Intuitively, she could tell that the writer was working with potentially life-altering material. Very gently and invitationally, she encouraged the writer to sit with her words a bit more. She pointed to specific spots in the writing that felt especially intense, asking questions such as "Do you see? Where this is White hot? … Do you *see* it? Do you *feel* it?"

In the months after writing that essay, so many things in the writer's life started to shift. She called off her impending marriage, quit her job, and found herself on the verge of a whole new life of her choosing.

Her story does not surprise me at all. Writing helped this writer dislodge deep-seated truths and inner knowings that allowed her to become "unstuck," not only within the piece she was working on but in her life as well.

It is worth noting how Miriam encouraged the writer to pay attention to both her own body and the body of the written work. These promptings encouraged body awareness (see Chapter 5) and provided gentle facilitation of this liberatory experience.

Sometimes, that's all it takes: drawing a star next to a powerful sentence in a student's work, asking "Is there more here?" A mentor of mine, the late great poet Baron Wormser, famously encouraged his students to "linger; dwell; stay" in certain spots of their drafts for these very same reasons. As he said to me once, those places are "where the good words come from." I've found that if a writer is ready to go to that deep place and if they need to, then they will. If you can sit beside them, that's even more ideal, because—if you pay close attention and try to attune to the subtleties, if you tap into your own literate sensibilities in order to read the writer's body language—you can usually tell how ready they are. Do they look away, glance down, tense up—or do they squint, sigh, make some fleeting eye contact, nod, roll out their neck, or laugh?

It takes restraint, though, to do this work in a way that honors the writer's autonomy—restraint of the sort Miriam displayed when she *knew* intuitively how much lay beneath the surface of her student's writing. She also knew that it would make the writing better if the student just *went* there, right into the heart of what she, as yet, was holding back.

But Miriam did not overstep, charging in with the intention to liberate this writer from the trappings of her life. She did not force the woman to have this transformative experience, for the sake of the writing or even with the idea that doing so would have a positive effect on the student writer's overall well-being. Instead, Miriam carefully made space for the possibility of liberatory experience but ensured that the writer held the power—the power to propel this experience for herself.

Miriam freed herself from her apparent role of helping her student write a well-crafted, publishable piece of writing and, instead, helped the writer claim space for the writing to get messy. She offered the student a chance to make the writing even messier. Because although we as writers always have that chance, that choice, we sometimes need someone else—a teacher, maybe, who is willing to shed any persona that resembles the all-knowing, answer-holding guru—to step in and remind us that things do get messy sometimes and need to. Expecting the cleanest piece of writing possible is not only unrealistic but potentially detrimental to our larger intellectual and emotional processing.

While it's possible to think this scenario is *way* too personal or not even appropriate to consider in the context of middle and high school, I think most of us who have taught writing for some time have encountered something similar: the sense that there is so much more beneath the surface of a student's writing, that there is so much more to mine. Sometimes, these encounters set off an alarm bell; we seek out the student's counselor or call home. Sometimes, we might feel inclined to avoid what we're sensing or encourage the student to write in a different direction. Other times, we might want to vehemently encourage the writer to write more, to be bold and courageous, to *go there*.

The point I'm trying to make in this section is just as much about protecting the student's well-being and safety in the face of these potentially liberatory experiences as it is about nurturing them. In fact, helping to protect a student's well-being *is* the way to nurture them, because the kind of liberatory experience I'm advocating for is the kind that attunes to the writer's needs and keeps them firmly within their own agency and power.

That brings us to trauma.

## Trauma-sensitive

One of the most crucial characteristics of a healing-centered approach is trauma sensitivity. A trauma-sensitive approach maintains an active awareness of what trauma is and how it can reside and be expressed through the body.

For teachers, trauma sensitivity involves recognizing that a degree of personal and collective trauma is always present and possible within the classroom. And with that awareness, making choices that aim to ensure the psychic and affective safety of each student. Can such safety ever be fully ensured? No. But we have to try anyway. Such an approach is essential not only for mitigating and preventing harm but also for creating a conducive space for healing.

## Trauma in the Body

Trauma is not just something that happens to a person but the lasting impact that remains in its wake, that lodges itself in the mind, spirit, and body.

We all have different bodies, which means that the same event or experience can affect different people in radically different ways. What causes trauma for one person may not become trauma for someone else.

What that means for us, as teachers, is manifold. To begin with, we can assume that many of our students are holding some degree of trauma. We can also assume that we won't always know why. And it's important to understand that we don't need to know why, in order to be trauma-sensitive.

It's also important to understand that trauma is not a deficit; it is a critical safety and survival skill, where the body responds as a protective mechanism against a challenging or harmful occurrence—or series of occurrences (Menakem, 2017). Think of the students bracing themselves in the face of racist, ableist, or classist comments, assumptions, expectations, or representations. And then consider the toll it takes on the body over time.

While we should assume that some degree of trauma is likely present in our classroom, we don't need to know the nature, scope, or cause of it to be trauma-sensitive, nor do we necessarily need to know which students in our classes have been traumatized. In fact, this ambiguous understanding is the very reason why a trauma-sensitive approach is so important to embody as a characteristic.

So many times, I've heard colleagues say, "If only I'd known" or "Why didn't their guidance counselor tell me?" after they put a zero on student work, or doled out a harsh punishment, only to later learn that a student was reeling from the death of a family member or recovering from an act of violence. I know I've thought or said something similar myself. "Why didn't they tell us?"

But the fact is, we won't always know. The students' loved ones, let alone their guidance counselors, may not know. The students themselves may not know that they are experiencing or holding trauma.

Working in my school's writing center, I have had the opportunity to re-encounter my previous students in later years—especially senior year, when they are working on college essays. I can't count the number of times I've conferenced with students writing about terrible experiences—a serious illness, a death, an act of sexual violence—that they endured years earlier while they were students in my class. In many if not most cases, I didn't know at the time. No one knew, not until much later, when the dam holding back the emotion broke open.

Almost always, I think: "That explains it." The sudden distancing. The head down on the desk. The grade plunging. The edge, the attitude. There is almost always in retrospect a perfectly visible sign.

That is why it's helpful to consider an inclusive definition of trauma that captures both acute, isolated experiences of trauma and ongoing adversity that creates chronic, toxic, and traumatic stress (Tayles, 2021). A broad understanding of trauma allows teachers to recognize how ubiquitous trauma and adversity are in our students' lives and places the focus on the *response*—such as hyperarousal (fight or flight) or hypoarousal (freezing or numbing)—rather than the specific nature of the traumatic experience.

No matter the cause, we can learn to read the possible signs, especially since it is usually beyond the scope of our training or purview to determine whether or not a student is experiencing or has experienced trauma. The root cause (and our own sense of whether it constitutes trauma) matters less to our response than our recognition of the need for accommodation. Assuming that most students carry, or have experienced, some degree of trauma can help teachers avoid or mitigate the risk of retraumatizing students or misinterpreting students' behaviors—head down on desk, sharply worded response—as intentional hostility or lack of engagement.

## Understanding Collective Trauma

As educators, we are entrusted with the care of students who have faced systemic injustices as a result of their identities and positionalities, whether based on their race, gender, class, ability, neurotype, language, citizenship status, religion, or some other category. It is our job to understand in a broad, encompassing way what those injustices are and how they operate in large and invisible or subtle ways and to spend significant effort imagining how these collective injustices might personally affect the young people in our care.

The truth is, we don't have to call something trauma—we don't have to know or decide whether or not a student's experience "deserves" that label—in order to make space for the likelihood of it and create an environment safe for those who may be holding it. An environment safe enough, even, that they may be able to move toward healing it.

But we do need to *understand* trauma—particularly the ways in which it can be layered with individual *and* collective experience. What I mean is that it's not a reach to assume that every child with an identity that has been marginalized—our Black students, our Brown students, our bilingual students, our neurodivergent students, our LBGT students, our queer students, our undocumented students, our students from impoverished families—may very well be carrying trauma from the experience of growing up in a society hostile to their humanity (Menakem, 2017; Page & Woodland, 2023). And on top of that are all of the individual traumas that can come from being a person alive in a world full of pain, hardship, and interpersonal harm.

What we really need to reckon with are the layers that can come from schooling experiences themselves—racism, bullying, and microaggressions from peers but also ostracization and shame that can come from the classroom: from feeling (or being told) that they aren't smart enough if they fall short of expectations; from sensing that the teacher doesn't like them or believe in them; from being punished or constantly spotlighted for behaviors that are rooted in trauma—or in cultural identity in a way not palatable to a White-dominant, monolingual, heteronormative environment.

Too often, traumatized students who need support, care, and true advocacy are misperceived as damaged, difficult, or defiant, which leads to castigations that inflict further trauma (Dutro & Caasi, 2022). Even—and sometimes especially—people who offer kindness or support may be seen as threats to a body that is in a state of fight, flight, or freeze. The traumatized person might wonder: can I trust that this person really cares? What happened the last time I did?

Racism, sexism, classism, and ableism compound this effect, because the threat responses may be constant and chronic. Will this person judge me? Will this group of people insult me? Ignore me? Hurt me? Am I safe here? Will I be punished for being myself? It's harder for a body with a constantly overactive sympathetic response, on guard for the next aggression, to find adequate relief from the parasympathetic nervous system that doesn't result in utter collapse (head down on the desk).

It's harder, in other words, to settle the body. An unsettled body tends to resist efforts at healing, instead retaining what Reesma Menakem (2017) refers to as "dirty pain," which is marked by avoidance and aggression—defense mechanisms for a body that is unable to find balance between hypervigilance and rest (p. 153). The presence of "dirty pain" can impede the very healing that some writers may be seeking when they find themselves called to write.

The causes and effects of unmetabolized trauma are important for us to understand as educators who may find ourselves caught off guard when overtures of compassion are met with hostility, resistance, or evasion. Or when students who choose to write about a difficult topic suddenly find themselves triggered toward anger or avoidance in the process.

## Trauma-Sensitive Writing Instruction

In a learning environment, a trauma-sensitive approach includes developing strong relationships with students that allow for "safety cues" to be communicated. Doing this effectively requires that the teacher attend to their own emotional state before and while engaging in communication with students (Tayles, 2021). What does this mean? It means trying to be steady enough in our affective responses and reactions to help students find their own sense of equanimity.

This steadying also involves remaining aware of our own social privileges and biases—including how our various positionalities may be interacting with our students'.

As teachers, we inherently hold an upper hand in the power differential based on our role in the classroom. This makes sense, as we are the responsible adults in the room. But it's worth remembering that we make so many of the most impactful choices for the class experience, including decisions like the degree to which we force participation or lecture at length, subjecting students to a barrage of information without any reprieve, which itself can be a type of trauma (Pennebaker & Smyth, 2016).

Power differentials in the classroom are compounded between teacher and student if we also hold other identity-based privileges. As noted above, students of color are taught by a predominantly White teaching workforce in the United States which is its own form of collective injustice and challenge for students of color (Haddix, 2015; Muhammad, 2020).

On the flip side, a teacher's identity may place them in a position of vulnerability as well. One of my participants, Marie Rose, described the emotional labor of preparing herself—and her students—for the experience of talking about race in a class where she, as the teacher, is the only Black person in the room, saying: "I understand that all of you are White students, and I'm a Black woman teaching this class, and this is how it makes me feel to show up and teach this today." Recognizing how she might feel triggered, frustrated, or drained, she prepares herself *and* them accordingly, first and foremost by calling their attention to the fact of her identity in their midst.

Such an approach takes, to my mind, an admirable amount of self-awareness, emotional intelligence, and composure. Marie Rose's approach laudably models the type of self-inquiry and self-check-in that can help each student find compassion and grounding within themselves in the midst and anticipation of potential provocation. Yet it's important to note the inherent inequity and injustice of this emotional labor. Such a circumstance raises the question: what systemic supports are (or are *not*) in place for teachers like Marie Rose, whose identities may be marginalized because of race, class, ethnicity, gender, or any other category?

As Tayles (2021) notes, "Instructors *and* students must feel some level of safety and security before they can engage in the risky and daunting work of learning and writing" (p. 106, emphasis added). A trauma-informed approach recognizes and honors this fact in a way that transcends surface-level encouragements, scaffolds, or modifications. Instead, it embeds and embodies trauma awareness and sensitivity throughout every choice and facet, and that includes the teacher's well-being as well.

This isn't about superficial self-care, which I've seen prioritized mostly under the impetus of how teacher well-being impacts students. Yes, a teacher's well-being will impact their students (Nankin, 2016), and, yes, that is a good reason to care about it. And, yes, the teacher in a secondary setting is the responsible adult in the room. But if the effect on students is seen as the sole or even primary reason to care about teacher well-being, doing so does nothing but reinforce a false dichotomy between students' and teachers' needs and desires. It sends a harmful message about whose needs really matter in the necessarily communal and relational space of a classroom.

While we, as classroom teachers, may not have the capacity, authority, or means by which to impact teacher well-being at the systemic level, we can at the very least validate the core importance of our own and each other's well-being and advocate for it when and as possible.

## The Inevitability of Trauma Narratives

I'll take a moment here to again share the famous words of Maya Angelou, in her brilliance: "There is no greater agony than bearing an untold story inside you" (Angelou, 2019).

Writing can be an enormously powerful way to heal from trauma. For me, writing has always been a way of amalgamating what I'm going through, what I've been through, and what has "happened" to me with who I am, how I want to experience life, and who I want to be. It's almost like I can't begin to heal from something *until* I'm ready to write about it. That's because it's usually easier for me to tell my stories through writing than directly to a person. When I talk to other people, I feel the need to make things sound pretty or acceptable or clear. I don't want to confuse people or mischaracterize what I mean. I worry about what others will think of me or feel around me. I worry that I'll upset them—that my turmoil will infect them and then there will be two of us for me to worry about. I immediately invalidate or downplay my feelings: "It wasn't that bad. It's not a big deal. I can handle it."

This self-invalidation has been a particular struggle for me in dealing with chronic pain for more than two decades. "Tell them how bad it is," my husband has urged me before every doctor's appointment. "I will. I'm going to be super clear this time," I promise. And then I watch myself from out-of-body sitting on the cold papered table saying things like, "I mean, a four maybe? It's not like I can't walk. I mean, most of the time, at least." When I was in labor with my second child, I called the doctor to inform her, because I knew it was time, only to hear her say, "You sound too friendly to be in labor." Thankfully, by then, I knew myself and my body well enough to get in the car anyway. Hours later, I was told without a doubt that I had made the right call.

Through writing, it's like I'm telling my story to myself, and this feels easier, even if it's messy. Often it feels necessary, like I'm bursting with it, like I need to see the words phenomenalize on the page in order to face their truth, however partial, muddled, ambiguous, or unformed. The agony of the untold story, as Angelou reminds us, is just too much.

As an English teacher, I've frequently borne witness to this bursting. It is embedded into the job. Yes, I tend to be a teacher who feels comfortable with vulnerability, who is no stranger to discussion or even demonstration of complex emotions in the classroom. That tendency does hail me in as a receptive audience for painful narratives. But I know, from talking to enough teachers for whom encountering these stories in their to-be-graded stack is just about their worst teaching nightmare come true, that most if not every teacher of writing will encounter a trauma narrative in some form at some point.

There are clear and well-established health and emotional benefits to writing about difficult experiences, especially if writers can find enough distance and detachment to analyze their emotional reactions and expressions when they show up on their page. Doing so, however, can exacerbate the pain in the short term, especially if that analytical perspective isn't reachable (Pennebaker & Smyth, 2016). Depending on a student's developmental maturity, distance from the experience, emotional stability, and—perhaps most importantly—support systems in place, engaging in such writing can be destabilizing or disastrous. We, as our students' teachers, are an integral part of their support system. So, what do we do when and while students are writing about trauma?

I address this more elaboratively in Chapters 4 and 5, so for now, I'll say that aiming to embody a stance of trauma sensitivity is essential to both our readiness and our response.

## Restorative

The word "restorative" these days is freighted with loads of connotations and misconceptions. It is often equated with an alternative form of punishment or discipline—one that, in some people's eyes, relieves a "perpetrator" from accountability and, in other people's eyes, does just the opposite: it reinforces accountability through a focus on restoring relationships and community.

The latter is closer to where I stand. The way I mean the phrase in this text, restorative experiences are those that reaffirm, re-establish, and repair what has been damaged or lost, including identities, relationships, and connectivities within the self, within communities, and between people and the rest of the natural world. The word "restorative," in the Indigenous tradition from which this use derives, is about nurturing and reconnecting with what is already present but may be latent or forgotten (Topa & Narvaez, 2022). It is also crucially about restoring from the effects of violence and systemic harms—a process that begins with naming and becoming more aware of these ruptures, abuses, destructions, and injustices (Smith, 2021).

It is important to note that restorative practices are not necessarily geared toward reconnecting with individuals, groups, or communities that have harmed you. Some relationships are truly past the point of repair. Instead, restorative practices can be about restoring the selves or the communities that have been impacted by harm.

A restorative approach to writing, specifically, can help writers connect with themselves through reflection and creative expression. It can help them connect with others through communicating ideas, emotions, memories, questions, and knowledge.

Writing is also restorative when it can serve as a mechanism of inquiry, helping writers become more critically conscious of themselves and the world around them, shining a light on a connectedness that is severed by systemic forces such as racism and socioeconomic injustice and further fragmented by denial, unawareness, and silence.

## Restoring the Relationship with Writing

So what would it mean for a writing process itself to be restorative? For one thing, a healing-centered approach can restore a lost joy for writing, a loss that can stem from a lack of inspiration or narrow academic expectations. Even for those who love to write, when we're asked to write in the same ways over and over, we can find ourselves disengaged from the very impetus that compels us to write.

An even greater source of rupture, though, is shame. One teacher I spoke to, Maeve, discussed how a negative comment from a professor in college left her "paralyzed to write" for many years; it was only decades later, in (perhaps ironically) her visual arts Master of Fine Arts program where the focus was not on writing, that she rediscovered a love for writing when a professor encouraged her to "write and write" in whatever way she pleased. Her teacher then read her writing and pointed out the most interesting passages, without any editing or assessment. Feeling seen and heard in this way allowed Maeve to feel connected not only to her teacher but also to her experience as a writer, which had been ruptured and fraught for many years.

For some people, though, writing in such a free-flowing manner, and having that writing be read by an audience, would be enormously difficult and stress-inducing. High school English teacher Giuseppe told me that, when he writes, he wants "100 percent of the audience to 100 percent get it 100 percent of the time." Even though he knows that expectation is "completely unreasonable," he continues to blame himself entirely if communication fails. As a writer, he believes his "disregard for audience is never appropriate." When I asked if he truly meant *never*, he repeated, "*Never*."

Knowing Giuseppe well enough, I would safely guess that he does not hold his students to such an egregiously harsh standard. And yet one may wonder: can they feel it? I say this as someone who is chronically self-flagellating, who has caught herself many times unwittingly projecting her own worried perfectionism onto her students.

I would argue that restoring his relationship with writing, for Giuseppe, might require restoring his relationship with his perceived audience but, perhaps most importantly, with himself. Write to please yourself is what I would suggest if I were asked for advice in a case like this. Write in a way that aims for clarity in *you*, that allows *you* to understand *you* and your ideas and feelings more clearly. Tap into that larger purpose and let it guide you.

Taking space to write with *less* audience awareness might counterintuitively help him reconnect with writing and ultimately communicate his ideas to others more effectively as well. Without seeking external validation, he might be able to practice seeking and receiving his own, to ultimately find that clearer message he is chasing.

## Restoring the Relationship with the Self and Others

Writing can also help restore the writer's relationship with the self in general. In a busy, fast-paced, noisy world crowded with information, hot takes, and travesties juxtaposed or interspersed with absurdity, writing gives us a chance to slow down, be mindful, reflect, and hear our own thoughts, to attune to our own feelings and senses.

This restoration of self can include the parts of ourselves that are fragmented by culture and society.

Marie Rose, a teacher of graduate education classes, told me about her process of working on two novels related to her connections to the land of Haiti. She grew up in the 1980s, during the height of the AIDS epidemic, which was a scary time to be Haitian, she said, as the Centers for Disease Control and Prevention declared Haitians to be part of the "4H Club"—heroin users, hemophiliacs, homosexuals, and Haitians—identities that were seen as risk factors associated with the autoimmune disease. Meanwhile, her parents were contending with having to flee from their beloved homeland, ruled by a violent dictatorship, and she was wrestling with what it meant to feel such a strong connection to Haitian culture and identity without ever having been to the country.

Creative writing gives her a chance to reconnect with the place of Haiti, with her extended family, and with a part of herself that may be less conscious for her on a daily basis. "It makes me think about how all of this is emerging because it's within me all the time," she mused. "I'm still making sense of it, reconciling with that lived experience, and how that experience shaped who I am."

Such rumination is not limited to her creative writing; it has also been present in the reflexive parts of her scholarly writing, where she has critically examined what it meant for her to grow up Haitian in America. Allowing herself to mine this terrain in all forms of her writing has facilitated a restoration of her connectedness to parts of herself and her identity she felt disconnected from, which is inherently healing in the sense of the word as *a movement toward wholeness*. It enables her, now, to guide her students in writing about their own often bifurcated identities and complex histories.

Writing can also help restore a person's relationship with others—if not externally, then at least internally. Lucy, a high school English teacher, said fiction writing has similarly helped her to connect and reconcile with her ancestry. Writing a fictional novel inspired by her grandmother and some long-held family secrets has meant grappling with her own anger, pain, and frustration and ultimately healing those wounds within herself and within her relationship with her deceased grandmother. The process of writing, in fact, both required *and* aided in this. As she worked to understand the semifictional character, she found grace for the real person as well.

What's happening here with writers like Marie Rose and Lucy may feel far afield from the type of writing we see or assign in our secondary classrooms. But I include these examples to suggest the true range and dimension of restorative possibility that writing holds. We can approach writing with a full understanding of its capacity to restore a writer's relationship with themselves, with writing, and with their own histories, families, communities, and memories. We can believe and thereby make space for that potential by inviting students to reflect on their identities and memories to the degree that they wish; by providing opportunities for them to practice exploring their own interests and inclinations through writing, to see where they lead; by affirming them in their pursuits, without interrupting a process of healing that is much larger than our class and its objectives and may more fully come to fruition years after they've left our classrooms.

And isn't that what we're really doing? Preparing them for life beyond their secondary education? Doesn't that end mean a whole lot more than making sure they're ready to write a perfect research paper in college?

When we see a digression in student writing that feels far afield from the apparent topic or our expectations, we can pause before we shut the digression down. Some important processing may be taking place. We might even express interest or encourage the digression to happen, either in the space of the assignment or elsewhere.

The restorative experiences I describe here represent a glimmer of what's possible when writers—no matter their age—are given a chance, and the support, to follow their intuitions and pursue what they feel called to understand and express.

## Transformative

The word "transformative" is listed here last by design, because in some ways I see it as the least mandatory. I make this point not to diminish the importance of transformative experience or to deny the fact that endemic changes large and small are *necessary* for our classrooms and systems. Instead, I am suggesting that, without a healing-centered approach, a leap to make writing a transformational experience for students can be dangerous. It can reinforce deficit notions, implying that our students need to change in some fundamental way, or it can inadvertently pressure us, teachers and students, to feel that everything we or our students write needs to be grand or groundbreaking.

An approach to writing that is humanizing, affirming, empowering, liberatory, trauma-sensitive, and restorative does not *need* to be so ambitious as to require some sort of radical transformation to occur as well. We don't need our students to change. We don't necessarily need to change ourselves either. Transformation and change are not synonymous, of course, but sometimes equated. Healing requires not so much changing ourselves but, more so, changing the conditions that surround and affect us so that we may become more fully ourselves—the selves we want to claim and be.

All of this said, with all the other characteristics present, I'd argue that a healing-centered approach to writing is likely to lend itself readily to transformative experience too—for the individuals practicing and experiencing it and even potentially for the system within which it is occurring. And that transformative experience may well be the fullest extension and greatest manifestation of a healing-centered process.

### Personal and Social Transformation

As I define them here, transformative practices and experiences are those that disrupt the status quo, break norms, and create new forms, opportunities, or pathways. In a classroom context, transformative practice includes looking critically at and subverting, rather than adapting to, conventional pedagogical approaches while inviting student self-determination.

In my view, a healing-centered approach to writing can transform the writer's relationship not only with writing but also with themselves, with others, with society, and with the rest of the natural world by promoting reflectiveness, action, and connection. The process of writing can break open new consciousness and awareness, while the product can communicate in a way that transforms not only minds and hearts but also policies, systems, and outcomes.

For many of the teachers I talked to in my research, reconnecting with writing was personally transformative for them. One found a new sense of community and connection through publishing her fiction online, which provided a helpful emotional outlet for her in the face of burnout. Another rediscovered confidence in her own voice through an experimental writing practice that inspired her to create extracurricular social-emotional learning workshops for middle school students that incorporate journaling and writing from the senses.

For high school English teacher Giuseppe, the most essential writing has a social conscience and purpose, with the capacity to transform the way people think and act. In that sense, writing can make an impact on the structures within society itself. Giuseppe's philosophy of writing influences the way he teaches writing. He encourages his students to write about social issues they care about and to speak out and take action through emails and letters. Despite the opportunity it creates, however, this philosophy leaves him feeling disillusioned when he's required to teach in forms that feel devoid of social purpose.

### Personal Growth as Social Growth

Asking students to write with honesty and authenticity about their own lives, experiences, opinions, observations, and identities is an approach that sometimes garners a reputation for being "soft" and unrigorous, yielding empty navel-gazing. But when done with purpose and intention, personal writing can be some of the most challenging and transformative writing possible.

In Marie Rose's Identity and Belonging class, in which her students are required to write reflexively about their own identities and positionalities through a researched lens, she said students have referred to it as the hardest class they ever took, as they comment, "I never had to confront myself. I never had to think about how I impacted others."

Being real with her students, opening up to them about the impacts of her own hybrid identity, and sharing stories of times when her own assumptions or stereotypings caught up to her gives students tacit permission to feel that they could be vulnerable as well. In effect, it transforms the norms of behavior in the classroom in a way that allows her and her students to transcend the status quo.

Intense honesty is transformative in any writing format because it is *not* the norm. Vulnerability is frightening for many people because it can be disruptive and uncomfortable. But that very messiness and discomfort are exactly what give the writing process its potential for healing.

Learning to write is not just—or even primarily—about skills; it's about being able to write with a complex perspective and with a larger purpose. According to Ernest Morrell (2003), a college writing course has no greater cause than to help developing writers become "engaged citizens and transformative intellectuals who see writing as a tool, if not *the* tool of social change" (p. 23). How might our secondary education classrooms prepare our students for such an expectation?

For one thing, we can help enrich and extend their sense of purpose for writing *beyond* merely getting a grade or finishing the task. We can encourage them to identify at least one additional purpose that is really their own, that they personally feel connected to. That purpose might be to finally finish an essay on time, to write something they feel proud of, to experiment with a new style or approach. Or the purpose could be related to the content: to learn about how federal immigration policies impact their local communities through research and analysis, to argue their impassioned stance for or against generative AI use in schools, to advocate for gender-neutral bathrooms.

A transformative approach to writing in the secondary education classroom can provide space for students to discover, hone, and activate a larger sense of purpose while equipping these writers with the confidence and support needed to pursue these aims. A transformative approach can create conditions in which pain can turn to insight, insight can turn to wisdom, and that wisdom can be shared—in service of ourselves and our healing but also in service of our communities and toward the world we and our students want to live in.

## References

Angelou, M. (2019, September 7). *There is no greater agony than bearing an untold story inside you*. [Status update]. Facebook.

Angelou, M. (2025, February 10). *Dr. Maya Angelou on National Freedom Day, we honor the signing…* [Video]. Facebook. https://www.facebook.com/MayaAngelou/videos/2876835225852129

Camangian, P., & Cariaga, S. (2022). Social and emotional learning is hegemonic miseducation: Students deserve humanization instead. *Race, Ethnicity & Education*, *25*(7), 901–921. https://doi.org/10.1080/13613324.2020.1798374

D'Agostino, S. (2023, June 5). *How AI tools both help and hinder equity in higher ed*. Inside Higher Ed. https://www.insidehighered.com/news/tech-innovation/artificial-intelligence/2023/06/05/how-ai-tools-both-help-and-hinder-equity

Dutro, E., & Caasi, E. (2022). The complexities of trauma in responsive teaching. *Language Arts*, *99*(5), 358–362.

Enriquez, G., Gill, V., Campano, G., Flores, T. T., Jones, S., Leander, K. M., McKnight, L., & Price-Dennis, D. (2024). Generative AI and composing: An intergenerational conversation among literacy scholars. *English Teaching: Practice & Critique (Emerald Group Publishing Limited)*, *23*(1), 6–22. https://doi.org/10.1108/ETPC-08-2023-0104

Freire, P. (2000). *Pedagogy of the oppressed* (30th anniversary ed.). Continuum.

Haddix, M. (2015). Preparing community-engaged teachers. *Theory Into Practice*, *54*(1), 63–70.

Herman, D. (2022, December 16). The end of high-school English. *The Atlantic*. https://www.theatlantic.com/technology/archive/2022/12/openai-chatgpt-writing-high-school-english-essay/672412/

hooks, b. (1994). *Teaching to transgress*. Routledge.

Jones, S. P. (2022). The language of curriculum violence. *English Journal*, *111*(5), 15–17.

Kim, G. M. (2021). What's in a name? Language, identity, and power in English education. *English Education*, *53*(3), 224–231.

Menakem, R. (2017). *My grandmother's hands: Racialized trauma and the pathway to mending our hearts and bodies*. Central Recovery Press.

Morrell, E. (2003). Writing the word and the world: Critical literacy as critical textual production. Paper presented at the *Annual Meeting of the Conference on College Composition and Communication* (54th, New York, NY, March 19–22, 2003).

Muhammad, G. (2020). *Cultivating genius: An equity framework for culturally and historically responsive literacy*. Scholastic Inc.

Nankin, I. (2016). *Breathe for change: Changing the world, one teacher at a time* [Doctoral dissertation, University of Wisconsin-Madison]. ProQuest Dissertations & Theses Global.

Page, C., & Woodland, E. (2023). *Healing justice lineages: Dreaming at the crossroads of liberation, collective care, and safety*. North Atlantic.

Pennebaker, J. W., & Smyth, J. M. (2016). *Opening up by writing it down: How expressive writing improves health and eases emotional pain* (3rd ed.). The Guilford Press.

Prilleltensky, I. (2008). The role of power in wellness, oppression, and liberation: The promise of psychopolitical validity. *Journal of Community Psychology, 36*(2), 116–136. https://doi.org/10.1002/jcop.20225

Smith, L. T. (2021). *Decolonizing methodologies: Research and Indigenous peoples*. Bloomsbury.

Tayles, M. (2021). Trauma-informed writing pedagogy: Ways to support student writers affected by trauma and traumatic stress. *Teaching English in the Two Year College, 48*(3), 295–313. https://ezproxyles.flo.org/login?url=https://www.proquest.com/scholarly-journals/trauma-informed-writing-pedagogy-ways-support/docview/2526905410/se-2

Topa, W., & Narvaez, D. (2022). *Restoring the kinship worldview: Indigenous voices introduce 28 precepts for rebalancing life on planet Earth*. North Atlantic Books.

# 4

# Embodying *Why*

## Values and Priorities of a Healing-Centered Approach

While I would not personally believe any attempts to capture the precise figure, it's undeniable that we as teachers make an inordinate number of decisions per day. We also grapple constantly with the cognitive and emotional dissonance of somewhat competing priorities: student well-being versus student "progress"; curriculum standards versus student engagement; differentiated instruction versus pacing expectations; and maintaining "rigor" versus providing support. These are just some of the broad categories that don't necessarily need to oppose one another but sometimes do.

The reality of these paradoxes became abundantly clear to me (and, I'd guess, to many of us) during the Covid-19 pandemic that began in March 2020, when a slew of our unquestioned habits and responsibilities were suddenly unreplicable as we taught from our kitchens and dining rooms. *What really matters here?* we were forced to ask ourselves. *What is really at stake? What is non-negotiable, and what can we do without?*

A couple years later, I pursued these questions formally through my dissertation research because their rhetorical nature no longer satisfied me. Back in the classroom, with the return of

DOI: 10.4324/9781003752721-4

the relentless bell-to-bell decision-making, I wanted consistency and the kind of inner guidance that was so much easier to hear and rely on in the slowness of the pause the pandemic foisted upon us. I needed real answers, even if they were only well-researched postulations.

As my inquiry progressed and crystalized, a goal formed: to identify what a healing-centered approach to writing is and how to enact and foster it for our students. I concluded that the most effective—maybe *only*—way to truly enact it is to *embody* it. This embodiment involves being clear about not just *what* a healing-centered approach to writing is but *why* it matters.

To embody an ethos means to take on not just its characteristics but its values and priorities. In this chapter, I outline four core values and priorities for those of us who aim to embody a healing-centered approach to writing: (1) psychic and affective safety, (2) belonging, (3) belief in the writer's abilities and possibilities, and (4) positive experience. Bringing these values and priorities to the center of our practice does not mean nothing else matters but can help us make decisions that align with what, at least to my mind, matters *most*: creating spaces where humanizing, affirming, empowering, liberatory, trauma-sensitive, restorative, and transformative experiences with writing are possible.

## Psychic and Affective Safety

The Greek word *psyche* most closely translates to *soul* or *spirit*, but it also captures the abstract concept of *mind* that transcends the physical *brain*. If we care about the safety of a whole person, we cannot neglect the psychic dimension—no matter how strange that phrase might sound in an educational context.

The psychic (mind/soul) element can be seen as part of a person's larger affective experience—meaning how a person is *affected* by the people and things around them, based on factors such as their mood, personality, identities, physical attributes, needs, or experiences.

Writing is a vulnerable act where the self is on display and up for scrutiny and evaluation, no matter how personal the subject matter. Even if not intended as such, criticism of someone's *writing* can easily be internalized as criticism of the *writer*. I talked to one teacher, Giuseppe, who is well aware of his strong writing skills but no longer chooses to write in forms beyond social media snippets after being told too many times that his writing is "too much." "It feels like a gut punch when anyone tells me that my writing is too much," he said, "because it makes me feel like *I'm* too much." Now think of students who are told that their use of language is wrong if it doesn't entirely conform to the rules of standardized American English. That their ideas are too obvious, too simple, too cliché. That their sentences don't make sense.

And it's not just the skills or execution that can elicit strong responses like the "gut punch" Giuseppe described. It's perhaps even more prominently the content.

The writing process, ideally, engages the mind comprehensively and intensely on a topic. But some topics can trigger a stress response that can cause trauma or retraumatization—and it's not always easy, for the teacher *or* the student, to predict which topics will do so. While a Black or Jewish student is most obviously vulnerable to topics such as the Tulsa Race Massacre or the Holocaust, any student might find themselves emotionally distraught upon learning and writing in detail about human atrocities of the past, especially when these travesties illuminate the true impact of injustices that endure in the present, such as racism and antisemitism, or genocides occurring today.

Close-reading and analyzing a book like *The Catcher in the Rye* might provoke a student who has lost a loved one or struggled with their mental health, while a student reflecting on the elusiveness of the American Dream in *The Great Gatsby* might find themselves ruminating on their own family's financial woes. I've had countless students shut down or stall out on a writing project not out of laziness or procrastination but because some aspect of their topic panged against a fear, anxiety, insecurity, memory, or fraught relationship in their life. It doesn't always make "sense" in an obvious way, to them or to me, nor does it have to, for the impact to be intensely real.

## Safety or "Coddling"?

The risk of causing psychic and affective harm always outweighs the benefits of pushing a student to their limits.

But prioritizing safety of any kind over intellectual "rigor" is not always a popular stance. Some see it as a form of coddling that promotes mediocrity and a lack of accountability. As teachers, we may feel pressured to keep the focus on "grit" and "resilience," to avoid "dumbing down" our teaching.

But as countless scholars have established, "rigor," "grit," and even "resilience" have become politicized terms that, on their surface, may seem harmless or helpful but can perpetuate racism in the classroom, when applied without critical context.

"African-Americans are resilient and gritty because we have to be to survive, but it is misleading, naive, and dangerous to remove our history on both sides of the water from the conversation about grit," writes Bettina Love (2019, n.p.). The legacy of African Americans' remarkable resilience in the United States dates back to the colonial days of the early 1600s, when African people were violently ripped from their homelands, to be tortured and enslaved, and forced to endure horrific conditions. Extolling the real virtue of resilience without at least equally confronting the unjust conditions that require resilience, and from which that resilience was born, propagates a harmful status quo.

In schools, an emphasis on resilience and grit keeps the focus on what students (and, in some cases, teachers) need to do to cope with unfair, inequitable, or unsustainable policies and practices, rather than placing the onus on the system itself that needs to change—along with the people who uphold it. Dena Simmons (2019) writes: "Schools and districts have spoon-fed lessons on grit to mostly students of color, suggesting that we must 'fix' them by making them grittier so that they can adapt to—rather than disrupt—racism and inequality in schools" (n.p.). In this sense, the word itself can feel like a dog whistle.

*Rigor*, too, is a loaded word. While often intended to mean academic challenge and integrity, it has connotations that usually equate with long-held standards of demand and performance that date back to a time when education catered primarily to White male students of the middle to upper classes (Jack & Sathy, 2021). If rigor means a 10th grader reading 40 pages a night, or a seventh grader being assigned an at-home essay due the next day, consider: which of your students might find that challenging? If these students are told that all they need is "grit" to keep up, which of these students is favored? What realities might such an admonishment ignore?

While an assignment given to a full class may be the same, the students' experience of that assignment is not. A child living in a short-term foster home being encouraged to interview their parents for a class assignment will not receive that assignment in quite the same way as someone going home to a loving family they have lived with all their lives. The affective atmosphere of a classroom or school hits individual and groups of students differently (Dernikos et al., 2020). Whose identities are represented in the books we read in English class? How are those identities portrayed? Whose writing is held up as a model?

The affective atmosphere in a classroom also prominently includes the teacher. How a student feels in the room with the teacher depends on not just who they are and what they do but also who that *student* is—what kinds of experiences they've had with teachers or even certain personality types in the past. Maybe the teacher reminds them of a mean uncle they have. Maybe overtures of kindness feel triggering for a student who has trouble trusting adults after being let down too many times. Maybe an English language-learning student feels that their hyperarticulate English teacher is judging their speech patterns, because that's happened to them before.

Psychic and affective safety means being aware not of what these variables definitively *are* but that they may exist in ways we cannot always see or anticipate.

### Students' and Teachers' Needs Are Interrelated

And then there is the students' effect on the teacher. We, too, come into the classroom with our own unique challenges, triggers, and backgrounds. We then take in and often carry our students' stories and pains and fears with us throughout our days.

This effect is compounded by the fact that student writers often use writing as a way to process complex emotions and will especially do so if they perceive a sensitive audience in their teacher. In the midst of this, how do we care for our own psychic and affective safety?

Miriam—who has taught creative writing for decades—emphasizes the importance of maintaining boundaries. That includes teaching students to assess their own boundaries as well. She frequently tells her undergraduate students, "Please don't write about anything for workshop that you're not ready to talk about in a somewhat distanced way." Yet students—especially young students—don't always know how ready they are or how they will react to other people's responses to their work, including a teacher's.

Any teacher who has helped a high school student with their college essay can likely relate to this tension between the content of the material and the craft of the writing. Even with an explicit focus on craft, the writing is still personal and needs to be handled as such. Students will frequently write around their trauma, channeling their stories into abstract metaphorical language that they feel very attached to but that remains inaccessible to their reader. "I'm not sure I know what's happening here," I might say gently.

In cases like these, I try to help the writer understand how they could be keeping their readers too far at bay; I might gently encourage them to consider being a tad more direct or even writing about something else entirely. But I also remind them that it is *their choice* how much they wish to share, and how explicit they choose to be. I assure them that it is their choice to remain as abstract as they wish, even if it means losing certain readers. I try, most of all, to pause and tune in to what is happening for the writer. Why are they writing about this? How is it affecting them? How comfortable do they seem with the idea of opening up further? How important is this piece to them? What is more important? That the writing be clear to a reader or that they write this truth they need to write, in the exact way they wish to write it? The answers are never 100% clear. But I'd rather err on the side of protecting the writer's authority to choose than risk causing damage.

No matter how discerning we feel we are or try to be, ensuring psychic and affective safety is never a perfect science, and the capacity for harm is always present.

### Safety as a Condition for Challenge

In my view, establishing safety is the opposite of coddling; instead, it is the basis for true, deep, and probing intellectual and emotional challenge. When writers feel safe enough to take an honest, critical look at themselves and their surroundings, they can start to consider how their own identities are shaped and perceived by, but also how they impact, the larger social world of which they are part.

For Marie Rose, a first-generation Haitian American and first-generation college student, learning to show up as her full authentic self in academic spaces "has been a journey." Now, she sees doing so as necessary to her pedagogy:

> For me to ask my students in my identity class to talk about their positionalities, creating environments where they have to talk about times when they included or excluded others, as a faculty member, I have to show up and be ready to do the same, and that's not something

> we're trained to do, or something someone *should* do because they feel they *have* to do, but it really has to come from the soul level, because students will know if you are BS'ing in class.

Showing up authentically involves adopting a regular practice and habit of self-reflection and inquiry. It might also mean being more vulnerable with colleagues, with friends, with family, and being willing to take risks in our conversations and relationships so we can learn about ourselves and each other.

While Marie Rose teaches in higher ed, it's worth asking: how might such vulnerability show up in an eighth-grade history classroom? In a 12th-grade English classroom? In *yours?*

## Belonging

"Belonging" has become a popular, you might even call it, *buzzword* in education in recent years. We've somewhat moved on from "inclusion," partly in the cowardly flight from DEI (Diversity, Equity, and Inclusion) and all that the acronym was supposed to represent and address and partly out of recognition that we and our students need to feel more than that our presence is allowed and tolerated. We need to know in our hearts and minds that room does not need to be made for any of us because we are already meant to be here, in community with one another.

But creating a sense of belonging for everyone requires more than just saying "you belong"; it means showing that truth in every facet. That includes writing instruction.

We can foster belonging for students through their writing by giving them the liberty—and helping them develop the capacity—to *choose* which parts of themselves, or which refractions of their voice, to bring to bear. It means being a receptive audience on the other end to listen for what they have to say.

That might mean giving students plenty of opportunities to write without overly dictating tone or formality—in other words, open space for reflective freewriting where they don't have to think about grammar, punctuation, spelling, or clarity; where they can talk to us or themselves on the page, in a voice that feels natural to them, and we can respond as *humans*, not evaluators.

Fostering belonging in writing can also mean inviting students to draw on their cultural heritage, multiple languages, interests, and identities—ensuring that they frequently have the opportunity and choice to do so, even if not in every assignment.

But to fully understand why belonging matters to writing, it is important to understand when, how, and why some situations can create the very opposite.

## Anti-Racist Writing Pedagogy and Belonging

To prioritize belonging requires an inherently and explicitly anti-racist approach (Inoue, 2016). It roots out harmful practices in every realm of teaching and learning, including the comments we make on students' papers, such as feedback that tells them to "go to the WC [Writing Center] to learn English," an actual teacher comment Morrison and Tonry (2021) expose and critique in their article, "Racism in the Margins" (p. 86).

Anti-racist writing pedagogy reckons with the fact that a comment like, "Go to the writing center" could have a harmless impact on a White student whose first language is English but is freighted with racialized implications when wielded upon a Black or Brown student whose writing does not conform to the dominant standardized American English. It reminds us to pay attention to who is in the room with us, what we may not know about their identities, and how our words, assignments, responses, and approaches might differently affect each one of them.

But anti-racist writing pedagogy is also concerned with more than interpersonal relations. It's also concerned with how we present and ask students to engage with content in our classroom. It requires us to evaluate what we ask our students to write about and how.

When I started teaching high school at age 30, after a decade of teaching college, I spent my last month of summer reading and rereading canonical texts I hadn't encountered in years—*The Catcher in the Rye, The Great Gatsby, The Crucible, Fahrenheit 451*. The one book by an author of color that I needed to prepare lessons for was Richard Wright's *Black Boy*.

What I felt in that month of successively devouring all of these books, with their outsized influence on American culture and generations of students, was a remarkable heaviness. It caused in me a kind of deer-in-the-headlights freeze-up. Despite any individual value they held, I felt overwhelmed by the subtle and overt violence and trauma pervading each of these texts. Encountering this intensity and volume of personal and social strife wasn't "normal" to me yet, or anymore, since my own high school days of reading "the canon."

When my classes reached our unit on *Black Boy*, I was struck early on by how many of my mostly White students wrote about racism as a relic of the past, with sentences essentially saying, "This goes to show how bad things were before we fixed racism." After responding to each one of these comments piecemeal, with prompting questions such as, "And where do we see racism showing up today?" I realized I needed to take a more holistic approach.

I needed to do more work up front. I needed to make my own stance clear, not just to educate and help deepen the thinking of all students in the class, not just to stave off ignorant or racist comments that students might make in their writing or in class discussions, but to ensure that students of color weren't finding themselves in a place to either (a) write something that bypasses, erases, diminishes, or negates their own experience and awareness because they think it's off-topic, irrelevant, or contrary to the "right answer" I might be looking for or (b) exhaust themselves with the hard work of illustrating the ongoing realities of cultural and systemic injustice rather than allowing that truth to be embedded within the place that we start from.

As we continued reading the memoir, I began to incorporate secondary texts, asking students to make connections between these texts and our primary source. We went back in time and read excerpts from Frederick Douglass's *Narrative of the Life of Frederick Douglass, an American Slave*. We went forward in time, listening to and reflecting on songs like Sam Cooke's "A Change is Gonna Come," a Civil Rights anthem recounting the singer's experiences of discrimination growing up Louisiana, along with Bob Dylan's "The Lonesome Death of Hattie Carroll," which tells the true story of the titular Black barmaid's murder at the hands of a wealthy White tobacco farmer's son who received a six-month sentence after beating the woman to death with a cane. Both songs were released in 1964, decades after the incidents Wright recounts in his story.

And then we went further forward, reading excerpts from Ta-Nehisi Coates' *Between the World and Me*, which illuminates the racism he faced growing up in the 1970s-'80s and up through the present day, while connecting it to the racism he was aware that his son would be facing at the time of the book's publication in 2015. We also looked at Peggy McIntosh's (1989) "White Privilege Checklist," so that each person in the class could self-reflect on the impact of race in their life in the present.

By the time students got to the final writing project for the unit, they were more prepared to analyze the text on a deeper level; they had a fairer shot at *not* writing something denialist or racist, and they could make deeper and more complex connections between the memoir and the "real world" around them—almost always part of the stated goals of a strong literary analysis. And I gained a new layer of understanding about the difference between teaching about race and fostering racial literacy.

The following year, after a reduction in force, I switched to a different school, with different books to teach, including Harper Lee's *To Kill a Mockingbird*. Lee's novel is one that I feel I can't teach responsibly without asking students to interrogate *why* this novel about racial injustice written by a White woman is so widely read, sometimes ranked above the Bible in terms of influence on American culture.

After reading too many essays about what a Civil Rights hero the main character Atticus is and how special his children are because they aren't growing up racist like their peers, I now ensure that students have closely read and written about the scene where Scout says, "Well, Dill, after all he's just a Negro," when her friend is crying after Tom Robinson is degraded by the prosecutor while on trial for a crime he didn't commit. We also closely study the scene when Atticus calls his rabidly racist neighbor, Mrs. Dubose, "a great lady" and a model of courage for her children. We do this not to entirely undermine the positive work Atticus is doing as a character but to complicate and disrupt both the racist/not-racist binary and the problematic overemphasis on the "goodness" of the White characters in the book whose not-racism is not nearly enough.

Similarly, with William Golding's *Lord of the Flies*, after reading too many papers extolling the character "Piggy" as being the most intelligent character on the island, the voice of reason, the one the children *should* have allowed themselves to be led by when stranded on the uninhabited island, I make sure that my students have read and written about the climactic scene before his death when he cries, "Which is better—to be a pack of painted Indians like you are, or to be sensible like Ralph is?" I ensure that we have read about the racist history of the word "savage" as applied to Indigenous peoples, so when they write essays about the book, they can think twice (or more) about what they mean when they use the term in their own analysis. They can critically analyze the novel's use of the term and avoid reducing the text's meaning into another false binary, in this case between "civilization" and "savagery."

And all of this is so-called "rigorous" learning, because it pushes student writers to analyze beyond the written text, to apply context to critical analysis, to synthesize outside knowledge and new learning with close reading and interpretation, and to evaluate the larger significance and implications of the text they are writing about.

### *Belonging as a "Writer"*

In addition to ensuring that students feel they belong in the writing classroom, we can help them feel like they belong *with* the writing; we can help make it possible for them to see themselves as writers. Writers are people who write.

Many of the teachers I spoke to in my research process are also people who write, but not all of them feel comfortable calling themselves "writers." One person I spoke to said that, at one point, she didn't feel like a "real writer" because she primarily wrote academically and not creatively—not in a way that made her "soul feel free."

With extensively published teachers like herself questioning their ability to claim the title of *writer*—wondering if they are *entitled* to write in the way their soul feels called to—it's not hard to imagine how a middle or high school student would find themselves silenced and held back, like they don't belong in a room full of "writers." Like they don't belong seeing themselves as such.

When we provide students with space to write autonomously and freely, when we frame writing as a series of choices they have (or *get?*) to make, when we take them and their words seriously and respond with authentic interest, we may help them feel like they *and* their words belong.

## Belief in the Writer's Abilities and Possibilities

What does it mean to truly *believe* in our students? To believe that they are more than capable of producing a meaningful piece of writing, something that they can be proud of and maybe even enjoy. Something that *we* as their teachers (and primary readers) can be proud of and enjoy as well.

Passively, we might all say or presume that we believe in our students' ability to do well. But—and this might be more radical than it even sounds—I'd argue that it's the equivalent of a shrug and a sarcastic "Anything's possible," unless we are actively *practicing* and *prioritizing* that belief—and not just in *some* of our students but in *all* of them.

I'll admit my bias here is shaped by my own relentless optimism. I *expect* to see people's best selves, and as a result, I feel like I often do. Am I disappointed sometimes? Of course. I'm aware of the quote, "Expectation is the root of heartache," falsely attributed to Shakespeare, and I know that a chorus of other quotable quotes supports it. But despite the truth in these words—and maybe it's because heartache is already a close companion of mine—the risks that come with these high expectations are ones that I reflexively sign up, over and over, to take.

## Belief and Support Go Hand in Hand

With each of the values and priorities listed in this book, I try to consider the good, well-meaning opposite. In this case, it might be "support." Support comes in the form of scaffolding, modifications, and moderated expectations. Every student faces different challenges when it comes to writing, and some face more than others. If we set our expectations too high and just convince ourselves that students can do it, we may be setting them up for failures that can further deplete their confidence and our own.

But as a writing center teacher for many years, I have seen many assignments so overly scaffolded to the point where students no longer feel that the words—let alone the ideas—are their own. This has led me to wonder: do we as teachers expect or even *want* them to be?

Zaretta Hammond (2021) writes, "Too often, when we deem students behind academically, we increase compliance measures and actually decelerate learning. We over-scaffold rather than coach students to engage in productive struggle to process the content" (n.p.). Scaffolds are important and helpful, and I am a late-stage convert to their consistent use, having *increased* my use of them in recent years while working with a school-avoidant population but also with so-called "Honors" students as well. Trauma and neurodivergence can make writing extremely difficult, and some students benefit from an intense level of guidance that allows them to fill in blanks with their thinking, taking structure and organization off the table so that the skills of comprehension and analysis can be isolated.

Yet this same neurodivergence that craves structure can also just as easily yield frustration with the appearance of box after box or blank after blank to be filled in. For some students, that so-often-dreaded blank document is *much* more appealing—especially when they are given lots of leeway in terms of what they're expected to produce.

In some cases, offering scaffolds with the option to bypass them entirely is enough. In the best cases, I've been able to sit with students and add scaffolds (in the form of sentence-starters and blanks) on the spot, as needed, while we write an essay together, sentence by sentence. Such an approach allows the student to see how a piece of writing can emerge organically, and it frequently allows me to back off as the essay takes shape and the writer finds their own rhythm with it. For a handful of students with whom I worked intensely over a longer span of time, I found that repeated instances of this approach allowed them to gain autonomy and confidence, as they began to anticipate next steps on their own.

The danger in too much scaffolding, however, is how it can reinforce the idea that there is one rigid way to respond to a prompt, one rigid way to structure an essay. It also eliminates the delight of the unexpected, the possibility that can emerge when all of the scaffolding is dropped, a prompt is offered, and we essentially say to ourselves, "Let's see what they come up with. Let's see what they do."

Yes, sometimes what they do is *nothing*. But even that helps us learn about who they are, how they write, what they might need, and what might emerge when we step far back, encourage, and somehow make it clear that we *expect* that they will produce something interesting. Especially when we respond accordingly, with interest.

## The Realities of Self-Doubt

Every writer I know contends with self-doubt—with the feeling that what we have to say is not unique or interesting or important, with the feeling that we may not be able to finish or even start a project and that it won't be good enough if we do. Sometimes these doubts are simply rooted in a natural insecurity. But often they stem from past comments we've received, from teachers or other readers—from external judgments that may not even align with our own visions and goals as writers.

Ethan, a high school Social Studies teacher, described his experiences with writing as a "rollercoaster." In high school, he enjoyed writing on his own and kept a journal, especially during a family trip to Portugal, where he reflected on his ethnic heritage and identity, making sense of its hybridity.

His relationship with writing changed dramatically after receiving an F on his first essay in college. He was advised by the teaching assistant (TA) who graded the paper to visit the university's writing center, which he did. Her most prominent directive was to eliminate traces of his voice in the writing. "Her advice was, you shouldn't *have* any voice," he said with a laugh. "'Your opinions as the author don't matter.' So that was very important. That stood out. And I thought, 'Well that's how I'm going to teach my students.'"

After consistently meeting with his professor and his school's writing center, Ethan became adept at this "objective" style of writing and considers himself a very "capable" academic writer now. For years, he taught students to write in the exact way in which he was taught. Now, after Covid and with the emergence of generative artificial intelligence (AI), he has started to reimagine his approach, allowing students to use personal pronouns in their writing when relevant and experimenting with less traditional or conscripted approaches. He also assigns writing projects with a degree of openness that allows for the unexpected, giving students a sense of control, with almost an underlying assumption that they will be able to come up with something great. Perhaps uncoincidentally, he has begun journaling again and has even experimented with some creative writing on his own.

For all of us as teachers, it's worth asking ourselves: if a student isn't conforming to the exact expectations laid out, what *else* might be there, latent? Instead of immediately rejecting what has come in, let it inform you. Honor what the *writer* might be trying to do and help them to explore what is *possible* in the writing. Yes, maybe you can let the student know how the writing has *not* achieved the expectations you outlined, but you can also consider the fact that these averted expectations might not be a terrible thing, because maybe something *else* is happening. Just because a student doesn't conform to a certain standard does not mean they don't have great *ability* in writing.

His professor's comments made Ethan doubt himself as a writer for many years and led him to teach writing in a way that felt rigid and restrictive for him as a teacher and for his students as well. As he gained more belief in his own writing skills and found the norms of learning disrupted by factors such as Covid and AI, he embraced an opportunity for change that his students now benefit from as well.

## Eschewing Prognosis

While the limitations that some writers face are certainly real, it is dangerous and harmful when a teacher or anybody equips themselves with the authority to determine a writer's potential and ability. No matter how certain we might feel about the insurmountability of a student's challenges with writing, we need a degree of restraint around ascribing any kind of firm prognosis. People *remember* being told things like "Your writing is weak" or "Maybe writing is not your thing."

In *Braiding Sweetgrass*, Robin Wall Kimmerer (2022) writes, "It is the duty of birds to sing, and the rest of us to receive the song as a gift" (pp. 263–264). The same ethos can be applied toward teachers of writing. What could change if we viewed our role in this way—as helping student writers find their song and hearing it as a gift?

With regard to your own relationship with writing, I assume that you can at least to some degree relate to self-doubt, because it's part of the human condition but also because writing is *hard*. It requires a lot from any of us, even if our skills are quite strong.

That said, if you're reading this book, I also assume that you—at the very least—never gave up all hope with writing. You never completely lost faith in its importance.

> Who helped keep that alive for you? And how?
> Who made you feel heard?
> Who made you feel like they *wanted* to hear what you have to say?
> What kind of difference did that make for you?

I'm sure, if you are a teacher of writing, that you have been able to offer this belief for many of the student writers who have passed through your classrooms. But we might push ourselves to ask:

> Who else can I do this for? Who else might really need it?
> How can I adjust my regular stance so that anyone who needs this receptive and encouraging ear can more readily receive it?

## Positive Experience

Schools, let's face it, are dreaded spaces for too many students. You might have your own memories of feeling tortured by a boring lecture or much worse: being targeted by racists or bigots or being constantly in trouble.

Even those of us who loved to learn might have found ourselves frequently disengaged. In *The Message*, Coates (2024) writes of his schooling experiences as a kind of "bait and switch," where his love for learning was stifled by an emphasis on following directions and sitting still. He describes riffling, as an adult, through his old school artifacts in his parents' house and realizing how long he'd held onto the shame of feeling that something was wrong with him. Teachers were rankled by his messy handwriting and restlessness and wrote comments like "wastes time" in his report cards. He reflects, "Sometimes I wonder how I got out—that is, how in god's name a child who could barely write a sentence in a straight line would become a writer" (pp. 65–66). And not just any writer—one who is a #1 *New York Times* bestselling author and National Book Award winner.

My own school avoidance started in elementary school with a similar frustration. Sitting at a desk all day, doing activities I didn't care about—or worse yet for me, being asked to socialize—left me asking for breaks every day, as I rationed out opportunities to go to the water fountain or the nurse. By high school and college, I found it easier to skip out entirely. I still did my work but often in a space and at a pace of my own choosing.

In *Imagination: A Manifesto*, Ruha Benjamin (2024) calls U.S. schooling a "pressure-cooker of stressors" (p. 38), where the imagination is stifled in favor of testing and standards, and social dynamics foster disconnection and widespread mental health issues. "What, then," she asks, "would liberating imagination look like? Schools could grow our hearts, not just our minds, helping us reimagine who and what we value" (p. 41).

> What better way to foster such reimagining than through writing?

A healing-centered approach to writing can bring enjoyment to the forefront for writers. It emphasizes opportunity within the *process* of writing and focuses less on the product than on the *experience* of creating the product.

My third-grade daughter's recent writing experience comes to mind here. In a small group, she and her peers wrote and produced a play, designing costumes and making props and ultimately performing the play for their class. They'd finished a long unit on frogs, so they were instructed to incorporate details about the amphibians into their play. The culminating event was called the Freaky Frog Fest, where they celebrated each other's creations and, as she recounted to me later, laughed joyfully the whole way through. When I asked her how the performance went, she said something that was, to me, unexpectedly profound: "Great! But what I really liked was making it."

No, writing isn't always a fun Freaky Frog Fest. Yes, it is often hard work. Prioritizing positive experience doesn't mean bypassing the challenges; it means trying to ensure that the end result is not all that matters.

"Positive" can mean different things to different people, but I chose the word deliberately here for its variability and expansiveness. Although some people may never *enjoy* writing, "positive" doesn't just mean enjoyable; it can also mean *meaningful*, *cathartic*, or *interesting*.

The phrase "positive experience" is meant to help us pause and weigh the costs and benefits of our choices and actions against a priority other than "producing high-quality work" or "mastering the standards." It compels us to ask: What might the student *feel*, both during and at the end of this process? What memory will this process yield for them—one of apathy or one of inspiration? One of shame or one of affirmation? One of dread or one of joy?

## "Writing" Beyond the Essay

How many of us have introduced a writing assignment to our classes, only to be met with a series of groans? "Another *essay?*" "I *hate* writing!"

But what if writing meant more than just another essay—or even just another short story or poem? What if writing meant processing, expressing, and sharing what you know, think, feel, or have learned in a way that makes the most sense for *you* as the author? What if part of the challenge was figuring out what that is?

With such an aim in mind, high school Social Studies teacher Ethan and his curriculum partner completely redesigned a research project they had been assigning for years in their Advanced Placement U.S. History class. While students were no longer required to write a formal academic essay as in years past, they were required to write reflections and research memos along the way.

Initially, Ethan and his partner worried that the project would be seen as less serious than when a long, formal research paper was required, but those fears were allayed early on. "If anything, it was harder to come up with those easy-way-outs," he recalls. "If someone did something that was mediocre, it was much more clear. As opposed to the research paper where mostly they looked the same."

The teachers quickly noticed how engaged their students were by being given so much freedom and choice in topic *and* form. That engagement wasn't always easy or fun—just the opposite. Some students became *so* invested in the process that they admitted, in the end, that it was a lot harder than writing "just another essay." Yet it was still "positive," because they cared and they learned and they likely grew and they ultimately experienced something (positively) memorable.

### Joy in Liberatory Experience

While school is, yes, a source of dread for many students, for many others it is an escape, a reprieve, a place of solace and comfort.

For one teacher I spoke to, school is where a sense of wonder was instilled in her. At home, life was traumatic and challenging, but in school, she was given a chance to use her imagination in whimsical ways—to look out the window and describe the rain, for example, with whatever words she could find. Those memories shaped her approach to teaching and compelled her to ensure that she was bringing a similar magic into her own approach as well—for any student who needed it.

People of any age can rediscover such magic. After Maeve's teacher in her photography program asked her to write and write and write, with no pressure at all to make it good, Maeve rediscovered a joy in writing that she hadn't felt since she was a child. She began writing stories, poems, journal entries—whatever felt right—and while academic writing continued to be a challenge for her, that feeling of challenge no longer dominated her relationship with writing. In turn, as a workshop leader, she is now able to help her middle school students untighten the strictures of writing and unlock joy in their process as well.

Think of your favorite or most "positive" experiences with writing. What shape did the writing take? Who was there? What were the instructions, requirements, or prompts? What kind of guidance was offered? What did you discover? What did you feel? How might you infuse such positive experiences into your teaching of writing today?

## References

Benjamin, R. (2024). *Imagination: A manifesto*. W.W. Norton & Company.

Coates, T. (2024). *The message*. One World.

Dernikos, B., Lesko, N., McCall, S., & Niccolini, A. (2020). *Mapping the affective turn in education: Theory, research, and pedagogy*. Routledge.

Hammond, Z. (2021, June 22). Liberatory education: Integrating the science of learning and culturally responsive practice. *American Educator*, *45*(2), 4.

Inoue, A. B. (2016). Foreword: On antiracist agendas. In F. Condon & V. A. Young (Eds.), *Performing antiracist pedagogy in rhetoric, writing, and communication* (pp. xi–xx). WAC Clearinghouse. https://doi.org/10.37514/ATD-B.2016.0933.1.2

Jack, J., & Sathy, V. (2021, September 24). It's time to cancel the word "rigor". *The Chronicle of Higher Education*. https://www.chronicle.com/article/its-time-to-cancel-the-word-rigor

Kimmerer, R. W. (2022). *Braiding sweetgrass for young adults: Indigenous wisdom, scientific knowledge, and the teachings of plants*. Zest.

Love, B. L. (2019, February 13). "Grit is in our DNA": Why teaching grit is inherently anti-black (opinion). *Education Week*. https://www.edweek.org/leadership/opinion-grit-is-in-our-dna-why-teaching-grit-is-inherently-anti-black/2019/02

McIntosh, P. (1989). White privilege: Unpacking the invisible knapsack. *Peace and Freedom Magazine*, 10–12. https://med.umn.edu/sites/med.umn.edu/files/2022-12/White-Privilege_McIntosh-1989.pdf

Morrison, G., & Tonry, K. (2021). Racism in the margins. *Writing Program Administration*, *44*(3), 85.

Simmons, D. (2019, October 1). *How to be an antiracist educator*. ASCD. https://www.ascd.org/el/articles/how-to-be-an-antiracist-educator

# 5

# Embodying *How*

## Processes and Practices of a Healing-Centered Approach

The critical question is always *how*.

Whereas the previous two chapters in this book define *what* a healing-centered approach to writing is and *why* it is valuable to embody one, this chapter examines *how* that can be done by outlining seven processes and practices to support such a stance: (1) "grace and space," (2) body awareness, (3) contemplative inquiry, (4) arts-based engagement, (5) positive identity engagement, and (6) communal experience.

I chose the words "processes" and "practices" as intentional alternatives to a focus on "product and perfection."

If you asked me ten years ago if I valued the final written product over the process that created it, I would have said, "Of course not." If you asked me if I expected perfection of myself and my students, I would have vehemently said, "No."

But did my actions and habits align with these denials?

Was I staying up late into the night striving to do something *other* than perfecting my lessons?

Was I writing line-by-line comments and paragraphs of feedback on student drafts in order to suggest something *other* than that their final products should be perfect?

DOI: 10.4324/9781003752721-5

Writing instruction that focuses more on the fruits of experience—the *process*—rather than the externally appraised merits of the outcome—the *product*—is more likely to foster a similar mode of being in students. Likewise, emphasizing *practice* can help teachers and students resist the many pressures to *perfect*.

A finite view of learning aims for a student or teacher to produce perfection—to achieve "mastery"—by the end of the unit or class, or to come as close to it as possible. What would it take to achieve that end? What sorts of goals could be set? Likely, the focus would be on constant evaluation, with the goal of improving performance.

A view of learning as infinite and unfinished, in contrast, emphasizes process and practice over product and perfection. It renders learning limitless and undefined—a scary prospect for anyone looking to meet benchmarks of 100% but an enthralling one for anyone energized by the infinite possibilities of learning and growth, willing to value and reward risk-taking and innovation over compliance and adaptation to a dominant standard.

And isn't that what it takes to write? An understanding of the infinite choices we have—over our words, our syntax, our structures, our details, our facts, our ideas—along with a willingness to choose, to *try?*

The following is a list of six broad strategies that, when practiced in process, can serve the infinite nature of learning in a way that is also fundamental to writing. Within them are countless opportunities and possibilities to personalize and individualize the ways in which they can fit into your own classroom and approach.

## "Grace and Space"

"Grace and space," for writers, is about having room to experiment, to make mistakes and try different approaches. It can involve finding liberty within constraints or finding an opportunity for personal expression and creativity within an assignment or within one's life.

In a classroom, "grace and space" can include holding capacity for the frustrations and challenges of the writing process itself, in order to help student writers find their own ways through them.

"Grace and space" was an explicit agreement in my previous classroom, where I worked with a small group of school-avoidant students. When I first proposed it, one student in the class experienced what appeared to me as a visceral reaction upon hearing the phrase. She dropped her shoulders, gazed toward the ceiling, and exhaled loudly, groaning, "Yes, *please!*"

I followed up by asking her what she took the phrase to mean.

"It means *give people a minute*," she retorted without a moment's hesitation. "Let them *be!*"

Many of the other students nodded in agreement, a rare moment of validation and solidarity for this student from the rest of the class.

Giving "grace and space" can be challenging in any classroom environment but especially in one rife with personal difficulties and collective traumas. For our group, it involved trying to practice *pausing* before responding or reacting. On any given day, someone's loud foot tapping could trigger another student with sensory sensitivities to the point of explosion. Or another student's remark about the way depression shows up in a short story could be taken personally by someone struggling with their own mental health, and they might storm out of the room, swearing or flipping someone off on their way.

When an incident like this occurred, we would talk about choices and strategies for next time. How could "grace and space" come into play? It could mean tolerating the discomfort caused by the tapping, if we imagine that the tapping person may be feeling anxious and may not realize they are doing it. It might mean giving some time to see if the tapping will stop before asking politely if the person could please cease the repetitive motion.

In the case of the comment about the short story, where the stakes are arguably higher, "grace and space" might mean the offended person takes a moment to consider that the remark was not ill intended or targeted. Or it might mean giving *oneself* the grace and space to pause, breathe, and then assert the concern. Grace and space would also involve me as the teacher talking about the importance of *sensitivity* when discussing charged topics, because we never know what someone else is dealing with or how our words will land.

It's important to note that "grace" does not mean allowing harmful, racist, and violent language or actions to go unchallenged; it does mean taking an intersectional approach when determining how to respond.

As teachers, we have a responsibility to ensure that the inherent dignity of all people and the realities of systemic injustice are not denied or framed as matters of opinion (Jones, 2022). We also have to remember, and explicitly point out to our students, that what is personal to one person in the room may simply be an intellectual exercise for another. We, as teachers, need to actively teach this concept to our students just as much as we encourage them to participate and speak up in class discussions. We can guide them to ask themselves: who is in the room with you? If you're debating a topic with someone else, consider: does this issue personally affect me? Might it personally affect the person I am debating? If so, might I bow out, step back, accede, or even admit my own ignorance if that's the case? (Oluo, 2019). We can also ask ourselves the same questions when instructing on a sensitive topic.

## "Grace and Space" in the Writing Process

So how does "grace and space" apply to writing specifically? Well, writing is hard. It requires us to be vulnerable. It brings many of our own personal, academic, and social issues to the fore.

For me, as a teacher, "grace and space" means recognizing that, where there is vulnerability, there is going to be some degree of resistance and avoidance. Resistance and avoidance frequently show up as defensive postures, argumentative stances, and seemingly rude or combative attitudes, all of which stand in the way of our teaching and the student's progress—the more so when we misunderstand these behaviors and experiences.

"Grace and space" means asking ourselves: what lies beneath or beyond these behaviors? How might I appeal to and draw out the more receptive aspects of my students' selves beyond these resistant parts? How might I better connect with the parts that might learn, open, grow, and connect when they feel safe enough to peek out?

I think, here, of the student who arrives to class every day when we are working on a writing assignment and puts his headphones in, slumps down in his chair, and tunes out completely. I check his document, and it remains untouched. I ask him why, and he stares at me blankly. "I'll do it at home," he grunts. I offer him help and he says, "I'm all set."

I'm thinking, too, of the student who copies and pastes large chunks of their work, previously from some random internet source and now from ChatGPT or another AI tool, but staunchly denies doing so.

Or the student who makes rude, snippy, or snide comments during instruction, who laughs with their friends to distract them from the lesson and their work, to make a show of how unseriously they take it.

These behaviors have appeared and reappeared over the years in my classrooms and in the classrooms I visit as a support specialist. Over the years, I've learned to see them as flags alerting me not just to some underlying *needs* but also to an opportunity: for movement, for change. These behaviors communicate: *I'm uncomfortable.* They spark, for me, a curiosity: *why*? Almost always, what I find is a story; in regard to writing, it's often a story about a fraught relationship with writing that long predates my meeting the student. The longer I can maintain curiosity over frustration, the more likely

I am to either learn the story or sit beside the student in their discomfort and gently, persistently help them see another way through it.

### "Grace and Space" for the Product

Beyond the process itself, "grace and space" also involves suspending or loosening the reins of expectations for what student writing might look like, in order to leave room for exploration and invention.

For high school Social Studies teacher Ethan, the redesigned Advanced Placement (AP) U.S History research project he and his curricular partner launched resulted in many students switching gears at several points in the process. The project built in grace and space for this exploration and enabled the students to practice extending grace and space to themselves. In their post-project reflections, students noted that the freedom they were given was both frustrating and challenging. Students experienced this room for exploration as a positive challenge rather than a leniency or slacking of perceived "rigor."

Assigning the more open-ended project in the first place demanded that Ethan and his partner make space for change as well, after ten years of teaching the project in the same way. Being willing to try something different means giving ourselves the grace to make mistakes, to feel like a beginner and suspend our feelings of expertise, to suspend the need to *know* how something will likely turn out. In Ethan's case, making space for his own exploratory approach, and extending himself the grace to test out his ideas while being uncertain of the outcome, helped him cultivate a stance in which he could support students in doing the same.

As teachers, we typically control many of the conditions and limitations that student writers contend with. That said, we have only so much control in the face of curricular and policy factors. The task, then, is to tease out where space exists within the constraints for additional grace—for students and teachers alike.

### Strategies for Implementing "Grace and Space"

- Ease expectations that students will learn to write "perfectly."
- Identify opportunities for experimentation and low-stakes writing experiences.
- Provide a degree of choice (in terms of topic, form, and process) whenever and wherever possible.
- Guide and support students in the process of making decisions about topic, form, and process.
- Recognize how and why a writing process can yield resistance in student writers.
- Offer leeway with page requirements, formality, language, deadlines, and other expectations as needed and whenever possible.

## Body Awareness

"I will not write unless I am swaddled in furs," writes John Babbott (2014) in his humor piece for the website McSweeney's. "I will not write unless I am oriented perpendicularly to a large window." And: "I must have fuzzy slippers" (n.p.).

Babbott's popular essay means to call upon the trap I imagine every writer and student on the planet has either fallen into or taken great (literal) pains to avoid: the perceived need to create the ideal conditions in order to write. The piece is funny in its adoption of a nauseatingly pretentious voice—the voice of a person one might call, as the essay presupposes, a "diva," who has "only written three times over the course of [his] career" but claims that these three pieces "have changed the landscape of contemporary artart" (n.p.). He therefore requires that the Motel 6 where he is staying accommodate his bowel movement schedule.

But despite the ironic evisceration of its own narrator, the essay has a dimension of wisdom in addition to its wit. The essay reminds us that the body and its comfort *matter*.

Writing comes from the body. From hands that hold the pencil or type. From a brain that processes information and ideas and codes it into language to communicate. From a nervous system, too, that decides—autonomically—if it wants, or is ready and able, to engage with a topic or any aspect of the writing process, particularly within a physical place and time. When we ignore the discomfort of the body, along with the possible sources of that discomfort, the vulnerability required to write may be (or feel) impossible to access.

Flexible seating has become a popular new addition to schools in recent years. In my current role as a literacy lab specialist, I am fortunate to work in a space filled with grant-funded furniture that kids actually enjoy sitting in (my own children helped me to pick the pieces). There's a cushy square mat that some like to call the "dog bed," where students can essentially lie on the floor with a lap desk; there are what some like to call the "ADHD" chairs, where kids can sit cross-legged with ease; there are stools and fold-up desks for those who want to maintain an upright posture; there are blow-up chairs, for those who like to sit close to the ground, with their legs stretched out on the floor.

When students step into the room for the first time, they tend to look around amazed: "Wow," they say, "this space is cool." I smile and tell them to choose a seat—whichever they'd like—and I observe as they consider their options, sometimes plopping down into one that feels too cushy, another that feels too rigid, before settling like Goldilocks into the one that feels "just right."

It is, for me, a literal dream come true. In high school, I used to flee the classroom as often as possible—by the time I got my driver's license, that meant leaving campus entirely—in no small part because of the hard chairs. I had always been relatively thin, but my eating disorder rendered me downright bony. Regardless of my body's state, I never liked sitting at a desk chair. My best work was always done at home, in a quiet room with soft music playing, propped up on a bed or a couch with pillows surrounding me. (It still is.)

Being able to facilitate a comfortable space for students who need one is the type of opportunity that drew me into teaching. At the same time, the relief I see on so many students' faces serves as a reminder of how ill suited the physical school environment usually is for so many of them—and for their bodies.

## The Nervous System's Impact in the Classroom

So, what can we do, short of (or even in addition to) buying new furniture and setting up alternative spaces?

For one thing, we can invite students to notice how they feel in their bodies as they write. We can encourage them to stretch, to breathe, to shake out their shoulders and roll their wrists throughout the process or before they sit down to begin doing so. I often demonstrate these moves theatrically—shimmying my shoulders, rolling my neck, saluting the sun, hopping in place—to make them laugh but also to invite them to remember, and relax into, their own bodies; to feel less ridiculous about moving them in healthy ways while they're in school.

When student writers are writing creatively or given lots of choice in terms of topic or approach, we can also help them learn to attune to what their bodies feel called to write about. Neuroscience refers to this ability as *interoception*—awareness of our internal signals. *Exteroception*, on the other hand, involves awareness of the sensory experience around us (Treleaven, 2018).

> How can these understandings be utilized in a classroom, where students may not have an abundance of choices over topics and form and where teachers as well may have limited ability to offer options in the physical space?

Exteroception can involve noticing what music, what chairs, and what type of physical environment and conditions help you write and determining how much agency you have to alter any of these conditions.

Interoception might involve noticing which aspects of a topic capture your interest most. Noticing how a sentence you wrote makes you feel, internally. Noticing what energizes you as opposed to what draws you away.

In my own classes, I have always tried to give students as much choice as possible—which may sound great but can be overwhelming for some students. In fact, offering choice is a deliberate aspect of challenge I like to weave into my classes. To support students, I also try to provide them with as much practice as possible with choice-making. If they watch a video, for example, I ask them to "freewrite" about what stood out to them most, before asking any specific comprehension or analysis questions. Often, their "reading checks" are similar: *What interested you most? What did you think, wonder, or feel while reading these pages?* These questions ask them to make choices, even though they're not called choices, because they require students to recognize what appeals to them and to articulate that interest onto the page.

I also regularly ask students to reread what they wrote—even if it's not much—and to star, circle, underline, or highlight anything distinct. "This might be a word, a phrase, a sentence—anything that leaps off the page from the rest," I say. Sometimes I elaborate: "It might be something that feels particularly true or interesting or well phrased, or it might be something that surprised you when you wrote it, for any reason. It could even be the thing that feels the most cringy. But don't cross it out! Sometimes what's cringy is what's most interesting, too."

This regular habit seems simple but has become a cornerstone of my practice because it fosters awareness in students of the *life* that their writing can take on with attention. It helps them attune to the energy in their words and to follow that energy accordingly. Sometimes, one word they circle sparks a whole new idea. Very often, one sentence they underline becomes the opening words of an essay, short story, or poem they eventually write.

Gaining such interoceptive awareness within the writing process can not only help students move past writers' block, build confidence, and yield greater autonomy in their own choices. It can also help maintain their psychic safety as well.

The stakes for this body awareness are high. As noted earlier in this book, some students find themselves drawn to writing about trauma or challenging experiences in their lives. While such writing can be transformative and healing, it can also be destabilizing. With creative writing especially, I encourage my students to notice what they feel drawn toward writing about and to be vigilant while they're doing so. "If it starts to feel like too much, take a break," I say, as a deliberate understatement. "You can always switch gears or come back to it later."

## The Looming Presence of "Teacher"

In order to understand the relationship between writing and the body (including the mind) that is doing the writing, it is important to understand how that *bodymind* (as the concept is sometimes called) is affected by the presence of others (Maté, 2022). For teachers, that means recognizing how our students' bodies and minds might be affected by the proximity not just of their peers but of *us*.

The mere fact of our being a teacher means we are embodying a role—of authority, of power—that some students may not feel comfortable with. Overtures of kindness and helpfulness may be met with distrust by a student with trauma who, in some cases, may be less accustomed to compassionate relations.

Racial dynamics within the classroom further heighten the need for body awareness, not only because of the potential presence of historical and intergenerational trauma within the students' bodies, along with the collective trauma that people of color may have incurred as a result of pervasive, systemic racism, but also because students of color are taught by a predominantly White teaching workforce in the United States. For me, as a White teacher, this fact leads to a tension between the need for critical and cultural humility and a tendency toward self-flagellation and self-erasure.

At the same time, I realize that the solution to the potentially harmful effects of my presence as a White person is *not* to make myself scarce and disappear and avoid relationships or interaction. It means doing the inner work of contending with my own racialized identity and settling my own body in the moment (Menakem, 2017). So how do we do this? First off, we pay attention to our own body's signals and responses. We pause, we breathe, we notice, we confront ourselves with questions like: do I find that tone rude because it doesn't fit with what was considered acceptable in my home and school growing up? Do I find that sentence flawed because its syntax is constructed in a way I'm not accustomed to? Am I assuming I understand my students' struggles and experiences because I've read some books about the experiences of Black and Brown people?

Ultimately, body awareness requires a practice of humility, which does not mean diminishing ourselves and our own wisdom. It *does* mean recognizing the limits of our awareness (Page & Woodland, 2023). It *does* mean being mindful of how our physical presence may *speak* to our students—and how *theirs* speaks to *us*.

## Attending to Signals of Dysregulation

For us as teachers, an important part of body awareness in the classroom is noticing symptoms of dysregulation—in our students, yes, but also in ourselves.

The need for such awareness is magnified in highly charged environments like the alternative school where English teacher Giuseppe taught before finding himself in a state of burnout that caused him to leave his job for a different one. For him, being in a trauma-filled environment where, in his words, "everything is always on fire all the time" led him to internalize student behaviors such as being late to class as personal slights, which took a physical toll on his body. He could feel himself tensing up. "I scowl in some way," he admits. "I've caught myself saying to myself … *Bro, watch your tone*. My tone will sour … I get sardonic, I get caustic… and even though I know that's not good for relationship building, even though I know it's not going to fix the situation, it's like … a coping mechanism? Or a response I learned from my father."

Gail Boldt (Boldt et al., 2015) describes this phenomenon as a "negative affective response" that is "largely out of our control" and "largely beyond the reach of our political convictions" (p. 439), which explains why there is such a disconnect between Giuseppe's professed values as a teacher and the reactions he observes in his interactions with students. He *wants* to be a teacher who honors his student's autonomy, who shares power with his students, who does not punish them for behaviors that are rooted in the oppressions of schooling. But he also catches himself reacting under stress in ways he can't entirely control. Body awareness helps Giuseppe notice and, ideally, interrupt the autonomic response his body has to perceived disrespect in the high-intensity environment of his classroom.

Regulation, ideally, is not about control, which is what makes it an imperfect word to describe what we may be aiming to do: pause. Care for our triggered bodies and minds in ways that we have practiced and that we know work for us, instead of the ways we are sometimes instructed to do so through canned strategies featured on a pamphlet or handout. Notice our physical reactions as information and take the time we need to respond in a way that aligns with our values.

When we are ready, we can process that information more thoughtfully, especially if we are able to recognize patterns over time and interrogate their cause. What unresolved issues in our selves keep flaring up, and why?

But that intellectualizing can happen later. In the moment, body awareness can ground us, keeping ourselves psychically safe and hopefully better preventing us from unwittingly inflicting harm.

## Strategies for Implementing Body Awareness

- Notice students' facial expressions and postures as they write or as they learn or talk about writing.

- Notice what physical conditions (i.e., lighting, music, and seating) facilitate students' writing.
- Provide options with regard to the physical conditions for students while writing (i.e., lighting, music, and seating).
- Notice which parts of a student's written product feel most potent or significant (i.e., words, phrases, and sentences that "leap off the page").
- Point out the most potent or significant parts of students' writing.
- Encourage students to practice a habit of noticing the most potent or significant parts of their writing and what they feel compelled to write about.

## Contemplative Inquiry

How do you feel about a noisy classroom?

Do you see it as a place of lively engagement, collaboration, and fun? Or is noise a sign of chaos and a lack of discipline?

How did you feel being in a noisy classroom as a student? How do you feel when you are in a noisy classroom, teaching? How do you feel when you walk by one?

The answer likely depends on the nature of the noise; is it focused noise, exerted on the task at hand, or is it emanating from distractive and erratic behavior? Are you the one having fun, or is it someone else?

But, in the most general sense, it also depends on our own dispositions and neurotypes. That's true for us as teachers, and it's also true for our students.

Contemplative inquiry, in *part*, is about providing a steady, consistent opportunity for *silence* in the classroom. Silence that isn't one-sided—teacher speaking, students listening—and silence that isn't funneled in with high-pressure assessment either. Silence that is more about *presence*—being present with ourselves and with our subjects of contemplation. I don't mean silence all the time. I mean deliberate, structured, intentional dips into silence for the purpose of authentic reflection, exploration, and, at times, probing inquiry.

Silence of this sort is so conducive, and maybe even essential, to writing. It is hard, or nearly impossible, for some writers to write without silence. Silence is also uncommon in schools—and not just in schools but in our modern lives. Silence, in this sense, can be a gift.

That gift, admittedly, is not always well received or easy to access by students who may be accustomed to scrolling through reel after reel as their friends chat around them and a television or music from a Bluetooth speaker plays in the background. I argue that it takes practice—with respect to writing, practice that is intentionally embedded into the process.

## The Benefits of Consistent Reflection

Practice in contemplative inquiry can come in the form of regular journaling or "freewriting." Journaling is a rite of passage for many people and a formative experience if not a regular practice for many writers. It certainly was for me. Often, throughout my schooling, I wondered if I could find a bridge between the kind of writing I did in my journal and the kind I was being asked to do for school. The answer usually seemed to be *no*. When I would write sprawling introductions or digressive paragraphs in the middle of my essays, they were not exactly welcome—in no small part because I didn't know how to make them work fluidly with the assignment in front of me.

Journaling is sometimes encouraged or required in an educational context, but even if not, regular reflective writing opportunities—what I couch for my students as "freewrites"—can be beneficial for fostering essayistic reflection and contemplative inquiry. To my mind, a freewrite is not concerned with grammar, punctuation, spelling, clarity, or cohesion but allows the writer to be random, digress, and try out any style that they wish.

Whereas in the past I would have described "freewriting" in the way Peter Elbow (2015) advocates—writing as much as you can, without thinking or lifting your pen, without editing yourself at all—now I have taken to letting students know that this "freewriting" opportunity is provided to help them cultivate a practice, and they have options for how they might use it. They can draw, list, or even stare into space as long as they are quietly trying to do nothing else but engage with the questions or prompts provided.

In this sense, "freewriting" can be viewed as a form of mindful contemplation—what poet rupi kaur (2022) calls "a form of deep listening where you let your thoughts flow out onto paper in real time" (p. xii). When the skill is cultivated through regular practice, such exploratory writing can provide an ongoing opportunity for silence and solitude, for internal questioning and introspection, within a classroom that is likely otherwise filled with externalized voices and activity.

Writing, in a school context, is often viewed as a space for *presenting* (rather than grappling with) knowledge, ideas, and questions, but a designated space carved out for journal-style reflection—ungraded and perhaps even unread by the teacher—can help students connect with their own thinking, feeling, and being, even or especially as it relates to academic content.

Regular journaling or "freewriting" has always been a mainstay in my own classes. My aim is to help students grow comfortable with their own writing voices, to practice thinking through ideas by writing them out, letting the mind do its work on the page (Lopate, 1995). I hope for my students to experience those moments of discovery and inspiration that can come from spontaneously engaging with words as they enter the mind. I hope they may grow comfortable with the messy voice that plods through the murky waters of thought until it stumbles upon clarity, startling itself with the discovery of insight. I hope they might see how much more valuable, how much more precious, that gem of insight is than the "perfectly" grammatical sentence that dresses up an empty idea. I hope for that insight, their own gems, to form the center of gravity within their writing, instead of its being driven by their allegiance to some nebulous idea of what I, as their teacher, am looking for them to say.

This is all to suggest that a regular, consistent practice of free-writing can help student writers build autonomy and agency and authorship as writers. It can help them find ease and fluency within the ungraded space of a reflective, open-ended response.

And it's not just for the purpose of reflection itself (which is valuable in its own right). It's not just an "add on" experience, separate from the rest of what we teach. These reflective opportunities can help students process challenging information and concepts and can also help them produce a more complex, interesting, and sophisticated written product. Reflective writing can be downright *rigorous* if that's what you're after.

## Embracing Essayistic Reflection

The word *essay* comes from the French word meaning *attempt*. As a practice, essayistic reflection leans into the concept of experimentation, encouraging writers to *try*—to test something out on the page, not needing to know if it will work out perfectly. It invites the writer to actively engage with a question and follow a line of inquiry through digression, responsiveness, and intellectual risk-taking, rather than allegiantly hammering home an argument from a position of authority and knowing.

Ironically, the word *essay* is laden with connotations of the very opposite: with the need to answer a question definitively, to unequivocally "prove" an argument with laser-like focus, with a clearly defined thesis and a stack of paragraphs, each one defending a supporting point. Yes, this paradigm reflects one form of the essay, the one most often assigned in school—and the one dreaded by many.

But we can also expand our view of the essay—or an essayistic approach—to include the non-linear and the digressive, the inherently imperfect and inconclusive. That very imperfection and inconclusivity is what can give the essay, as both a process and a product, its power and capacity to foster deep inquiry and learning.

An essayistic process is more about engaging with questions than answering them. When I taught at the college level, I would offer my first-year literature classes a variety of essay topic options to choose from—some quite specific (i.e., analyze the author's use of symbolism in this story or that) and others strategically open-ended. One of my favorites: *What does this story reveal about what it means to be human?*

Without fail, each semester, I would have at least one student who chose this latter prompt thinking it would be easy. "She can't tell me I'm *wrong*" is what I imagined them thinking.

And then they would embark on the journey of writing the essay, encountering the guidelines (substantiating evidence, sound argumentation) and eventually bumping against the realization that such an open-ended inquiry is actually very hard or, at least, very hard to do *well*. They'd come to my office hours and admit as much. I'd smile and convey some variation of "I'm glad you came" and help them work through the difficulty. I'd encourage them not to flee the situation and switch gears completely but instead to embrace the ambiguity, wielding their skills of close reading, analysis, and interpretation and honing them further while doing so. Very often, the students would finish with a product they felt proud of—and, quite certainly, with the experience of a process they learned and grew from.

What I was asking students to do with that question was not just to write an *essay* but to write *essayistically*. It was hard for them to do, and as I realized the first time I assigned the prompt, it was hard for me to teach them, too. But well worth it.

## The Place for Contemplative Inquiry in the Classroom

At the secondary level, I feel obliged to step in far before a student finds themselves floundering like the undergraduates I described above. Still, I like to provide these expansive offerings for students who want to reach for them—or for those who need to learn the hard way not to underestimate the challenge of a gaping open question.

I also try to help students gain facility and familiarity with this type of essayistic reflection by providing them with regular low-stakes opportunities to practice it.

At this point, I don't know how I could teach writing—or, really, *anything*—without providing space and options for contemplative inquiry. This may be due at least partly to my own predilection toward peaceful silence. I'm an introvert at heart; I think best in silence. I *feel* best in silence.

It may also be due to my neurotype, which is easily distracted and overwhelmed in noisy spaces. Schools tend to foster, encourage, and even thrive on social engagement. But for some of us, it's just too much.

When I started teaching high school, I wondered if I would ever be the teacher whose room exuded waves of laughter and animated conversation. The contemplative stuff? I was really good at fostering that. Not so good at creating a party. Many students commented on how peaceful my classroom felt, how much they enjoyed the freedom of the freewrites. Some expressed relief that they'd found such a placid retreat in the midst of their raucous day. But I could tell that some students, accustomed to being in the center of lively interactions and spirited debates, did not feel entirely comfortable in this culture of quiet. I was glad that some students were finding a rare place that suited their preferences, but I wanted my classroom to be a place where any and all of my students could thrive.

Now, my teaching approach is more balanced between the social and the solitary, between the tumult and the quiet.

But I also make sure to carve out space for contemplative inquiry, and I find opportunities to elevate these practices as well. For example, in the course of a unit, I might collect several "freewrites" and require, at the end, that students choose one from which to build a formal response. I want student writers to know that reflection and contemplative inquiry are real work—this work is about them and their minds, and it has real value. Space to hear themselves think and feel can be a hallowed one within their learning.

### Strategies for Implementing Contemplative Inquiry

- Offer open-ended questions as prompts and provide time and space for students to respond informally.
- Invite and welcome digressions and emergences in teaching.
- Utilize mindfulness exercises, including journaling and mindful movement, to inform and reflect upon teaching.
- Allow and encourage students to digress in their writing/process when possible.
- Point to and help students notice emergences in their writing.
- Guide students in the use of mindfulness exercises as part of the writing process.

## Arts-Based Engagement

"The impulse to do and revere art is an ancient need—whether on cave walls, one's own body, a cathedral or a religious rite, we hunger for a way to articulate who we are and what we mean."

So writes Toni Morrison (2019) in her essay "The Habit of Art."

As teachers, we know those students for whom art is the only way. They draw intricate landscapes and portraits in their notebooks during Science lectures. They come into Social Studies yawning after spending late night hours at play practice. In English class, they write elusive, poetic essays that are far too long or short, and they forget to incorporate quotes. (Yes, I was the latter.)

Too often, students like these find that their grades do not reflect their aptitude or effort. Too often, their strongest competencies are underutilized. Their strongest skills are seen as peripheral, not academic enough. The question I encourage us as their teachers to consider is not only what can we do *for* them but also what can we learn *from* them? What can we learn from *their* needs and abilities? Too often, their particularities become typecast as deficiencies in the classroom, but I believe that instruction designed with these learners in mind can actually enliven our instruction and even challenge other students who have grown too comfortable with conventional structures.

If Toni Morrison is right, as she tends to be, are we missing an opportunity to channel this "ancient need" in our classrooms?

### The Healing Capacities of Art

Art, the way I see it, is inherently healing because it does not force cohesion. It acknowledges the inevitability of fragmentation and thereby honors, represents, and potentially restores us from the fractures. What I mean is that it helps us to bring disparate pieces together into a new *whole*. It can help us to *feel* whole, even when we are in pieces. Art is what Julia Cameron (2016) calls a kind of "spiritual chiropractic," aligning the overtaxed body and mind with the deeper soul dimension, the *psyche*. It moves us toward a new connectedness, a new wholeness—which is exactly what healing is: a movement toward wholeness.

But what place does any of that have in a classroom outside of the arts?

I would guess, not much of a place, in most current classrooms. Or not as much of a place as it could—and, dare I say, *should* have.

Arts-based engagement as part of a writing practice involves drawing on the capacity of art to enliven the senses and activate the soul dimension, to help us imagine alternative ways of being in the world with each other (Greene, 1993). Art inherently emphasizes process. It not only allows for but *requires* us to practice tolerating and even embracing the messiness of the unknown. It invites the writer to engage in a non-linear and exploratory process of constant trial and error, a continual re-envisioning.

Zaretta Hammond (2021) refers to arts-based methods as "studio habits" that allow for "cognitive chewing" and "productive struggle" (n.p.). Learning behaviors like these expand neural pathways in the brain and are especially essential, she argues, for students who are historically marginalized, as they empower students toward their most authentic strengths in a way that rigid pacing guides and excessive scaffolding that lower expectations never will.

Yet "productive struggle" runs counter to the ways in which many, if not most, people experience, teach, or have been taught to write. I've had many students come to meet with me in my school's writing center, saying, "I'm really struggling," and I'm tempted to say, "That's great!" (Depending on the context, sometimes I do.) Learning happens in struggle. Growth happens in struggle. Discovery happens in struggle. A painter stands back from their canvas and asks themselves what's missing. A musician listens for the wrong note that found its way into the measure. Novelists pore over each draft, trying to figure out what they overlooked from their character's story. All of these moments require sitting with frustration and uncertainty while resisting the trappings of impatience, self-doubt, panic, and capitulation.

What helps mitigate some of this uncertainty, or builds a tolerance within those less practiced or comfortable with it, is a strategy like a design constraint. I have a colleague who frequently calls for her students to use a very specific number of images or metaphors in certain pieces she assigns. While a move like this can seem formulaic, it becomes that exact type of design constraint that some students need in order to make something artful. And often, the writers will go well beyond the required minimums to produce something lovely or inspired. No stop sign appears, and they keep going.

Even people who are non-artistically inclined can benefit from arts-based engagement. Promoting and fostering an arts-based approach to writing, in this sense, can present an opportunity for any writer to tap into the primordial need for expression that Morrison describes and heal a part of the self that may not otherwise have had the space to do so.

## The Work of Cultivating Imagination and Emotion

While some students may dread them, many students associate creative writing opportunities with "fun."

But they aren't always fun.

In my experience, simply offering students the opportunity to "be creative" or make choices without consistent and deliberate support and guided practice will not immediately, or even often, yield the creative freedom that teachers and even students might expect. When this immediate outpouring of creative expression does not occur, people—including teachers and the students themselves—might cast the matter off with such thoughts as "Well, I am/they are just not naturally creative" or "I/They just don't like creative writing … it's not my/their 'thing.'" Relatedly, creative writing is often deemed to be non-essential, something that cannot be taught. It's seen as too personal and therefore difficult to assess (as if all writing isn't).

Instead of abandoning the practice of creative writing altogether, we should ask ourselves what larger factors may be at play when students struggle with creative activities. One factor is the consistent messages they may internalize, from a young age, that emphasize a "right" and "wrong" way to do things. As one of my research participants said to me, "Good kids do this. Bad kids do that." "Girls wear this. Boys say that."

In addition to an overemphasis on "right" and "wrong," the challenge to engage in creative, arts-based practice stems from an undervaluation, restriction, and repression of imagination in schooling (Greene, 2008). When imagination is relegated to elementary-school playtime, individuals and collectives may find it difficult not only to write creatively but to think creatively and to imagine their way toward alternative ways of being. An arts-based approach engages, nourishes, and strengthens the imagination, which is vital to the type of transformation we need to sustain our humanity within the many systems that work against it.

And it's not just the imagination that is underutilized and underdeveloped. It is also the genius of emotion.

Most writing done in schools is academic, and academic writing favors an "objective" and intellectualizing approach. Emotional and embodied ways of knowing are marginalized or purposefully excluded from the process, most noticeably through admonishments against the use of first-person pronouns or phrases such as "I think," "I feel," or "I believe."

The role of emotion in learning is steeped in power relations. Historically, emotion has been seen as "beneath" logic, as a less evolved aspect of human nature than cognitive reasoning, elevated in status only when it is associated with intelligence—namely emotional intelligence as a tool that can be used for productivity or career success.

Nonetheless, emotion—as many of us know and believe—can give us important information and understandings that cognitive ways of knowing cannot. It can help us understand, for example, why some writers and writing instructors have strong emotions in relation to writing. Students and teachers alike may find themselves drawn toward or repelled away from certain styles and forms of writing (Ahmed, 2014). Take a moment to reflect: What types of writing do you most enjoy? What do you most avoid? How might these natural aversions and predilections show up in your own teaching?

Students and teachers, as we know, might even find themselves turning away from *all* types of writing. Maybe they've never been exposed to or invited to write in a form that aligns with their own preferences, their own organic communication style. Maybe they've been told they don't write well. Maybe they fear the vulnerability necessary to artistic writing.

Ahmed (2014) writes that "attention to emotions allows us to address how subjects become invested in particular structures such that their demise is felt as a kind of living death" (Ahmed, 2014, p. 12). In other words, emotions can help us understand what makes change so hard. How certain policies, practices, tools, and strategies become so entrenched that we feel we can't work or teach without them. Can you think of any such "structures" in your own teaching practice or school? Structures that, if they were to crumble, it would feel like a living death? This phrasing may sound dramatic, but how many of us have heard someone joke—or joked ourselves—that you can pry this or that assignment, teaching practice, class activity, or policy from our cold, dead hands?

Change is hard, especially in a profession that is inevitably *always changing* its expectations of us. The sociopolitical pendulum is always swinging and smacking us back and forth. We have our valid reasons for feeling a certain way in the face of this phenomenon. But Ahmed's point is worth heeding: when it comes to our teaching, what are we emotionally invested in, and why? What does it feel like when we're asked to change that thing in some small or large way, and why?

### Strategies for Implementing Arts-Based Engagement

- Use poetry and art as prompts for writing.
- Experiment with alternative pedagogical approaches and techniques.
- Allow students time and space to experiment with a variety of possibilities and options for writing.
- Create design constraints to promote and make creative writing accessible.
- Provide low-stakes opportunities for risk-taking.

## Positive Identity Engagement

If a person senses that they may be negatively perceived or associated on the basis of their identity, they will become vigilant until a lack of threat is detected. That is the theory behind Geoffrey Cohen and Julio Garcia's (2008) Identity Engagement Model.

If the threat is confirmed through situational cues (i.e., a lack of representation or the perpetuation of stereotypes), the person will decide whether or not it's worth coping with the threat. If they decide that it's not, they will check out, shut down, avoid, or otherwise flee.

The impact of this phenomenon is especially present in schools, which fit into the category of "chronically evaluative social environments" that Cohen and Garcia (2008) say heighten the threat of internalized judgment (p. 365).

It's easy to imagine how the effects of negative identity engagement might play out in a secondary classroom: a student stops handing in work, cuts class, acts out, or isolates themself from their peers. But what is the cause?

To begin to address this, we can ask ourselves: what are the "cues" in our own classrooms that might make some students feel threatened? These might include our own race, gender, or neurotype. The demographics present in our room. The pattern of students we typically call on, praise, or reproach. The histories we teach, the authors we assign, the scientists we feature on our walls. Some of these factors are within our control. Many aren't.

So what can we do to reassure a sense of safety in the face of these variables? How can we try to reaffirm that it's worthwhile for our students, and their identities, to risk engagement—*and* ensure that it is indeed safe for them to do so?

One way is through actively practicing "positive identity engagement."

While negative identity engagement is clearly harmful, the antidote is not to ignore or dismiss identity. Just the opposite. "Colorblind" stances, for example, can convey a message that one's race or culture is inconsequential and not worthy of consideration (Pimentel et al., 2016). They can promote a sense of erasure and homogenization that compels students to flatten their linguistic, cultural, and familial identities in order to fit in and excel (del Carmen Salazar, 2013).

Instead of aiming to be identity-neutral, we can positively and actively engage identity by not just allowing but encouraging students to bring their own backgrounds, interests, and experiences to bear in their schoolwork—and being a receptive, encouraging audience for them when they do so.

But how?

## Inviting Identity In

Writing assignments that invite students to actively reflect on and examine themselves as social beings can positively engage their complex, intersecting identities rather than ignoring, dismissing, or harming them. The experience of doing so can be affirming and restorative, especially for students who may have complex or hybrid identities.

Social-emotional learning and theater teacher Austin's identity project is an explicit example. In September of the year in which we spoke, they invited students to take a silhouette of their faces and fill it in with their identities, following some scaffolding and teaching about what words such as race, class, gender, ethnicity, geographic region, and religion really mean. "We also talked about values—personal values, school values, hobbies," they said. "Whatever they chose to make bigger inside the drawing was something more important to them." In late March to early April, students revisited the drawings and did some journaling about what stayed the same for them and what had changed. This step occurred after these upper-elementary students had completed two important projects: the creation and production of a collaboratively written play and a poetry translation project using heritage languages from their families.

While journaling about the experiences, one student wrote, "After doing the play, I feel like I'm not shy anymore, so I can take shy out of it." Another student, who wrote a poem about making maqluba with his parents, said he would now make his Palestinian heritage bigger in his silhouette.

The project not only honored students' identities but helped to actively shape them through the students' mindful intentions and reflections.

## "Positive" Cannot Mean "Bypassing"

"Positive identity engagement" does *not* mean bypassing or overlooking what is difficult for students to confront. White students, for example, can be invited to reflect on their social positionalities and privileges in a developmentally appropriate way, with support from teachers who have done the same (Muhammad, 2020).

While interrogating identities in the context of power, privilege, and historical suffering can be painful, challenging, and vulnerable work for teacher and student alike, we do our students a disservice by not providing them with a safe space for this work and potentially miss an opportunity for transformative experience ourselves. Confronting ourselves and our roles in society is not easy, but avoiding this inquiry out of fear can lead to denial, ignorance, and harm.

For several years, I taught an Identity, Culture, and Society unit in a 10th-grade Honors English class within the predominantly White and relatively affluent school in which I work. The culminating assignment was an essay that required students to incorporate both textual analysis and personal reflection. While the expectation was never that students needed to write explicitly about their identities, and they were always offered the chance to write more generally about their observations of some aspect of culture or society they were interested in, at least one student per year would resist the assignment on the grounds that there was nothing "special" or "different" about their identity; one student even wrote in a pre-writing proposal, "I'm just normal," with a self-deprecating implication that this was boring, but without the self-awareness to recognize that the comment was perpetuating Whiteness and monoculturalism as a norm.

Another student expressed that it was "unfair" to be given this assignment, because he (a White male) had never experienced any identity-based discrimination or hardship and would not have anything to write about. This response compelled me to critically reflect on *why* this student equated the academic exploration of identity and culture with discrimination and hardship. It also forced me to recognize that questions of identity, culture, and society did not either appeal or seem relevant and accessible to many of my White, monolingual, or relatively monocultural students, which if anything made me sense an even greater need for the assignment. Disrupting the comfort of those who, like fish in water, have always experienced their identity as a "norm" can be a powerful way to foster critical thinking.

Yet, despite the many transformative pieces of writing I'd received, where students admitted to never having considered, for example, their ethnic heritage and the ways in which they repressed it in order to assimilate into their school and town environment, I realized that I needed to consider how some students may have felt pressure to disclose and examine aspects of their identity that they did not want, or feel inspired or prepared, to examine.

While most if not all of the apparent resistance or hesitation to the assignment came from White students, I had to remain aware that my students who may already have felt marginalized would probably be less likely to express their hesitations, and so my instruction and guidance needed to explicitly remind students of all the options at their disposal—for example, the fact that they were free to examine subjects of identity, culture, and society that they observed around them or in media. I also worked to conference and check in with each student throughout the process.

My responses to resistant comments such as the ones described above, on the other hand, were always geared toward helping students see that we are all social beings, socially situated, and therefore worthy of contemplation within a sociocultural context—perhaps even more necessarily so if we had never felt the need to stop and engage with such inquiry before.

Inviting writers to explore their own interests, ideas, feelings, memories, experiences, and questions, in addition to their social identities, is a way to help them complicate their sense of self. It can help them to avoid overly identifying with or fearing external perceptions imposed by others.

It's also a task that needs to be taken very seriously. Students should never be required to disclose, present, or reflect on any aspects of their personal identities that they don't feel comfortable sharing. Personal reflection and sharing can be invitational rather than compulsory, with multiple, expansive options for entry offered.

At the same time, we can try to cultivate a sense of safety for students by remaining aware of how we talk about different identity groups and markers, and how we do or do not represent them. We can be mindful of who is present in our room—what we know about their identities and what we *don't* know. We can also consider our own identities and how we might bring those forth more intentionally, in order to model the type of engagement and reflexivity we wish to invite for our students.

### Strategies for Implementing Positive Identity Engagement

- Offer students frequent opportunities for writing in first-person voice (via formal or informal responses or assignments).
- Encourage students to identify connections between academic subject matter and personal interests, knowledge, and experience.
- Create opportunities or options for students to reflect on and write about their identities in a manner of their choosing.
- Share personal connections with students in a relevant way.
- Identify opportunities to connect academic subject matter to your own personal interests, knowledge, and experience.

## Communal Experience

Writing is frequently viewed as a solitary endeavor. Stereotypical images of the writer closed up in a dark attic, tapping on keys under lamplight, peaking out three times per day for meals, are all too vivid in our collective imaginations.

But the point of writing, so often, is just the opposite: it's to reach out and *communicate* with others, to connect through words and ideas across time and space.

The communal aspect, however, can feel too abstract for some writers, too *later*. Even those of us who love to write, who choose to write as part of our living, who make the *choice* to embark on the multi-year journey of writing a book or a play, who relish the moments of solitude that produce written material, can find it lonely and isolating. *Will anyone ever read these words?* we wonder. *Will these pages matter to anyone? Does anyone besides me care about this topic? Will anyone want to hear what I have to say?*

Now, let's think about middle and high school students, most of whom are constantly connected to one another through texting, social media, or gaming; most of whom are used to receiving an *instant* response to their words and ideas and who are ready to supply one in return.

It may well be that a traditional writing process—of drafting and revising in silence, with time to hear and formulate their own thoughts with care—offers a welcome reprieve for many of them from the rapid-fire exchanges that may dominate their social lives. Even if unwelcome, such a process may prove rewarding or strangely satisfying. Many of us would say it is necessary. Sometimes you get what you need.

But that doesn't mean it's easy, and that doesn't mean it's how things always need to be.

## Writing Together

As I envision it here, communal experience as part of a writing process and practice is about engaging the social self through joy, through connection, and through socially oriented activity.

One of the most explicit examples of communal writing I've encountered came from Austin, who writes a collaborative play with their students each year in their social-emotional learning classes. They described it as an experience of sharing ideas and, together, finding the right words to help students articulate their visions, voices, and personalities.

While Austin takes the lead on storytelling and structure, they typically defer to students in matters of syntax and word choice. "When a kid disrupts the language and puts it into incorrect grammar I think, 'Great, because that means it's going to flow out of your mouth correctly, right? And that people will receive it. Because the way I write it on the page is going to be really flat and static, and you're going to bring it to life.'" The form of collaborative writing Austin described reflects a true synthesis of their and their students' voices coming together to produce a product meant to be shared and enjoyed with an audience.

A spirit of collaboration can also enrich and enliven an individual writing process. For us as teachers, that might mean grounding our feedback in a mutual desire to help the writer fulfill their vision, rather than imposing our own. When we model this approach, we can also help students do this for each other.

With my own classes, especially with creative writing, I try to encourage students to see peer review as an opportunity to help each other identify *opportunities* within each other's work. When responding to your peer's writing, I advise that the first step is *always* to name what resonates most for you. What's working? Where are you pulled in? What are you interested in? What do you enjoy?

Then, what questions do you have? What do you want to know more about? Where in the piece are you seeking more clarity?

Only after these two steps does the reader then move toward: what else might you try here?

I try to remind them that the goal is not to "fix" each other's writing, and it's certainly not to tear each other down. The goal is to honor the work—and each other—enough to identify possibilities and help the writer see them, too.

And this is not a touchy-feely, "too nice" approach. It is serious work that serious writers undertake with and for each other.

## Writing for a Receptive Audience

Research has long shown that writing for a so-called "authentic audience" is an important motivator, maybe even a crucial component of learning to write well. Such an awareness is what leads many of us, as writing teachers, to assign letter-writing activities—to senators, community newspapers, family members, celebrities, authors. We encourage students to enter contests, and sometimes we require that students read their work aloud to their classes, school communities, or families. They compile portfolios to be presented and scored by adults other than their teachers. All of these experiences help them *remember* that the point of most writing is to communicate with others. The message needs to land.

*Forgetting* about audience (or taking it for granted) is what leads students to write without context or clarity about books or historical periods because they know that we, as their primary readers, have read the book, know the background, or can easily guess what they mean. Forgetting about the audience's needs is what leads them to, as a smart colleague of mine observes, "throw spaghetti at the wall, hoping it will stick."

*Remembering* audience is what leads them to write powerful and stylistic college essays, as they envision a bored or skeptical admissions officer on the other end of their missive whose attention and endorsement they desperately want. It's what leads them to write clear and moving statements to administration or the school newspaper about pressing issues in their community—such as overly restrictive cellphone policies or rampant bullying—when they really want to see something change.

The idea of an audience—of actual people receiving and responding to our words—is helpful to writers at every stage and level. Writers' groups can be so powerful for this reason. As adults, when we don't have a teacher, editor, or publisher awaiting our words, it can feel hard to self-motivate or keep the momentum going on a project. Writers' group meetings can be fun, too, just like book club meetings are. There was a time, for me, when I would barely write at all if I didn't have a date on the calendar and a small group of friends asking, "Are you coming on Wednesday? Where are your pages?" Open mic nights, too, are a testament to how lively group celebrations of writing—from the most polished to the most unfinished—can be. Strangers come together to cheer each other on and test out new material, and unexpected friendships can form in those spaces.

So how do we replicate that enthusiasm, that joy, that immediate affirmation in our classrooms?

I've always wanted to be the kind of teacher who could return students' full drafts very quickly after they'd written them, while they still cared about the contents, with supportive and motivating comments for revision flooding the margins, but that has never been me. I'm a slow reader, with a busy life.

What has worked in place of that paradigm is to offer quick writing prompts that are more about ideas than about form, more about *what* they have to say rather than *how* they say it. I can read responses like these rapidly and star, circle, or underline what stands out to me, with a personalized response—a question, a comment, a "Yes! Great point!" or "I'd love to hear more!" Over time, this habit can remind student writers that someone *wants* to hear what they have to say, someone *wants* to hear and understand more.

Also helpful is creating a culture in the classroom that is ready to *celebrate* writing. Especially in my creative writing classes, I frequently invite—and strongly *urge*—students to impromptu share at least one sentence, if not a full paragraph or the entirety, of what they wrote during a freewrite with the class. The purpose of this experience is *not* to offer feedback but to honor and encourage the writer. Feedback can come later.

No matter what the students share, I clap enthusiastically, inevitably inspiring the whole class to join in as well, until it becomes an expected, if cheesy, practice in the classroom. Often, I ask the student audience to note at least one specific aspect they enjoyed—a word choice, an image, a sentence, a detail. Sometimes this request elicits an awkward silence, but after repeated iterations, I almost never have to jump in myself to get us started; a student will almost always step in with something to offer. Over time, it becomes easier for students to do this for one another—to be a positively engaged audience. It takes some distress tolerance on my and their part, but the moments of awkward silence eventually minimize.

Routines like these prime students for our final experience of the class, where students prepare a "formal" reading—a full poem, a paragraph from an essay, a few pages from a short story—and deliver it to an audience, their class, that has learned from experience how to be celebratory and receptive. They cheer for one another and readily uplift specific elements they enjoyed from each reader's piece.

## Writing for Fun

Let's face it. The joy we glean from writing, if any at all, is not always in the process of doing it. It's often in the response.

One of my favorite memories as a teacher occurred when a group of teaching artists visited the high school where I work as part of our involvement in the Poetry Out Loud program. Poetry Out Loud is a recitation competition, historically sponsored by the National Endowment for the Arts and the Poetry Foundation. The teaching artists came to us with the intention of inspiring our students to perform and write their own spoken-word poetry, but they also involved *teachers* into the process.

We gathered in a too-small room, with students and teachers in chairs and on the floor. The artists performed their own spoken-word pieces and then offered us prompts that they participated in as well, showcasing the messy process of creation and displaying the raw beauty of what it can evoke. They put us teachers on the spot, too, asking us to write poems and share them without any time to edit and modeling a celebratory spirit when we did so that made the risk feel truly safe and joyful. Students laughed and clapped and cheered us on and then began writing their own poems and raising their hands to share as well.

Every year, on the day before winter break, teachers in my school host recreational sessions for students that are supposed to be fun or engaging. My go-to offering is a collage poetry experience, where students can sit in comfortable chairs, drink tea or hot chocolate, eat snacks, and experiment playfully with magazines, fabrics, scissors, and glue to make projects that will never be graded. They laugh and chat and share materials and experiment and *make* and seek opinions and start over and maybe produce something that moves them and the people around them as well.

Is collage poetry typically the most signed-up-for session? No. That would be something like pickleball or movie-watching. But for the few students who do join, this communal experience of "writing" together is, I'd like to think, one we remember. And it's taught me that there is, indeed, a craving—and an educational, enriching value—for the type of experimentation and *joy* that can result from a writing process that *feels* good, together.

## We Need Each Other to Heal

Solitude, surely, is an important part of writing—one that many of us introverted writers relish and crave. It can give us a break from the roles we need to play in the world—student, teacher, daughter, mom, team captain, neighbor, oldest brother, little sister. But practicing writing as a process of communal experience does not need to be at odds with that solitude. On the contrary, such an approach can protect it. It can involve writing for and with the self in a way that restores a deeper connectedness to the larger social world. Ideally, it might join solitudes in a larger communal endeavor of meaning and connection.

Teaching is an incredibly social job. The social aspect is the hardest part of the job for me and almost drew me away from teaching high school after my first year. *So* many social interactions! *So* many relationships to maintain! And so little time for writing.

At a certain point, I realized that I *needed* to give myself time for creative or reflective writing in order to sustain my social battery and keep teaching but, more importantly, to stay in touch with my*self*. Now, I keep a journal in my school bag and try to take it out every morning, to write at least one sentence that captures how I'm feeling and what I'm thinking about, beyond the job I have to do that day. Every school break, especially if my own children are occupied with camp, I take myself to a coffee shop, put my headphones in, and write. There was a time when I had a shining half hour between the end of my work day and their pickup time, and I would take myself to that coffee shop and work on a novel project—an epistolary novel that enabled me to write in fits and spurts. For me, nearly nothing is as restorative as writing alone in a coffee shop. When I emerge from that state of concentrated silence, I am often all the more eager to connect socially with others.

## Communal Experience Is Healing

While writers' groups and writers' workshops can counteract the isolating aspects of writing, what other opportunities for communal writing might there be? What other forms might a communal writing experience take? How might communal experiences of writing meet the needs of those for whom writing is *too* solitary?

According to Four Arrows, also known as Wahinkpe Topa (Topa & Narvaez, 2022), "To build capacities for getting along with others in a kind, cooperative manner, you need to calm yourself, feel connected, and expand your imagination"—all practices that can be fostered through both a solitary and group writing experience. He cites several practices, which he defines as "routine Indigenous ways of being," that can aid in this process. These include "self-calming" and "social joy"—practices that "expand your communal imagination," helping people to remember and feel the interconnectedness among all beings (p. 180).

A communal approach to writing is, in this sense, inherently healing. The need for social connection is hardwired into our nervous system, which suffers without reciprocity—to the point, and as a result, of trauma (Maté, 2022). Communal experiences can aid in healing that trauma, bringing us into synchrony with others (Menakem, 2017; Treleaven, 2018). We literally need each other to heal. I mean that in both ways it can be read.

Healing includes—and can happen through—our relationships with writing as well. The relationship is reciprocal. I argue here that, through a practice of communal experience, our relationships with writing can help us move in the direction of healing our connectedness with ourselves, with each other, and with the rest of the world around us.

In a world that may feel like it's always on fire, why does writing matter? What difference can writing make? On some level, I ask myself these questions all the time. Including every time I sit down to work on this book. And defeated answers are what keep me away from writing.

What keeps me coming back is more than hope or faith; it's a deep belief in the power of *trying*. What keeps me coming back is a deep desire to not only see a better world but build it together with others. To contribute a thoroughly considered vision for a small piece of what that better world might look like, so that my piece might link up with someone else's.

There are many reasons we ask students to write, and I have expounded upon them ad nauseum in this text already. One critical reason is not just to reflect on and enjoy but to positively *impact* our collective experience.

### Strategies for Implementing Communal Experience

- Engage in generative or collaborative writing experiences with colleagues during professional learning or collaborative working times.
- Write along with students as they write. Share out when helpful/relevant.
- Offer students practice with sharing their writing in a supportive and scaffolded manner (on a volunteer basis, in chosen pairs or small groups, and perhaps eventually assigned).
- Guide students to respond positively to each other's writing (i.e., pointing out what they enjoyed or admired).
- Invite or create space for students to write about topics of social importance to them.

## Applying the Framework

In the following chapters, I apply the healing-centered framework outlined in the past three chapters to four different stories of four different teacher–student relationships. Each scenario illustrates how the framework can be applied and brought to life, in service of a healing-centered approach to writing.

All of the characters in these stories are fictional but very much "real" in the sense that they are an amalgamation of so many students and teachers I have taught or worked with in my 20-plus years of teaching.

In the first two, I present scenarios where things feel "stuck"—the writing, the relationships, the people. In the second two, I highlight examples in which things begin to get "unstuck." In all of these stories, I aim to explore some of the complexities, nuances, and challenges that can dwell beneath the surface of everyday interactions.

As you read through the stories of these teachers and students, you might consider: What sort of writing experiences might they benefit from? What would a healing-centered approach look and feel like for them? What characteristics might they embody in their writing experience, and how?

After each anecdotal description, I begin an analysis using elements of the framework, with an implicit invitation for you to continue this analysis, on your own or with others.

## References

Ahmed, S. (2014). *The cultural politics of emotion*. Edinburgh University Press.

Babbott, J. (2014, February 25). *I will not write unless I am swaddled in furs*. McSweeney's. https://www.mcsweeneys.net/articles/i-will-not-write-unless-i-am-swaddled-in-furs

Boldt, G., Lewis, C., & Leander, K. M. (2015). Moving, feeling, desiring, teaching. *Research in the Teaching of English*, *49*(4), 430–441.

Cameron, J. (2016). *The artist's way: A spiritual path to higher creativity* (25th anniversary ed.). TarcherPerigee.

Cohen, G. L., & Garcia, J. (2008). Identity, belonging, and achievement: A model, interventions, implications. *Current Directions in Psychological Science*, *17*(6), 365–369.

del Carmen Salazar, M. (2013). A humanizing pedagogy: Reinventing the principles and practice of education as a journey toward liberation. *Review of Research in Education*, *37*, 121–148.

Elbow, P. (2015). "Personal writing" and "expressivism" as problem terms. In R. T. Roeder & R. Gatto (Eds.), *Critical expressivism: Theory and practice in the composition classroom*. WAC Clearinghouse, Parlor Press. https://doi.org/10.37514/PER-B.2014.0575.2.01

Greene, M. (1993). Diversity and inclusion: Toward a curriculum for human beings. *Teachers College Record: The Voice of Scholarship in Education*, *95*(2), 211–221.

Greene, M. (2008). Commentary: Education and the arts: The windows of imagination. *LEARNing Landscapes*, *2*(1), 17–21. https://doi.org/10.36510/learnland.v2i1.270

Hammond, Z. (2021, June 22). Liberatory education: Integrating the science of learning and culturally responsive practice. *American Educator*, *45*(2), 4.

Jones, S. P. (2022). The language of curriculum violence. *English Journal*, *111*(5), 15–17.

kaur, r. (2022). *Healing through words*. Andrews McMeel.

Lopate, P. (1995). Introduction. In P. Lopate (Ed), *The art of the personal essay: An anthology from the classical era to the present*. Anchor.

Maté, G. (2022). *The myth of normal: Trauma, illness & healing in a toxic culture*. Avery.

Menakem, R. (2017). *My grandmother's hands: Racialized trauma and the pathway to mending our hearts and bodies*. Central Recovery Press.

Morrison, T. (2019). *The source of self-regard: Selected essays, speeches, and meditations*. Knopf.

Muhammad, G. (2020). *Cultivating genius: An equity framework for culturally and historically responsive literacy*. Scholastic Inc.

Oluo, I. (2019). *So you want to talk about race*. Seal Press.

Page, C., & Woodland, E. (2023). *Healing justice lineages: Dreaming at the crossroads of liberation, collective care, and safety*. North Atlantic.

Pimentel, O., Pimentel, C., & Dean, J. (2016). The myth of the colorblind writing classroom: White instructors confront White privilege in their classrooms. In F. Condon & V. A. Young (Eds.), *Performing antiracist pedagogy in rhetoric, writing, and communication*. WAC Clearinghouse. https://doi.org/10.37514/ATD-B.2016.0933.2.05

Topa, W., & Narvaez, D. (2022). *Restoring the kinship worldview: Indigenous voices introduce 28 precepts for rebalancing life on planet Earth*. North Atlantic Books.

Treleaven, D. A. (2018). *Trauma-sensitive mindfulness: Practices for safe and transformative healing*. W. W. Norton & Company.

# 6

# Case Study

## Esther and Maria

### The Student, Esther

Esther is a Black, Haitian American sixth-grade girl attending middle school in a predominantly White, affluent district. She takes the bus every morning from a nearby city, 15 miles away. When she entered kindergarten, her parents—Haitian immigrants who work in public service—enrolled her in an "open choice" program in the hopes that a series of well-funded schools would prepare their daughter for a life of social stability and financial security in their adopted country.

Esther is an excellent student, fastidious in all her efforts. She consistently completes her work and aims to please her teachers. She "hates" writing, or at least says that she does. Though she steadily earns Bs on most writing assignments, it takes her an enormous amount of time to complete each one because she labors over every detail and draft, trying to make it "perfect." Writing, in this sense, has never been enjoyable for her. Sometimes, she worries that her writerly voice isn't formal enough, that her vocabulary is too basic, and that her style dips too much toward the conversational. At home, her family speaks in mostly Creole. The writing she feels her teachers expect doesn't quite "flow"

DOI: 10.4324/9781003752721-6

for her as easily as it seems to for her peers. And there was that one time in third grade, which pops into her mind quite frequently, when she wrote "pwoblem" instead of "problem" on the board, and the whole class—including the teacher—laughed at her. She's not sure why she keeps remembering that moment. Way worse things have happened since then; she's heard the n-word spoken in her proximity more times than she can count. But something about that moment really stuck.

Speaking of her peers—socially, she feels somewhat separate from the other students. Because she lives in a different town, she doesn't participate in the same sports or after-school programs, and her parents don't socialize with other parents in the community. She wonders if her classmates judge her: for the clothes that she wears, the city that she lives in, the way that she talks, her lack of attendance at weekend activities. Well-meaning White friends and acquaintances have asked her embarrassing questions, like *Do they have schools in Haiti?* or *How do you make your hair look like that?* Less well-meaning kids, especially in elementary school, would snicker behind her back and laugh at the food she brought for lunch. Even her Black friends in this town are hard to relate to. In her eyes, they all live in mansions and spend their school vacations in places like Aspen or Nantucket. Teachers avoid pronouncing her last name; some of them seem to ignore her, while others are just a little *too* nice, always making sure someone is willing to link up with her during groupwork or downtime.

## The Teacher, Maria

One of Esther's teachers, Maria, is in her fifth year of teaching English Language Arts (ELA). As a first-generation Italian American, Maria can relate to Esther with respect to having grown up in a bilingual household with immigrant parents. Intuitively, she understands how a chasm can form when you feel like your family customs, traditions, and communication styles are so different from the ones you see around you. Her parents did not go to college and, growing up, she sometimes felt embarrassed by her own linguistic "slip-ups" in the classroom, where she would pronounce the word "hello" as "ello" or a word like "live" as "leave." Maria cannot, however, inherently relate to Esther's experience of being Black, from a family of non-European immigrants, and growing up in a lower-income city outside of her school district. Maria is White, raised fully immersed in a middle-class community, and her ethnic identity is not too visible or apparent on the surface. She tries to remain cognizant of these differences, to avoid overestimating her ability to relate to Esther. She knows how dangerous it is to assume that she can understand Esther's experience. The effect, however, is that Maria keeps herself a bit at arm's length. She wants Esther to feel comfortable around her so much that she makes herself less approachable and open than she could be. She holds back.

As a student, Maria was an underperformer; she experienced periods of depression and anxiety which led to her being school-avoidant. That meant not always, or even often, doing her homework, paying attention in class, or studying for tests. It meant skipping school, once she was old enough to do so; skipping classes in college. Despite all this, she ironically put a lot of pressure on herself to achieve; she was highly intelligent and usually could rally at the end of a term to pull her grades up if she was feeling well enough. Her bouts of overachievement, fueled by a deep perfectionism and desire to please her parents, to live up to their hopes and expectations—effectively balanced out the under.

Now, as a teacher, Maria overcompensates for what she sees as the deficits of her past. She tries to be perfect. She stays up late each night grading papers, planning lessons, and writing paragraphs of feedback on students' drafts. She is always trying to find new ways to engage her students, to make them *care* about reading and writing. She worries, at times, that her colleagues won't think she is a good-enough teacher—that they will somehow sense her inadequacy; that the students she passes along to them in seventh grade, for example, will wonder what went wrong, what she was doing all year, and why her students never learned to write the "right" way. She's always a little unsure of her own sense of what the "right" way is; Maria operates to a great degree on intuition. She tuned out a lot of her own schooling and feels she can't rely on it as a point of reference. She is also an avid reader and writer herself, so she draws from that well of experience in her teaching.

In part, Maria became an ELA teacher because she always loved to read and had aspired to be a writer. She majored in English and Creative Writing in college and had been working on a novel and a book of poems before she started teaching. The two fields of teaching and writing are vastly different but related. Maria pursued teaching with ambitions of sharing her passions with young people, aiming to be the type of teacher that she had needed as a child. And in many ways, Maria has succeeded at just that. Her students enjoy her class. They can tell how much Maria cares, and it makes them care, too. Many students have discovered an interest in writing from being in her class. They even write on their own; a small group of them have approached her about starting an afterschool Creative Writing club.

But Maria herself doesn't write anymore. She barely has time to read for pleasure. Conscientious students like Esther appreciate that Maria is genuinely invested in their growth, but Maria still feels like she could be doing more for them. She toggles between wanting to instill in her students a passion and interest in the subject matter, as well as confidence in their own voices, and wanting to equip them with the necessary skills to be "successful" as students. Sometimes the two priorities feel hard to reconcile. It makes her wonder: what am I *about* here? What is the real goal of my job, and am I doing it?

On top of that, so much class time is now eaten away by the need to prepare students for their standardized tests, by which she is evaluated. The district has adopted a new curriculum with challenging multiple-choice questions that almost all of her students seem to be struggling with. The questions drag down the students' grades and elicit a slew of parent emails and phone calls. Worse than that, they seem to deplete students' confidence. More and more of her students are saying, "I'm just not good at English class."

And then there's Esther. She's a hardworking student, who always does what she needs to do; she puts in effort, asks questions when she's confused, and is that true "pleasure to have in class" the report cards love to tout.

But Maria senses that Esther is not comfortable in class. Is it her? Is it the other kids? Is it the subject matter? Is it like this for Esther everywhere in the school?

In truth, for Esther, English class is her favorite. She loves the freewrites they do once in a while. She likes that Maria is not afraid to talk about race and other pressing topics that come up in the books and stories they read—at least compared with most of the other White teachers she's had. Maria also doesn't talk about racism like it's just something that happened in the past; she tries to make connections to the present day and has them read poems by people like Langston Hughes and Maya Angelou but also Amanda Gorman and Ross Gay. Esther also appreciates that Maria doesn't yell or constantly criticize the students—even "the bad kids—and call them out for every little thing they do wrong. The other kids are nicer in that room as a result, less defensive. Sometimes, Esther wishes Maria could be a little tougher on them—they do still get away with stuff—but at least Esther feels slightly less on guard in that room, less like she's just waiting for someone to say something mean or ignorant.

In terms of writing, Maria gets the feeling that Esther is holding herself back. Some of Esther's freewrites contain glimmers of a powerful writing style, interesting and candid, much less formulaic and stilted than the ones she uses in her essays. Maria loves it when she sees Esther incorporate snippets of Creole into her sentences, when she references home, when she reflects on what it feels like to move back and forth between her city and this town, when she brings her parents' dialogue to life on the page. She wishes Esther would share her writing with the rest of the class. She feels that they would learn something from it. Many students in the class do like to read their work aloud, and because all of the students have practice with peer review and frequent groupwork, their peers are generally supportive when people share.

But Maria would never push Esther to share unless she wanted to. She also wonders how much she should encourage Esther's unique style beyond these freewrites. How would other teachers respond to that real and honest voice coming through? Would they think it's too informal and blame Maria for leading her astray?

> How might a healing-centered approach to writing help Esther and Maria find a way forward?

First, let's examine what's at stake, and what seems to be impeded, for each of them.

## Esther and the Characteristics

In general in school, Esther is in an environment that appears to feel largely unaffirming of her and her racial and cultural identity. As a result, she feels that she needs to write in a way that is dehumanizing—rote and exacting and washed of any markers of individual voice. She follows every rule she learns with stringency, and so most of the writing she does feels laborious and tiring.

The freewrites she writes in English class, on the other hand, feel liberatory and give her a place to express herself without worrying about whether or not her grammar, punctuation, spelling, and word choice are in line with the teacher's expectations, with the typical norms that she has skillfully learned to apply but sometimes doesn't want to. The prompts are open-ended and give her a chance to say things she wouldn't otherwise say. She knows that her teacher isn't grading the freewrites, and sometimes not even reading them, so she can talk about how she feels treated by her peers or what it feels like to move between worlds. But she isn't empowered to take these freewrites seriously; they feel totally separate from the "real work" of school because they aren't graded, they happen sporadically, and they're not used in any way.

Whether or not she is experiencing trauma is not something Esther may have thought about before, and her teacher Maria is not in a position to assess that status. The core memory Esther has, though, of being laughed at in third grade when she slipped into her home language in class, could very well be a kind of trauma—the kind that gets retriggered by new instances of discrimination or flags of unbelonging she encounters. Menakem (2017) writes, "We can have a trauma response to anything we perceive as a threat, not only to our physical safety, but to what we do, say, think, care about, believe in, or yearn for" (p. 7). Her body remembers the feeling of embarrassment when a part of herself slipped through in a place where it didn't feel welcomed or appreciated.

Her mind, on the other hand, may be telling her to get over it. After all, that memory was not the worst case of discrimination she has faced. If she told anyone else that she still thinks about this moment, would they take her seriously? How seriously? Trauma sensitivity calls for us to take it all seriously. It calls for us to *not* make assumptions about what is or is not trauma; it calls for us to assume that anyone, and maybe even everyone, could be holding some degree of it.

So what would it take for Esther to have an experience with writing that is more healing-centered? An experience with additional capacity to be identity-affirming, restorative, and maybe even transformative?

## Maria and the Characteristics

In the midst of an increasingly standardized curriculum that is not intended to honor and nurture the individual humanity of each student, Maria is making some efforts to counterbalance the force of it in a humanizing way in her classroom by regularly inviting students to express themselves freely without constraints. The effect is that students are increasingly comfortable doing so, and people like Esther are beginning to open up and reveal some deeper layers of their identities and experiences. More and more students seem to crave these opportunities and are seeking them out, asking Maria if she will host an afterschool club to support their new or awakened interest in creative, reflective, and expressive writing.

And it's not just the offering of these opportunities that seems to be working. In Esther's case, it's also their consistency and the fact that Maria has dropped some hints that it's okay to write what you need to write. Outside of these exercises, her willingness to talk about racism and her representation of Black poets have felt affirming for Esther, enabling the student to take the risk of writing more personally about her own experience.

At the same time, Maria feels reined in—and unempowered—not only by the rigid expectations of the new curriculum, which require her to devote an abundance of time and energy to standardized testing prep, but also by the implicit expectations that she internalizes from her environment. Stephanie Jones (2012) refers to this phenomenon as the "nomos" of teacher practice, which consists of unspoken rules about how a teacher should be and behave—in my mind, further homogenizing a field already lacking in all kinds of diversity, especially race and gender. The "carefully sanitized discourse" (Jones, 2012, p. 135) Maria has been influenced by and called into adopting may be holding her back from utilizing her own background—her cultural identity, her mental health history, her school avoidance—as an asset in her teaching. Currently, she seems to experience these aspects of self as a source of shame.

Could the reason for this shame be, at least in part, that these memories hold trauma for Maria? Could it be that she has not fully processed their impact on her, on her identity, on her teaching practice, and on her life? Is it possible that she has not had the space, support, guidance, or inclination to critically examine how her former tendency to feel embarrassed by her own linguistic patterns, for example, was rooted in a larger repression of linguistic expression and identity that favors a White, middle-class, monolingual norm?

But maybe she has examined her own experience in the context of trauma. However, maybe she has not yet been able to reconcile that phenomenon with the fact and relevance of her own Whiteness; her Italian American family's racialization as such. In Menakem's (2017) words, immigrant groups such as the Italians, in the United States, were "inducted into the false community of whiteness" (p. 71) decades before Maria's family arrived here. But what he calls "white-body supremacy" doesn't just affect people of color; he writes, "the inherited trauma of white-body supremacy" is "embedded in all our bodies," (p. 10) and shows up in the form of "constricted bodies, frozen attitudes, and closed minds" (p. 104). That "constricted body" is what Maria feels when she is hyperaware of Esther's Blackness and her own Whiteness. Even though her recognition of the potentially unsettling nature of her presence may be helping Maria to approach Esther with sensitivity and grace, it is also keeping her at a distance from the young person in her care who might benefit from the extra nurturing and attunement that Maria feels too uncomfortable to extend.

As Menakem (2017) writes, "Once White Americans begin this all-important healing process, minds, nervous systems, attitudes, relationships, and culture can all have a little more room to grow and transform" (p. 104). How might a trauma-sensitive awareness enable Maria to give herself the grace to risk making an error in an effort to reach out more directly to Esther? To recognize how her own Whiteness is not only showing up in the classroom but impacting her practice and ultimately impeding a more affirming and liberatory approach?

There is also the matter of Maria's historical relationship with schooling, likely its own source of trauma—including the shame she felt, and still carries, from feeling unable to adapt to the norms of schooling as a result of her depression and anxiety. How might working to heal this part of herself and her past help empower her to be the kind of teacher she wants to be? The kind who is confident enough to make choices that align with her own inner knowing about what her students need, rather than making decisions driven by self-flagellation, fear of judgment, and a perceived need to conform?

Might she reallocate some of those hours obsessing over lessons plans or writing paragraphs of feedback on student papers to her own writing practice? Could she join in more frequently and authentically with her students while they're writing in class as well? Might that help her to restore her own waning relationship with writing as well?

Could she share a little more of her own struggles with her students? Could she share curated snippets of her own experience, to model vulnerability and connect with the class on a more human level?

How might these moves create a more ideal environment for transformative experience to occur? Could knowing it benefits her students as well give her the permission to extend this grace to herself?

## Applying the Values and Priorities

We can see that Maria believes in Esther's abilities—she recognizes her unique writerly qualities—but is she fully convinced of her possibilities as well? Or is she allowing standardized expectations to dominate her evaluation and assessment?

Maria is trying to create positive experiences in her classroom and is succeeding in many regards. Her students mostly enjoy being in her classroom and want more opportunities to learn from her. But Maria doubts herself and her practices. Her continued focus on her colleagues' perceptions, and her own potential shortcomings, are pulling at her and creating a competing priority that often wins. Her need to prove she is a capable teacher keeps her from prioritizing positive experience as much as she could.

Belonging is a value that matters to Maria, and it's what Esther is lacking in her general schooling experience—but Maria is too. She feels like an imposter in her school environment and role. Belonging matters for everyone in a community. How might Maria work toward fostering belonging for herself, and how might that help her foster belonging for all of her students, inspiring them to share their true selves as well?

On a related note, Maria's prioritization of psychic and affective safety is something that students like Esther can feel. Generally, kids are kinder to one another in Maria's room—or, at least, they don't seem to feel as comfortable being hostile, racist, or rude to one another. Maria's willingness to talk seriously about topics like racism makes it clear that she is thinking deeply and critically about injustices and inequities in society. How deliberate is this, on Maria's part, as a method for cultivating psychic and affective safety for students with marginalized identities? Could even more intentionality increase the psychic and affective safety of students such as Esther—whom Maria wishes might reach a point where they can share their critical perspectives not just in writing to her but vocally, with their peers?

## Integrating the Processes and Practices

So what processes and practices can be implemented, encouraged, or refined in order to support a healing-centered approach to writing, not only for Maria and Esther but potentially for all students in the space?

Contemplative inquiry seems to play a significant role in Maria's classes in the sense that the freewriting opportunities with open-ended prompts are creating impact; the students value them and use them for both critical and reflective thinking. They give students the "grace and space" to express themselves without at least external pressure to conform or perform. Some, like Esther, are using their contemplative practice space to write about their own lives and selves, a form of positive identity engagement. The practice of informal, exploratory writing also becomes a kind of arts-based engagement for many students who have discovered or reignited an interest in creative writing in Maria's class.

How might Maria provide a bridge between these freewriting opportunities and what she and students consider to be the "real work" of the class? What would shift or be enhanced if she managed to do so?

In my own classes, I have experimented with different approaches. In some cases, I have collected the freewrites and kept them in a folder, then returned them at the end of a unit or before an essay so they can revisit what they wrote and even respond to their own earlier writing. In other cases, I have asked students to select one or more of their freewrites to share with a peer for feedback before they expand or revise it into something more formal. In any case, my goal is to help elevate these reflective writing experiences and artifacts, and to illuminate their significance.

As for body awareness, Maria senses that Esther doesn't feel comfortable in the room, and that's probably a sharp instinct. Maria is also aware—maybe too aware—of her own embodiment as a White teacher and how that might be impacting Esther's comfort level. In a way, Maria is not feeling comfortable in her own skin, and Esther could very well be picking up on that.

Or not. It may not be Maria at all who is making her uncomfortable. Maria might need to ask herself: what else could it be? Who is Esther sitting near? Might there be a better spot in the room? By blaming herself, she may be missing a chance to see what else could be causing Esther's discomfort.

Communal experience is the height of what Maria ideally wants to achieve. She'd love to see Esther sharing her experiences and perspectives with her peers in an open and affirming way. She offers regular opportunities for students to share their work aloud, but Esther doesn't typically volunteer. While less so than in other classes, Esther seems to feel disconnected from her peers in English class. Maria, rightly, does not want to put Esther or any unwilling student in the spotlight. Perhaps Maria could find a way to encourage all of her students to be more vulnerable in their sharing. Positive identity engagement, in her class of mostly White students, might mean inviting them all to think, write, and share more about their own racial, cultural, and ethnic identities. She can also model it herself by finding relevant ways to talk about her own positionality, with phrases such as "As a White teacher ..." or "As an Italian American ..." or "As the daughter of immigrants ..." or maybe even "As someone who has struggled with depression and anxiety ..."

In closing, I'll say this: One might read the story of Maria, or encounter a teacher like her on a surface level, and think: she's doing great. Her students are mostly happy and engaged. Esther, too, is doing fine in the class. A look at her grades in PowerSchool would set off no alarms. Why center Esther's needs so intensely here?

And this question is what it's really all about.

We center the needs of those most at risk for marginalization because every person in the room matters.

We also center the needs of those most at risk for marginalization because, by doing so, we improve the conditions for everyone.

## References

Jones, S. (2012). Trauma narratives and nomos in teacher education. *Teaching Education*, *23*, 131–152. https://doi.org/10.1080/10476210.2011.625087

Menakem, R. (2017). *My grandmother's hands: Racialized trauma and the pathway to mending our hearts and bodies*. Central Recovery Press.

# 7 Case Study

## Lila and Dan

### The Student: Lila

Lila is a 10th-grade girl, White, from a middle- to upper-class family that speaks only English. She has always been a high-achieving student, at the top of her class. Her parents are highly educated, with degrees from "prestigious" universities and with successful careers as lawyers.

This school year, for the first time, Lila is struggling to complete her written assignments. Suddenly, she just can't seem to write at all. Her parents are alarmed by her grades; her teachers are frustrated by the tardiness of her assignments. Lila is a quiet, otherwise dutiful student, and her teachers did not at first expect to find her essays missing from the submission pile, unfinished or maybe not even started. Now, halfway through the year, they are "onto" her tricks: turning in blank documents, claiming not to know why an email didn't go through, feigning illness on major due dates. They see her moves as sneaky, and they are annoyed by her excuses. They sometimes chat about her behavior in the lunchroom.

It's strange, even to Lila, that she is struggling so intensely with writing because Lila always *loved* to write when she was

DOI: 10.4324/9781003752721-7

younger. She filled notebooks in elementary and middle school with stories and poems and ideas. She kept a journal and sometimes even liked to read her entries aloud to her parents; she wrote plays for her friends and family and assigned them all roles to perform.

In the ninth grade, however, something started to shift: writing became very *serious*. It wasn't at all *fun*, especially in school. Even though she understood that the type of writing she was asked to do—with thesis statements, supporting evidence, and clear claims—was very different from the freeform writing she did on her own, the pleasure she took in writing of any kind began to wane.

She did, however, begin to "master" the skills her teachers were looking for. This was clear to her because she consistently got checks on the rubric that read, "Demonstrates mastery," under categories like "organization" or "mechanics." Her friends would glance over at her desk and roll their eyes. "How are you doing that?" they'd remark. Her grammar, as one teacher noted in the margins, was "impeccable." These comments only increased the feeling of pressure. She knew she was a strong writer, but would she be able to maintain that level of achievement?

Now, in her sophomore year, even this type of academic writing, with clear guidelines and a formula she'd learned down to a tee, has become difficult—not because she doesn't know *how* to do it. It's like her body just won't *let* her.

Socially, too, things have changed. Lila sits in the library during lunchtime and avoids her usual group of friends that she has been close with since elementary school. In her eyes, they all seem so happy, adjusting to high school with ease, while she is constantly feeling out of place, exposed, as if they can see right through her. Like everyone can. She'd rather hide.

She's lost a lot of weight this year, too, and doesn't want anyone to notice. She wears oversized sweatpants and sweatshirts every day and ties her hair into a messy bun. She'd rather no one look at her at all.

## The Teacher: Dan

Lila's history teacher is Dan. He is White, too, middle class, hailing from a family of teachers, and grew up in a suburb two towns away from where he teaches. Dan is a popular teacher with a reputation for being tough but fair. "He works you hard, but you learn a lot," many kids say of him. "Tough grader." He's been teaching at the school for almost 20 years and is practically an institution himself.

Academic writing was always one of Dan's strengths as a student, and now he considers teaching academic writing to be the backbone of his success as a teacher. While some of his colleagues in the Social Studies department think it's not their job to teach writing, Dan brings writing instruction into the center of his practice. He sees the writing process as a way to teach critical thinking, a way of guiding students to analyze challenging subject matter by synthesizing disparate information and organizing complex ideas into a cohesive structure through an often painstaking process of drafting and revision.

Lila is now his student for the second year in a row. He is baffled by her ghost-like performance on writing assignments; last year, she performed as a star student of his—a model student. In fact, he frequently used her essays as anonymous exemplars for the rest of the class. Her older siblings were previously in his classes as well, and though they were also exceptional students, he believes Lila may be the strongest writer among them. It's always exciting to him when he encounters a writer of her caliber; he feels like he can mentor her in a way that doesn't reach most. All the more so, it frustrates him to see her struggling.

When a student like Lila is not doing well, it makes him feel that *he* is not doing well. And yet he isn't doing anything differently this year, and she managed to excel last year. Could it really be him?

## Identifying the Characteristics

In general, Lila's experience with writing in high school does not appear to feel humanizing. She has internalized the sense that there is a right and wrong way to do things; there are rules to master, and the rubrics used to evaluate her writing reinforce this idea. Even though she herself *has* been told that she's "mastered" the type of writing being asked for, and valued, in school, she does not feel free to experiment, take risks, or engage in the type of writing she has always enjoyed. She may be afraid that the expectations will continue to increase and she won't be able to maintain her status.

Dan's class is no exception—if anything, it's a prime example. Dan is widely recognized as being an effective teacher of writing, if "tough," because eventually, most of his students learn to write in the way that he teaches it. And the way that he teaches it aligns with the traditional, formulaic structures of academic writing in standardized American English. Students' perceptions that he is "tough" come, in part, from his grading practices. The "tough" perception, however, may also derive from the strict and relatively narrow standard to which Dan is holding his students. He expects them to align to it and will grade them down accordingly if they don't, sending the message that his class is "hard" (i.e., "rigorous").

Dan's approach is lacking humanization not just for students in their writing but also for himself. His acknowledgement that "he's not doing anything differently this year" is, in my opinion, the greatest clue. His teaching persona and modus operandi seem relatively locked into place—and certainly it works in many regards. But when a student like Lila isn't doing well, he both over- and under-attributes her performance to himself. By that I mean: he worries that he's not teaching as well as he usually does, but fails to imagine that he may need to shift in order to meet her evolving needs.

Lila has been affirmed in the sense that the checkmarks on the rubric tell her she's done things "right," that she's "mastered" the skills she is being taught. But these seeming affirmations actually make her feel added pressure; they further trigger her perfectionism and her doubts about whether or not she can maintain these high expectations.

It is possible, too, that these comments are in some sense *unaffirming*, because this way of writing feels so contrary to her natural inclination, but it earned her good grades and accolades. What if she were to take a risk and try something different? Deviate from the formulas and write in her own style? Would those affirmations disappear?

The seeming affirmation she has received is, in effect, unaffirming. The type of affirmation I'm writing about in this book is more than just telling student writers that they've done well or assigning them good grades. It's about giving them space to be themselves, to express their ideas, feelings, and questions with the grace and space to figure out what those are and how they want to express them. It's about finding their own sense of inner affirmation, according to the standards and expectations they hold for themselves, beyond any rubric.

So what would it take to make Lila's experience with writing more restorative? First, it's worth framing the issue in those terms. When a teacher notices that a student is uncharacteristically struggling to write and finish assignments, the response can move beyond punishments (late penalties, detentions) and frustration (judgmental assessment, comments in the lunch room), toward inquiry: what might be impeding the student's *relationship* with writing? What might need to be restored, and how?

For Lila's case, reflecting on these questions might start with trauma sensitivity. What else might be going on in Lila's life? Lila's distancing from her friends, skipping lunch, and wearing oversized clothing might indicate an eating disorder or some other mental health concern that may or may not have been triggered by a traumatic experience. Dan may or may not be aware of these changes. But if he or any of her other teachers talked to a guidance counselor, or Lila's parents, what might they learn—or not learn? What adjustments, in the meantime, can Dan make within his purview as her teacher—particularly with regard to writing—to help her cope through the challenges? Could she somehow be empowered (with support) to find her own way through these struggles with writing? Could she be freed from some of the rigid requirements in order to loosen up the stuck writing muscles? Could this bout of difficulty with writing be the type of crisis that catalyzes a transformative experience?

## Applying the Values and Priorities

In Dan's class—but not *just* Dan's class—Lila is interpreting a message that conveys: academics are paramount.

And, of course, academics are crucial. Dan's primary jobs are to teach his subject matter and to help sharpen students' skills.

But, ironically, that academic development isn't happening in Lila's case because, culturally, her teacher and school—in good conscience—are overprioritizing academics.

Lila is feeling out of place in high school, but more so, whole facets of herself do not feel welcome in her classroom—especially the creative and imaginative parts of herself who used to write stories and stage plays for her family and friends.

Dan, overall, is a strong teacher who "gets results": his students generally learn what he is trying to teach, and they respect and value him. But are there times when this emphasis on results takes too much precedence over other priorities, such as psychic and affective safety or belonging? Could prioritizing positive experience—inviting more variety, choice, or experimentation into the classroom—alleviate some of the pressure that students like Lila experience in classes like his?

As for prioritizing a belief in the writer's abilities and possibilities: Dan does believe in Lila's abilities. But has he truly considered and made space for her possibilities? Is there an opportunity to incorporate more open-ended writing opportunities, with fewer constraints, to see what she and the rest of the students come up with, when less *directed*?

It also stands to wonder: what about the students who *aren't* "mastering" the skills in the way that Lila did? Those students who are glancing over at her paper and saying, "How are you doing that?" Is there just as much belief in *their* abilities and possibilities? Is there a true openness to the chance that they could very well surprise him with their capabilities on any given assignment?

## Integrating the Processes and Practices

Have you ever felt the way Lila does—as if your body won't *let* you engage with something, someone, some activity? How about with writing, specifically?

The idea that the body won't *permit* you to engage with something is rife with the possibility of eye rolls and dismissiveness. But, in fact, it makes a lot of sense.

First off, we don't know if Lila is experiencing some sort of trauma or difficulty beyond academics, but it's entirely possible that she is. She's lost weight and is making visible efforts to hide her body and herself. In her writing, she is experiencing a kind of bodily shutdown—what neuroscientifically might be seen as either a "freeze" or "collapse" response. She used to write creatively and expressively but hasn't done so since the eighth grade. In the ninth grade, she focused exclusively on and "mastered" the art and craft of academic writing but now cannot seem to write at all.

As I discuss in earlier chapters, academic writing requires a kind of alertness of the nervous system that is starkly different from the kind that tends to produce creative or imaginative writing. Academic writing, in its reliance on critical and analytical thinking, activates and leans heavily on the sympathetic nervous system. In Lila's case, her sympathetic nervous system may have been in overdrive, locked into a hypercontrolled mode for so long that she has trouble accessing the parasympathetic response to balance it out. The parasympathetic nervous system is responsible for our "rest and digest" functions but also supports the spaciousness and feeling of safety required to be creative (Maté, 2022).

It's entirely possible that the reason Lila has been unable to access her creative and reflective writing practice for two years has much less to do with school than with something else going on in her life. Part of the cause may generally be attributed to her trouble adjusting to the pressures and expectations of high school, or it may be due to some specific incident or even trauma that has put her sympathetic nervous system (fight, flight, freeze) on constant alert, to the point where, now, she not only doesn't *enjoy* writing but can't seem to write in any form at all. However, the pressure to perform in a very specific way in her writing has certainly not helped.

Practicing body awareness here can, first off, validate the body's role in her ability to write. Her inability to complete assignments is not from laziness or a desire to flout her teachers' deadlines and rules. For her, it is a physical reaction that indicates a need for greater support and perhaps a different kind of scaffolding or modification.

Body awareness can also serve as a reminder to consistently offer different "ways in" to a writing assignment; to offer, when possible, a variety of choices in terms of form and style, and to provide regular low-stakes opportunities to practice writing in various modes. This strategy might include offering more reflective and contemplative writing opportunities or using arts-based strategies such as poetry writing or ekphrastic prompts that invite students to respond to photographs, paintings, poems, or other artwork with their own words.

Some teachers might also consider facilitating mindful movement or breathing practices to help students settle their bodies before or while writing. Even small reminders about finding a comfortable position, taking breath or movement breaks, rolling out the wrists, or rolling back the shoulders can help call attention to the body's role in writing. While Lila's struggles may sharply highlight the challenges of writing that live and manifest in the body, it is likely that such practices could and would benefit all students.

What Lila is struggling to offer herself in her writing is the "grace and space" to be less than perfect. To score less than "demonstrates mastery" on the rubric by trying something different, something she isn't sure that her teacher will "like." She would rather get a zero.

I would wonder, in this instance, if Dan, too, is struggling to give himself the grace and space to try new approaches in the classroom, to innovate and experiment with different strategies, assignments, and activities. He has found what he sees as a tried and true method for teaching writing. Is he willing to risk the vulnerability that comes with deviating from his usual practices?

Finally, while identity might not explicitly *seem* to come into play: what would positive identity engagement look like in this scenario?

Lila was, for a while, Dan's star student. Being the one in the class who scores the highest on writing assignments could very well have become part of Lila's identity—at least as prescribed and assigned by others. Did it align with her view of herself? Did it become something that grew to be such a part of her self-concept that she feared losing it?

In this regard, the narrow, seemingly positive view of Lila as a high-performing student may serve to be unaffirming—certainly of Lila's self-identity as the creative and imaginative playwright and poet who doesn't seem to feel a sense of belonging in her current environment.

According to Tema Okun's (2021) theory, both Lila and Dan (like Esther and Maria in the previous chapter) are contending with the effects of White supremacy culture, which dictates "one right way" to do things and upholds perfectionism. The first is "the belief there is one right way to do things and once people are introduced to the right way, they will see the light and adopt it," and if they don't, "then those defining or upholding the one right way assume something is wrong with the other" (n.p.). That "assumption" can come, for teachers, in the form of something so seemingly benign as a lowered mark on a rubric, which a teacher may feel beholden to assign, because the student did something essentially deemed "wrong."

Perfectionism, meanwhile, is not about excellence but rather about "the conditioned belief and attitude that we can be perfect based on a standard or set of rules that we did not create and that we are led to believe will prove our value" (Okun, 2021, n.p.). Before entering high school, Lila had her own well-developed and established relationship with writing. She had an embodied sense of what writing felt like, what it meant to her, and what its purpose was. That embodied sense was completely disrupted when she got to high school and learned that there were very specific ways in which she was expected to write. Surely, these rules were introduced to her earlier, but their dominance and increasing complexity in high school proved to be overwhelming for Lila. Dispositionally, Lila was accustomed to being a top student. Maintaining that status, it became clear, meant "mastering" these rules she was being taught. But at a certain point, her body was no longer willing to employ them.

Dan, meanwhile, is teaching writing in the exact way he learned to write, professing the values, standards, and expectations he was implicitly and explicitly taught were the "right" way, which most likely align with the curriculum materials used in his school and the way most of his colleagues teach writing. He may be taking his practice to another level, but that's likely being seen as a good thing; he's likely receiving accolades for this very "success." Would he have reason or inclination to stop and consider the possibility that such an approach is enacting White supremacy culture? Would he find it credible to believe that White supremacy culture could be harming a White student such as Lila? And yet, how might consideration of such a framing help him, and her, find greater movement within this moment of "crisis"?

As Oluo (2020) makes clear, White supremacy is not just "about Klan members and neo-Nazis," it's about "a society where White culture is normalized and universalized" (n.p.), and that culture includes language practices and expectations for written expression that have dominated for centuries in the United States. In Okun's (2021) words, they involve an overemphasis on objectivity, a belief and prioritization of "neutrality," and an overvaluing of ideas deemed "rational," along with a "shaming" of those ideas deemed "emotional" (n.p.).

In effect, these values, priorities, and expectations—no matter what you call them—are limiting Lila's sense of self and perhaps Dan's as well.

So, who is Lila, beyond this role of "star student"—compliant, high-achieving, and "capable"? Who is she beyond the sneaky, avoidant, or even "lazy" reputation she may be slowly gaining and defaulting to, now that her behavior is not aligning with her former image? How might Dan come to find out more about her identity?

And who is Dan, beyond the role of the good, "tough" teacher that students and teachers respect and take seriously? What would it look like for him to allow his classroom and teaching to get a little messy? Be a little less predictable? Bend in unexpected ways?

Who might they each become if they use this moment of challenge, and the confusion that arises from it, as an opportunity to grow? If they approach it as a *crisis*, as in "turning point"?

As Sean Ginwright (2022) reflects, "We are all flawed—and trying desperately to hide it. The truth is that the quality of our journey is not figuring out how to be perfect but rather reflecting on who we become in the process" (p. 16).

## References

Ginwright, S. (2022). *The four pivots: Reimagining justice, reimagining ourselves*. North Atlantic.

Maté, G. (2022). *The myth of normal: Trauma, illness & healing in a toxic culture*. Avery.

Okun, T. (2021). *White supremacy culture characteristics*. White Supremacy Culture. https://www.whitesupremacyculture.info/characteristics.html

Oluo, I. (2020, November 30). *Mediocre by Ijeoma Oluo* (excerpt). The Cut.

# 8

# Case Study

## Eddie and June

### Eddie

Eddie is a 12th-grade student, Cuban American. His full first name is Edmundo, but only his closest friends know that, and they invoke it only in jest, because they know that it bothers him when they do so. Even on the official roster his name is listed as "Edmund," and *no one* calls him that.

Eddie is not the most motivated student, least of all in English class, where he is constantly asked to do his least favorite thing: *write*. Writing, to him, is a pointless endeavor, especially now that he can just use ChatGPT to generate essays on command, with no real way for a teacher to prove he used it. Generative artificial intelligence (AI) is the way of the future, in his eyes, and conveniently so, since his writing skills largely plateaued in middle school. He's gotten pretty good at prompting, which he's been told by teachers and guidance counselors and other adults is a valuable skill in itself. Even his father encourages him to use AI for assignments. "My bosses want me to use it," he tells his son, "and your bosses will expect the same from you some day."

Before generative AI hit the scene, Eddie's mother would sit for hours with him, trying to help him with writing his papers

DOI: 10.4324/9781003752721-8

for school as best she could, while his father mostly sympathized with his son's challenges. Eddie's father is a successful auto mechanic who grew up in a small multigenerational household filled with many relatives, including his parents who did not speak English. He started working in a neighborhood body shop at age 12 and learned valuable skills that would never be rewarded in school, where he barely scraped by with his grades. He dropped out of high school at age 16 so he could work full time, though he eventually earned his GED at age 20, when his first son—Edmundo—was born.

Early into Eddie's senior year, something a little different happened. His Environmental Science teacher gave him a writing prompt that somewhat shifted his relationship with writing. This teacher's name is June.

## June

June is a Korean American woman whose family immigrated to the U.S. when she was a child. Like Eddie, she has an alternate name that reflects her heritage: Ji-Hoon. In college, June wavered between majoring in English or Biology, because she performed well in both subjects. She loved to write, especially fiction, but Biology seemed like a more practical choice, one that could keep more options open.

June never expected to teach, but in graduate school, she had the opportunity to work as a teaching assistant (TA) and surprisingly enjoyed the experience. Her main responsibility was to grade and conference with students on their papers, a task most of her peers dreaded; her classes in the Sciences tended to attract people whose relationships with writing ranged from disinterested pragmatism to outright loathing. The other TAs in her program dreaded reading student writing and didn't put much time or energy into the task. June, on the other hand, spent hours reading and responding to students' work. Her feedback was so helpful that students began seeking her out for extra help beyond the mandatory conferences. June thoroughly enjoyed sitting with these student writers and talking with them about their work. She loved pointing to specific places within their writing where she saw opportunity for growth and brainstorming ways to further develop, clarify, or organize their ideas in new ways. Witnessing a paper transform into something the writer could feel proud of became a mission for her.

Now, as a high school teacher, June uses reflective writing prompts in class to help students *connect* with what they're learning on a personal and social level—to see how terms like biobehavioral synchrony and neuroplasticity are not just definitions to memorize but important concepts that show up in their own relationships. Or to consider how population health is affected by more than genetics but also by social conditions and to imagine alternative ways of living and structuring society that could improve these outcomes. She brings her classes outdoors to write in their journals, encouraging students to use their senses to make observations about the natural world and to notice how it makes them feel. Often, she collects and reads their entries, but only when she tells them in advance that she will do so. Otherwise, she tells them her reading is optional; that way, if they really need to write something but don't want anyone to see it, they can choose to keep their writing to themselves.

## Eddie's Writing

The first journal prompt June gave to Eddie's class was to write about a place that you feel strongly about. "It could be a place you know well," June elaborated, "like your bedroom, your backyard, this town … or it could be a place you don't know as well, like a one-time vacation spot or even a place you've never been."

The phrase "*Place you've never been*" sparked something for Eddie: he immediately thought of Cuba. He laughed to himself silently as it came to him, because he'd never been to Cuba, but the place nonetheless loomed large in his mind, in his life, in his household, in his family. Old photographs of dirt roads lined with palm trees, colorful buildings with arched windows, and portraits of sprawling family weddings and patron saints adorned the walls of his home. Wistful cries for "la isla" rang through the rooms of his home along with the soulful voice of Benny Moré and lively rhythms of Celia Cruz's salsa music.

*Cuba,* he wrote. *Never been there, but I always been there.*

In his reflection, Eddie described his family dinners of ropa vieja and yucca con mojo; his grandmothers' stories of growing up on the island and playing in its dirt fields by the sea—stories he'd heard so many times that he felt as if he'd experienced them himself.

It felt good to write these details. Although they simply came from the reality of his life, there was something powerful about putting them on paper, putting this part of his life into words—naming it and claiming it. It made his experience feel meaningful. It made it a *story*.

When he turned in the handwritten page at the end of class, he felt a little uncomfortable. He'd just written what was true, without thinking too much about how it sounded to a teacher. She'd said not to worry about grammar, punctuation, or spelling, and so he didn't—he rarely did, but even less so than usual. But would she suddenly care about these things now that he'd turned it in? He shrugged internally. "She already knows I can't write," he thought. "What does it matter?"

This writing felt a little different, though. It was personal. He wasn't sure he wanted to see the same kind of criticisms or red marks he typically saw on his work in other classes in response to something so close to his heart.

At the same time, he sensed that this teacher might not do that. She was pretty chill, in his eyes—not so uptight like other teachers. When students pointed out typos in the assignments she gave out, she didn't get angry or defensive; she just laughed it off.

The next day, when he received his freewritten response back on his desk, there appeared no grade, just as promised, but a comment stretched across the bottom: *Loved reading this, Eddie! I can relate, with my Korean family's influence*. She had starred and underlined his opening sentence and scribbled beside it: *Great line*.

*Great line* was a comment like none he'd ever received from a teacher. It was short and vague, but strangely, it made him feel important—less like a student, and more like an equal. Because he *knew*, on some level, that it *was* a great line—because that line was *true*, and honest, and real, and he'd had the courage to write it. It might not seem like courage to someone else, but it was for him. He was usually very private about his life.

After that moment, without any word or fanfare and maybe even without any awareness of why, he started putting a little more effort into his writing assignments—and not just in Environmental Science. At first, it frustrated him that his grades in English class were still very low. But then, he decided to ask his teacher why. She told him to come for extra help, and—for the first time since teachers started advising him to do so in the sixth grade—he went.

A couple months into the school year, Eddie approached June for help with his college essay. June was surprised because, last she knew, Eddie wasn't planning to go to college. And, she was a Science teacher—not a typical first pick for college essay guidance. But she asked no questions on the matter, smiled widely, and said, "Of course I'll help you!" as she clasped her hands together near her heart. "I'd be honored!"

He laughed and rolled his eyes. Any other teacher, he wouldn't have believed, but with her, he felt like she actually meant it.

## Identifying the Characteristics

For Eddie, writing hasn't typically meant much to him. His lack of interest in writing made it easy for him to offload writing to generative AI when it became so readily possible to do so. Writing had never felt like a humanizing endeavor for him; why not let the chatbot have at it?

The journal assignment in June's class, however, was unexpectedly affirming. The simple prompt—*write about a place you feel strongly about*—was enough to shift something new into place for Eddie. He took it as an invitation to write about something that mattered to him: his culture and his family. He *liked* what he wrote, even if he was unsure that his teacher would like it, and was doubly surprised and affirmed when she recognized the value and promise within his words. When June wrote, "Great line," it was a way of saying: *I see you.*

This seemingly small moment was liberatory in the sense that it freed Eddie from a relatively fixed way of seeing himself and his writing. It empowered him to use his voice and inspired him to restore his relationship with writing by putting in more genuine effort and connecting with his teachers for one-on-one support. He began to take himself more seriously as a writer.

June's approach to teaching writing made space for such transformative experience, in no small part because she seems to have a discernibly trauma-sensitive approach. Eddie braced himself to see red marks and negative comments on his very personal journal entry, even though he was told not to worry about grammar, punctuation, spelling, or any other writing mechanics. While he may or may not be carrying trauma, her response ensured his psychic and affective safety.

June's written comments—*Loved reading this, Eddie! I can relate, with my Korean family's influence*—are mutually humanizing; she made herself a *person* to him and not just a teacher. In effect, the experience was additionally restorative because Eddie brought into the classroom a part of himself he may not typically draw on, reconnecting two parts of himself that are often split from each other.

## Implementing the Values and Priorities

June prioritizes psychic and affective safety in that she invites students to write personally about themselves and their experience, but she actively maintains a safe container in which to do so by setting parameters and boundaries around the experience. For example, if she is going to collect their journal entries, she lets them know in advance; otherwise, turning them in is optional. Her comments on these entries are not evaluative, because the purpose of the journals is not for students to demonstrate strong writing skills but rather to give students a place to connect with and process their thinking, feelings, and ideas.

In this way, June has made positive experience a priority in the class as well. She takes students outside to write with their senses and gives them space to explore within the realm of writing, without the pressures of grading and assessment. For Eddie, this approach made him feel comfortable enough to write personally about his culture and family in a way that wasn't typical of him, in a way that he recognized as being honest and truthful. The open-ended nature of the prompt, and June's warm and affirming response, sent him a message that this part of himself he shared did, indeed, *belong* in the classroom.

June's positive response to Eddie's quickly written reflection, to me, suggests an emphasis on belief in his abilities and possibilities; it indicates a stance that is "expecting to find the familiar profound," in the words of Wendy Bishop (2003), and an alertness to "that potential in student writing that is there, as yet unactivated" (p. 268).

## Integrating the Processes and Practices

In addition to extending grace and space for her students to write without the looming threat of criticism, June is extending herself the grace and space to be imperfect. Eddie notices how easily she is able to laugh at her own mistakes; she isn't afraid to express emotion ("Loved reading this, Eddie!" and "Of course I'll help you! I'd be honored!"), and perhaps it is her consistency that makes him believe her.

June is cultivating body awareness by encouraging students to write from their senses and attuning to the "body" of work produced on the page by marking off specific places where the writing resonates most for her as a reader. In terms of her own body, she notices the emotion that arises in her when she reads her student's work, and she uses that emotion to guide her response and interaction with him and with the piece.

Both of their identities are positively engaged in this instance. Through the open-ended prompt simply asking him to write about a place he feels connected to, Eddie finds himself writing about his family and culture in a meaningful way. He even smiles and laughs to himself as he does so. June, meanwhile, shares in his joy, reacting to his writing with alacrity and connection—she brings her own identity to bear, writing, "I can relate, with my Korean family's influence," to his reflection. This connection becomes an instance of communal experience.

While arts-based engagement may not seem to be prominent here, the exploratory nature of the prompts promote expression in addition to contemplative inquiry. Inviting students to write from their senses can also be an arts-based and contemplative practice that June is able to incorporate, through writing, into her Science classroom.

In my imagination of these two characters' journey together, I see Eddie writing a powerful college essay in which he revisits his original journal entry and takes it further, reflecting on the hybridity of his Cuban American heritage or on the role and importance of his Cuban culture within his life. I envision the two sitting together—June pointing out places where Eddie might spend a little more time, digging deeper, finding the refraction of his voice he chooses to use to express who he is and what he wants from his future, reflecting on which aspects of himself that he wants to carry forth. I see him writing the way toward both his next steps and a more integrated sense of self.

## Reference

Bishop, W. (2003). Suddenly sexy: Creative nonfiction rear-ends composition. *College English*, *65*(3), 257–275. https://doi.org/10.2307/3594257

# 9

# Case Study

## Mason and Tag

### Mason

Mason is an eighth-grade boy, autistic, with exceptional analytical skills but severe difficulties with written expression. In fact, he describes writing as physically *painful*. He didn't mind writing so much in elementary school, when it was about either learning the rules of grammar or writing whatever you want. Now, it's about doing both at once—writing the "right" way *and* having to figure out for himself what that will look like.

In the mainstream classroom, where he can more easily "hide" in a sea of others, he simply avoids writing at all costs. In his special education classroom, where teachers and paraprofessionals he knows quite well sit beside and try to guide him, he grows angry—sometimes explosively so—when he is asked to work on his writing. His support team feels torn between wanting to help him succeed in his subject-area classes and wishing his other teachers would be more flexible with his writing assignments. Does someone for whom writing is *so* challenging really *need* to write at all? Aren't there enough other ways to assess understanding? These are questions they ponder.

DOI: 10.4324/9781003752721-9

Yet these questions feel a little too "out there" to actually *ask.* Writing is a core skill in their school's curriculum—it's a requisite part of the standards—so *of course* Mason needs to do these assignments. And so, they help him—sometimes, they wonder, a bit too much? They provide him with a flurry of scaffolds, including sentence stems with blanks for him to fill in.

But the blanks overwhelm Mason as much as a stark-white page does. His teachers say they're meant to help, but Mason resents them (the blanks but also at times the teachers). The document looks messy, and he doesn't know what the teacher wants him to say to fill in the spaces. Looking at the page with all those words and lines makes him want to scream, flip a chair, and storm out of the classroom—something he has done several times before. And he *hates* when that happens. He feels terrible afterward and it's hard to walk back into the room. Last time he had such an eruption, he could barely look at anyone for weeks afterward.

So his special ed teacher types for him. She prompts the next word and the word after that. While she does so, he stares at the ceiling throughout the process. His mind wanders to other topics. He remains calm by squeezing a stress ball and chimes in on occasion, when his teacher repeats or rephrases her questions and gives him enough time to process and respond. Eventually, the essay gets written and sent to the subject area teacher. It's done. "You did it!" his teacher says excitedly, but he just sighs violently. She doesn't get it, is how he feels. This matters way more to her than to him.

At the same time, he feels relieved, mostly because his teacher will stop making him endure this belaboring process. She is relieved as well and gives him a break. They watch a funny video together featuring cats arranging themselves into odd postures as a reward for both of them.

## Tag

Tag is Mason's Health teacher. Tag is an artist, queer, who likes to write but is primarily a visual artist: collage, painting, and sculpture. In college, they took a couple of poetry workshops and then assembled a collection of their pieces to self-publish and illustrate, mostly to share with friends. They also participated in poetry slams at local coffee shops, just for fun. Generally, writing at a desk in solitude is not enjoyable for them; they prefer it when writing feels like a social experience—a chance to exchange ideas and express emotions through words in a creative way.

Health classes at their school are taken rather seriously, especially the end-of-year research process that happens within it. The intensive project is viewed as a pre-high school benchmark, a rite of passage for all students in the district. Students are instructed to select a health-related topic of interest to them, to study it thoroughly, and to present their findings in (almost) any way they wish. There is a high degree of choice around the "product" they create, including the most obvious choice: a research paper.

Some students take the research paper route because it feels like something they know how to do; the guidelines are clear, and Tag offers a quick review of "the writing process" while emphasizing that their writing skills are not the primary element being assessed. But many other students enjoy the fact that they *do* have the freedom to select something else—a painting, a play, a poster, and always with a written component, where they explain their choices, along with a short description of each source they used. When students identify topics they really care about, it can become a true passion project, something memorable that they recall years later and talk about even in high school: "Remember when you made that board game about cancer research for Mr. Quimbley's class?"

Tag likes to "prime" students for this experience by offering artistic options throughout the school year: *Illustrate your feelings about sleep; write a poem from the perspective of a dinner plate; act out a healthy response to a bully.*

Mason often struggles with these prompts, but because they are not scored and the stakes are low, his grade is not affected. Tag usually says, "Just do what you can!" Sometimes, what Mason can do is nothing. Other times, he comes up with something really interesting but usually in one short burst toward the middle or end of class—maybe a (relatively brilliant) sentence or a quick cartoon sketched into his notebook. "That's great!" Tag usually responds, and they mean it; they're glad to see Mason engaging at all. Sometimes, they wonder if they should be expecting, or "demanding," more of Mason. But inherently, these prompts are designed to be exploratory, open-ended, and without strict guidelines, so they have no specific grounds on which to push.

Mason appreciates this approach in his own quiet way. He likes being in Tag's classroom because he never feels put under a spotlight like he does in most places. While there is a lot of groupwork, which he typically doesn't love, there is also a lot of time for quiet reflection, and even if Mason doesn't produce much in that time frame, it does give him space to think, to *breathe*.

Sometimes, although he would never admit it to himself or to his special ed teachers, he even kind of *likes* some of the prompts. He especially likes how Tag will never call on him to share, although they pop by regularly to check in—but never in a loud or blatant way. Never trying to correct him or complain that he hasn't written or done enough. Maybe that's because it's "just" Health class, Mason reasons (it's not). Still, he wishes more teachers would give him that room to just *be*.

## Mason's "Writing"

Tag's classroom may have been a welcome reprieve for Mason from the pressures of expression he felt in other spaces. When it came to the big project, though, Mason shut down. Even for the brainstorming part, which was ungraded and done in class, he produced nothing. Tag felt thrown and confused; they'd always had what Tag saw as a solid relationship with Mason. What was happening now? Tag reached out to Mason's support team, but none of them could persuade Mason to talk about the project at all. The proposal deadline came and went, and the rest of the class had moved onto the research and planning steps, before Mason had even chosen a topic.

Tag knew they needed to try a new approach. They decided to hold a series of conferencing days with their students, with the aim of meeting with each person for up to 15 minutes. Not only would this benefit everyone, Tag reasoned, but they would also be able to work directly with Mason without calling special attention to him during class.

They began by asking Mason why he hadn't started. No reply. "Does this project feel particularly difficult?" Tag followed up. Mason gave a slight nod. "What makes it so hard?" No reply again, but Tag already intuited the answer: the project involved so much planning, so many choices, so much elaboration upon ideas. Even if it wasn't a typical "writing" project, it felt like writing in disguise.

"What topics related to health are you interested in?" Tag tried to ask casually.

Mason shrugged and glanced toward the left wall.

"Which of our units did you like the most?" Tag tried again, looking straight at Mason.

Mason turned his gaze toward the ceiling.

"Tell me this: what makes people healthy? And what makes people *unhealthy?"*

Mason snapped his head toward the right wall. "Pollution," he retorted. "Pollution makes people unhealthy. Dirty air."

"Yes!" Tag nodded enthusiastically. "Yes, Mason, that's so true." Tag recalled seeing Mason's face particularly alert during their unit on environmental health. It made sense that he would say this. "And what causes pollution?"

"Greedy companies," Mason spat, turning his chin upward. "Carbon emissions. Lazy people who drive everywhere."

Tag released a laugh. "Yup. That's all true. I agree."

Mason pinched the fabric of his jeans as he spoke. "People act like all it takes is recycling bottles and newspapers. No one even *reads* the newspaper anymore. It's not the papers. That's a *joke*."

"Tell me more," Tag coaxed.

Mason still would not turn to face Tag, but he looked down at his own lap and said: "It's the oil companies. The private jets. Gas pipelines running through poor towns on the rural plains. It's lead in the water in places like Flint, Michigan but so many other places we never even hear about."

Tag couldn't believe their luck to be present, to be witness, to this moment. The amount of words Mason had spoken seemed nearly equivalent to the total Tag had heard him speak all year. Sure, there were still no words put to page, but something had *happened* here. Some breakthrough of expression, at least in *their* relationship with Mason.

"Yes," Tag encouraged, "yes. This is such an important topic. Would you consider doing your project on this?"

Mason turned his head toward Tag now and gazed straight into their forehead. "I can do my project on this?"

"Yes, yes!" Tag emoted, wondering if they should tone down their enthusiasm a tad, so as not to scare Mason back into his shell. "I think the health impacts of pollution is an excellent topic."

"And how it's not all the same for everyone," Mason added.

"Right," Tag nodded. "That's right."

Mason nodded in return. "Maybe."

## Identifying the Characteristics

The most dehumanizing part of the writing process, for Mason, might be the feeling that it *must* get done at all costs. The blanks he sees on the scaffolds he's provided with overwhelm him. He feels obliged to fill them in almost robotically, but they feel devoid of a purpose other than completion. His support teachers are so desperate to help him finish the process so that he, and they, can move on because they see how painful it is for Mason. At the same time, they feel beholden to help him meet requirements that may seem typical or even flexible for most students but are egregiously challenging and triggering for Mason.

In Tag's class, writing feels slightly less painful because there is usually no set requirement in terms of length, and Tag does not react negatively when Mason writes no more than a sentence. The fact that he is empowered and free to take as much time as necessary, producing a sentence or a quick sketch by the end of the class without being chastised or prodded, affirms his need to process his thoughts in a way that works for him and his unique neurotype. While the plethora of choices offered for the research project may *appear* to be the most liberatory aspect of the class, it is this space Mason feels—"to just *be*"—that truly frees him to find his way.

Tag's trauma sensitivity comes through in the way that they check in regularly with Mason but take their cues from Mason as well; they don't call loud or blatant attention to the student while he works, and they give him plenty of wait time while conferencing together.

Mason's support team is also demonstrating trauma sensitivity in their awareness of how triggering the writing process can be for him. They understand the lasting impact of his outbursts—the shame these episodes create for Mason—so their well-meaning efforts to help him complete assignments are aimed at staving off an explosion. Their relationship with Mason matters, which is why—when they all finally endure through the end of the writing process—they simply watch a funny video together to reconnect, to restore the inevitable rupture that emerged. This rupture and release can be seen and heard through the violent, heavy sigh Mason releases in reaction to his teacher's joy upon finishing the assignment.

His support team does ask themselves an important critical question: does he really *need* to write, in all of these instances?—but they fear that the question is too "out there" to pose. They may not want to make waves or question norms so embedded that it would seem "radical" to question them. But what might be transformed if they broached this conversation more honestly and directly with their colleagues—teachers and administrators?

The answer is not necessarily that Mason shouldn't have to write, that the requirements should be seen as arbitrary or too challenging for him to complete. But the question itself can also help everyone think more intentionally about why—and to what degree—the written component of a learning process matters.

Take the case of the required Health research project—such an embedded part of the curriculum that every student in the district completes it. The *necessary* aspect of it was triggering for Mason; he felt the pressure, and it caused him to shut down. Tag, too, felt the pressure, because they didn't have the flexibility and authority to free Mason from the requirements entirely.

Because they noticed not just the shutdown in Mason's work production but also the rupture in the relationship, Tag tried a new approach, which turned out to be restorative: they initiated mandatory conferences with all students, a move that benefited not just Mason but the rest of the class as well. In this regard, remaining alert to Mason's needs, and their relationship with him, was transformative for Tag's approach with all students in the class.

## Implementing the Values and Priorities

We can see that Tag prioritizes psychic and affective safety in his classroom, at least with respect to Mason, because they give him space to process in the way that he needs to, without applying pressure or criticizing the pace of his work production. What's extremely telling, however, is that even when the pressure mounts in the face of this high-stakes project, Tag continues to prioritize Mason's psychic and affective safety above the need to make sure that Mason completes this curricular requirement.

As a result of this prioritization, Mason manages to have a positive experience in Tag's class, even with writing, although he won't admit it to himself or his support team. He also achieves a greater sense of belonging; while he might feel as if he needs or wants to "hide" in many of his "mainstream" classrooms, Tag makes sure that Mason feels seen. Tag attends to Mason regularly and gives him space in a way that is deliberate, not neglectful.

Perhaps above all else, we see the centering of a sincere belief in Mason's abilities and possibilities. Mason's challenges and limitations are very real, but Tag isn't looking to define them or let them shape Mason's experience. They remain genuinely excited to see what Mason will come up with, and they persistently encourage Mason with the patience to help him draw his ideas out.

## Integrating the Processes and Practices

Part of the grace and space that Tag practices involves body awareness. Tag is not detracted by Mason's lack of eye contact, heavy sighs, sharp replies, or physical signs of irritation. They understand how physically challenging it is for Mason to write, and they provide him with a wide berth in which to express that frustration.

Generally, Tag attunes to Mason's signals, recalling how alert his eyes were during a previous unit on pollution and noticing how he turns his head in a different direction when his interest shifts. They even consider how their own enthusiasm might "scare Mason back into his shell," demonstrating awareness of the affective conditions that may or may not keep Mason engaged.

This body awareness also enables Tag to positively engage Mason's identity, not as an autistic boy who struggles to write but as a passionate, socially conscious individual who cares about the climate crisis and its impact on communities.

Tag, as an artist themself, eagerly incorporates arts-based methods into their teaching. They don't just offer students the chance to create a work of art instead of writing a paper, they expose students to the artistic process and offer consistent opportunities to practice. While Mason may or may not choose to create something artistic for his project, the exposure to alternative forms of expression, and the exploratory approach they have been practicing all year in Health class, will likely aid him in finding his way.

What Mason seems to appreciate most about Tag's class is the space he's given to think, and to breathe, in quiet reflection. Tag does not rush Mason to respond to or deliver on a prompt. They understand that, when Mason is silent or not producing any writing, he may still be processing, and while the quantity of output may be small, the value is not.

Through the communal experience of sitting with Mason and attuning to his moment-to-moment needs, Tag helped Mason identify a purpose beyond just finishing the assignment so his teachers will leave him alone; they helped Mason tap into his intrinsic interest in the larger social issue of not just pollution but climate injustice.

In my idealized vision, based in part on my own experience with students like Mason, I see an opportunity for real movement here—a chance for Mason to articulate his thinking with clarity, if brevity, not just to his teacher but to his peers as well. Mason's avid sense of purpose can fuel an interest in audience: *What do your peers need to know about this topic, and why?* is a question Tag can remind Mason of throughout the process.

The sticking point might be form. While Mason is being invited to "write" in a form other than a paper, he might not know what else to choose. Perhaps a slideshow, in which he presents his argument—a "thesis"—in a sentence or two. Though elaboration is difficult for Mason, Tag might ask: *How are people going to know that you know what you're talking about?* to help prompt Mason to find evidence to support and illustrate his argument. If Mason were to channel the urgency he feels into a message he can deliver with intention to his peers, with Tag as a support helping him to find his way, it could be a healing experience. It could help him at least slightly reframe, reimagine, or restore his relationship with writing—with expressing himself and his ideas—and move his audience to care as well about his words and their meaning.

# 10

# Toward Embodying a Healing-Centered Approach to Writing

For my entire life as a writer and throughout my career as a teacher, I have worked deliberately toward embodying a healing-centered approach to writing—even if I never named it as such. While I may not have always gotten things "right," I am certain that *healing*, in the way that it is defined and outlined in this book, has been at the heart of the intentions guiding my practice. If an intention is truly "the healing process of a wound," then it is fair to say that this process is messy and imperfect, just as any real movement toward wholeness tends to be.

As someone who practices writing as an art, I see writing as a sacred space and act. This view sensitizes—some might say, over-sensitizes—me to the potential for psychic and identity-based harm within any kind of writing process. As a teacher of writing in a traditional schooling space, I often see—or *feel*—myself as an agent of harm, enacting and reenacting dehumanizing and demoralizing experiences with writing.

But that's just one way of seeing things. For many students, it just might not be that serious. Writing is something they can take or leave. They'll do it because they have to, and they won't particularly enjoy or hate it. Personally, as someone who was

DOI: 10.4324/9781003752721-10

school-avoidant, I am highly aware of how harmful traditional schooling spaces and practices can be for some people and how long it can take, and how hard it can be, to restore from their effects. As a teacher alert to the turmoil, I sense evidence of harm everywhere. As do-no-harm to my core, I am risk-averse when it comes to students' social-emotional well-being. For me, writing is 100% that serious.

And not just because of the risks involved but also because of the potential for missed opportunity. I have witnessed countless students find the power of peace, clarity, and voice through writing, even when they least expect it. Those are the moments I try to be ready for. Those are the moments I try to preserve and help make possible.

Because there is no way to fully ensure, contrive, or plan for these moments, the only sustainable way I've found to increase their likelihood is through embodiment.

## What Do We Mean by "Embodiment"?

Embodiment—in almost all the definitions I've read—involves a whole-self engagement of mind, body, and spirit. It stands in contrast with the disembodied experiences we sometimes find in educational spaces where knowledge is seen as an objective entity accessed exclusively through the mind, and where we who inhabit the space—teachers and students—are defined by our roles in the classroom: teacher as knowing authority and student as receiver of that knowledge.

Disembodied teaching, learning, and writing practices are those that ask us to put our desires, interests, identities, and complexities on hold in order to align, adapt, perform, and ultimately conform to a controlled standard. These practices dehumanize us because they reduce human beings to the realm of the abstract. They devalue essential elements of our humanity that cannot be measured by a standardized test; that cannot be appealed to through an inflexible, unresponsive, or scripted curriculum; that do not produce bell-to-bell teaching and maximum alignment to stated objectives written on the whiteboard.

Embodiment, on the other hand, engages the real bodily *presence* of teachers and students, in all of our complexities and possibilities. In her 1994 text *Teaching to Transgress*, bell hooks writes that, as teachers, "we are invited to teach information as though it does not emerge from bodies" (p. 139), and I think that's largely still true. Enter scripted curricula and inflexible pacing guides.

Recognition of this dynamic is growing, though, and has been for quite some time. More flexible seating options, kinetic activities, and mindfulness practices emerge every day. We teachers are encouraged to be "authentic" with our students and emphasize relationships.

Despite these shifts, the educational enterprise still cannot completely shake off the old models from our training, socialization, and systems. Why? Because these newly emphasized aspirations are tacked on to the ideal standard, with nothing else taken away from it. To varying degrees, we still need to ensure that students are "mastering" the content, hitting their "learning targets," and demonstrating they have done so in "the data," as measured by standardized testing mechanisms. We still need to maintain strong "classroom management" and uphold behavioral "norms."

Now, though, we are encouraged to do so in "restorative" ways while showing up as our genuine selves and building strong connections with our students. We are being told that doing so matters. That should feel great, no? It's what a lot of us have been hoping for, working toward, or even fighting for, no? But without the removal of anything else, without real change beneath the surface, without a clear definition or common understanding of words like "restorative," the push to "be authentic" becomes just another out-of-reach ideal to live up to (or not). Sometimes we are authentically burnt out. Sometimes we are authentically disembodied.

Embodiment takes work, often counteractive work that swims against the current. Sometimes it requires an overhaul. Like healing itself, embodiment is an ongoing process: never complete and almost always rife with challenges. Some of these challenges may be new, emerging through the process, while others cycle through us from our past. Expecting embodiment to be a neat, linear process that can happen for an individual without any systemic accommodation or community support is unrealistic and unsustainable. Disembodiment is not something that can be quick-fixed with any professional development session, product purchase, or one-off series of yoga classes.

Without acknowledging the very real barriers to embodiment, we are effectively gaslit by messages that appear to be inviting us toward wholeness, without any real support or pathway toward it.

## The Importance of Embodiment

Through my experience as a writer and teacher, I have cultivated a set of skills, strategies, and intuitions that can be difficult to name, precisely *because* they are embodied. For me, the work of teaching with a healing-centered ethic is always an art, and so there is no rigid guidebook; it is always a subtle negotiation among mind, heart, body, and spirit, which collaborate to make decisions in moments of encounter. In order to fully support students in a healing-centered way, these elements of mind, heart, body, and spirit all need to show up prepared and informed, which also means nurtured and cared for; respected and valued. For me, showing up "ready" is the essence of embodiment.

But maintaining such a stance is easier said than done.

For teachers, the mind is necessarily overloaded with complex intellectual tasks along with sprawling to-do lists. The body—at least my own—is taxed from standing for hours in front of a classroom, leaning over students' desks or crouching down beside them, lugging books and materials to and from my car and across the school, holding my breath too long in moments of stress, forgetting or finding no time to eat lunch, neglecting any semblance of an exercise routine, enduring too many hours without a bathroom break.

And then there is the soul, a word that feels almost alien in most discussions of teacher practice. hooks (1994) writes of this omission as an example of "the objectification of the teacher," in which there is "little emphasis on spiritual well-being, on care for the soul." Historically, the structures of education "denigrate notions of wholeness" by propagating the Cartesian notion of a mind/body division (p. 16). This duality may lead teachers like ourselves to compartmentalize, with the mind firing on all cylinders, the body performing all of its necessary functions, and the spirit saved for later.

Yet chronic compartmentalization, at least in my experience, is not just a pathway toward fragmentation but also a coping skill. Unhealthy or not, compartmentalization sometimes feels for me like the only way to get through the day. The trouble is, certain compartments—to uphold the metaphor—become junk collectors, rarely attended to until you really need something from them. And then, you are sifting through a mess. That "mess" for me takes the form of aching muscles struggling to form a downward dog pose in yoga class on the day after Thanksgiving, because I haven't practiced since August; closets overflowing with months of shoved-in items; countless text messages from friends and family left unread; a nervous system that can't settle enough to read a book for pleasure. But compartmentalization can get much worse than that, too. It can mean emotional exhaustion, burnout, or a health/pain crisis like the one I describe in Chapter 12.

Think of that junk drawer again. Assuming you might have one, too: what do you do when it gets too full, and you really need something from it? If I have the time, energy, motivation, and patience, I dump everything out and do a deep clean. More often, I find what I need quickly and relegate the clean-up process to an unspecified time in the future. Sometimes, I shake up all the contents in frustration to the point where I make a much bigger mess and can't even close the drawer back up. I might run out of time, without finding the item, and blaze forward into my day with a total disaster awaiting me the next time I need something from that drawer.

I've resigned myself to the fact that I will likely always have a junk drawer, just like I will always compartmentalize to some degree in order to stay grounded and leave one compartment messier than it needs to be. But being embodied, for me, involves recognizing the effects of this compartmentalization and attending to the contents to the extent that I can while giving myself grace when factors beyond my control conspire to make doing so seemingly impossible.

## The Challenges to an Embodied Approach

Personal healing as in a movement toward wholeness is made more difficult by the fact that we live in an ailing world over which we seemingly have little control. For many of us, the major disasters of war, disease, poverty, genocide, political chaos, and climate emergency persist in the outer layers of our everyday fragmentations that come from working longer hours for dollars that don't stretch far enough, a hypercompetitive culture of rampant consumerism, and an epidemic of distraction and depletion from overuse of technology and media inundation.

Contending—or, maybe more accurately, *not* contending—with all of these phenomena at once leads to disconnection: from ourselves, from each other, and from the rest of the natural world. "Disconnection in all its guises—*alienation, loneliness, loss of meaning*, and *dislocation*—is becoming our culture's most plentiful product," writes Gabor Maté (2022), leaving us "enfeebled" by "malnourishment of mind, body, and soul" (p. 296). Although Indigenous worldviews remind us of our inherent connectedness, compartmentalization feeds the illusion of separateness and prevents us from appreciating or being nurtured by that link. In turn, that fragmentation makes us unwell. Disconnection, in this sense, is both cause and effect.

So how *do* we nourish, honor, sustain, and foster synchronicity among our own minds, bodies, and souls? How do we support this process for others—including our students? In my view, all of this is exactly what aiming to embody a healing-centered approach entails.

A first step is to understand and address the barriers to such embodiment.

Embodying "for" a healing-centered approach to writing means grappling with the challenges *to* embodiment, which include the fact that so many of us have experienced writing predominantly in school settings. If we are teachers in a traditional classroom environment, the challenges are compounded by the fact that our role as teacher can work against our own embodiment. Too often, teacher embodiment is overlooked and taken for granted, if not actively counteracted by some of the challenges I list here: (1) maintaining a sense of purpose, (2) nervous system disruption, and (3) competing pressures and fragmentation.

I identified and outlined these categories based on conversations I had with several teachers who are writers in addition to being teachers or are teachers interested in healing-centered approaches to writing. Although they never met each other, I imagine all of us circled around a metaphysical table, engaged in lively conversation, enthusiastically and inoffensively interrupting one another to build upon each other's ideas, mutually determined to uncover new insights about what it means to write, why it matters, and how we might best preserve the most precious, sacred, meaningful, joyful, transformative, and moving aspects of the process for ourselves and for those in our care.

I talked to this group of educators not only about their practice as teachers of writing but about their own experiences with writing because I believe that (a) our own experiences with writing shape how we teach writing and (b) reflecting on our own experiences with writing can provide a window into our students' experiences with writing—either by contrast or through similarities.

## Maintaining a Sense of Purpose

The most obvious challenge to embodiment in the teaching of writing is: why bother? What is the *point* of teaching writing? What is the point of *writing?*

As examined in earlier chapters, these questions have become more commonplace and less rhetorical in our era of generative artificial intelligence (AI), causing students and teachers alike to interrogate the purpose of writing and of learning to write well.

Ethan, a high school Social Studies teacher, said a challenge for him is "to continue to think of new ways for students to 'write' in the age of A.I. that is not just forcing students to handwrite all their essays." Instead, he wants to teach and inspire them to use a multitude of media to express their thinking and knowledge and to see why it is important to use their own voices to do so—despite the temptations of AI. At the same time, he understands how and why his students who find writing difficult, boring, or too time-consuming see AI as an effective shortcut—a reason not to bother with writing.

English teacher Lucy spoke to me at length about the consequences of the fact that students in her school write mostly about books they didn't choose to read. "They don't like them," she said. "Therefore they don't like reading, therefore they don't read. And writing is so onerous. They associate every type of writing with writing literary analysis. And so then they say, I hate to write. So what's the point?"

Lucy added that this disengagement has often led her to wonder the same thing her students wonder: "What's the point?" Their apathy depletes her own sense of enjoyment and meaning in the process of teaching writing.

The depletion of purpose, in other words, can be contagious. While frustrated by the fact that "even the most willing and amenable" of his students still do not seem to enjoy the process, high school English teacher Giuseppe describes his own relationship with writing as "one of ambivalence and hesitation and utilitarianism only," despite feeling strongly driven to write in the past. He laments how the vast majority of his students—"younger people who have been inundated via an image-based communication system, mostly screens and their phones"—do not see much meaning in writing and certainly in editing. Yet, while he believes in the "civic importance" of written expression, he similarly does not feel a strong inclination toward the practice.

"If writing doesn't compel you, move you, to *do* something, why bother? I know that's a huge platitude, but that's how I feel," Giuseppe told me. For him, writing in forms beyond email, social media, and texting is something he is very good at, but he rarely feels the urge to engage in it, because it is not enjoyable, and there is usually no immediate audience to respond, validate, or take action as a result of the writing. On this level, he can relate to students who don't enjoy writing and see no point when the only purpose seems merely to be getting a grade.

Giuseppe added that even he has turned to ChatGPT for his own graduate school writing: "I found a lot of the assignments to be so vapid and a lot of the commentary so robotic and sparse that I didn't even waste my time on it." Many teachers—when confronted with a task that feels purposeless—may find themselves similarly relating to the very students they encourage not to use generative technology. With AI-generated feedback from teachers becoming increasingly common, there is a valid fear that the robots will essentially be in dialogue with one another.

Given how easy it is *not* to care about writing, I would argue that it is exponentially more likely that a writer will pursue and finish a writing project if it aligns with their embodied desires—all the more so if there is a cognitive sense of purpose and meaning in the act. In other words, the writing is more likely to happen if the body wants to do it, and the mind believes it is worth doing.

Sammy, a high school Science teacher who writes and publishes fiction frequently in an online fan-fiction community, does not question her purpose for writing; she views it as energizing, enjoyable, and a way to be social by connecting with others while exploring relationships through the mode of fiction. As someone who trains dogs recreationally and defines herself as the "head of a four-legged family" but lives with no other humans, this social connection is especially important to her.

What keeps her from writing, though, is not a perceived lack of purpose in the act of it but more so a general sense of purposelessness in her job as a teacher that has sapped her momentum for writing. With curriculum changes, and a correlating lack of engagement from her Advanced Placement students, she said, "It's been hard to feel like what I'm doing matters as much, and there's an aspect of self-esteem tied up with not just teaching but writing. Anything that's creative and coming from me, it's harder to believe in it." Her comments highlight important questions for us as educators: how does a student's general self-esteem impact their confidence in their writing? And how might increased confidence in writing potentially boost the writer's overall self-esteem?

When it comes to purpose, what I've found in myself is a tendency to veer radically between implicitly insisting to myself and my students that writing an effective thesis statement is the most important thing they could possibly learn and deeply sensing that a messy, exploratory process is worth more than any polished product.

The responsibility of teaching students to write well in forms they don't enjoy—forms that require an enormous amount of discipline on their *and* our part—can be daunting and requires a good deal of momentum and emotional investment. "Remember your why" deserves to be the Instagram punchline that it's become because it's probably the *last* thing we need to hear when we're truly stressed, overwhelmed, or burnt out. That said, the saccharine dictum raises a good question: what *is* our why? What are we truly trying to achieve when we teach writing? Which priorities and objectives are most necessary, and which parts might we release a bit in order to allow ourselves and our students to discover new ways? How can we tap into our individual sense of purpose in the teaching of writing to find more layers of personal investment in the process?

## Nervous System Disruption

Even—or perhaps especially—if someone feels a strong pull toward writing, if they believe in the power and importance of their topic or idea, if they feel strongly that they have something to *say*, they might still struggle to access the mental and emotional space most conducive to writing. One reason for that fact is the nervous system.

It is extremely difficult to write with an overloaded nervous system. Research shows that an overactive sympathetic nervous system—the one responsible for the on-alert, hypervigilant, fight-or-flight response that is overactive in so many of us—makes it challenging to focus, settle, and reflect. It also causes physical symptoms in the body, such as indigestion and pain, that can lead to distraction and discomfort. An overactive parasympathetic nervous system is not any more conducive to writing, as it can lead to emotional shutdown and cognitive disengagement (often known as "freeze" or "collapse") (Treleaven, 2018).

Finding enough calm, ease, and clarity in order to write is a challenge for many (if not all) writers, including so-called "teacher-writers." "If I feel unsettled or super busy, I can't write," says Marie Rose, a professor and researcher who recently began writing fiction. For her, a family member's illness, coupled with work responsibilities, makes it difficult to find not just the time for writing but also the right mental and emotional space for it—especially, creative writing, the type she most wants to engage in. "The majority of times, my mind is engaged with the writing that's expected in academia because that's my job," she told me, but "my soul wishes to write more freely."

This conflict between what the body and mind *have* to do, versus what the soul or spirit *wants* to do, creates a feeling of tension and frustration in the body—what might be termed a state of *dysregulation*—which in turn makes it harder to write. It is certainly something I have seen in students, even those who love to write, who *want* to write. "I had hours of math homework last night," they'll tell me, "so I couldn't work on my short story." Even if the short story is an assignment for a grade, they find it impossible to do the work, because the pressure of tests and assignments—things they "have" to do—weighs heavily over the things they *want* to do.

The *dread* that many students associate with writing is extreme in some cases. A popular brand of reels shared among teachers on social media caricaturizes the explosive reactions from students when asked to write a paragraph or even a sentence, but in my experience the exaggeration is not that far off, especially for students who are contending with trauma.

Giuseppe, who recently left a job at an alternative high school serving school-avoidant students, found that his students there had a vehement aversion to writing. "It's utterly impossible for some to write more than a sentence," he told me, and not because they don't have the ideas or skills but for at least two likely reasons: (1) they may have been told in the past that they are not very good at it and (2) writing requires a degree of vulnerability that is frightening or triggering for students who already feel such a heightened sense of vulnerability.

While Giuseppe can rationalize the reasons for this aversion, he admits that he finds it to be demoralizing, perhaps even contagious. When a student arrived ten minutes late to his English class, for example, he found it difficult to depersonalize, and it affected him physically. "It *feels* like they're saying, 'I don't give a f—. And, if *you* [the student] don't give a f—, I feel like, maybe what I'm doing doesn't matter." He realizes cognitively that a student in a constant state of fight or flight is likely not acting with that level of intentionality and is probably late for a variety of reasons that have nothing to do with their teacher. At the moment, though, "it *feels* like a punch in the gut."

Such personalization may be especially prominent for teachers when dealing with their own "life" issues. Having suffered two great personal losses, Giuseppe said that the school year in which we met had likely been the worst of his career. "While this year was the year more people told me I was a good teacher than ever before, I can't *feel* it," he said. "As someone who has always been told how good they are at what they are good at, when you are manifestly not doing well at the thing, it's like, soul crushing."

Dealing with significant life issues such as grief can make it hard for a teacher to settle their nervous system. For Giuseppe, this heightened state created a block that kept him from being able to perceive his own "success" as a teacher. That lack of resonance made him feel invalidated, which led to further dysregulation, making it harder for him to tolerate, grapple with, hold space for, and ultimately aid his students in settling their own nervous systems. In addition, excellence had become part of his identity, to the point where falling short of that ideal felt "soul crushing."

Recognizing the effects of our own nervous system imbalances can help us relate to students who are facing loss, grief, and other life challenges or who may not be living up to their own expectations for themselves. Students in such states may likely find it hard to access enough nervous system stability to write.

## Competing Pressures and Fragmentation

Several of the teachers I spoke with are people who love to write, who wish they had more time and energy for writing and struggle to make space for it in their lives. Stress, responsibilities, and competing priorities can make it difficult for anyone to write. For those who enjoy writing, it can sometimes seem like a luxury rather than a priority or important habit of well-being.

Miriam, who has published many works of fiction and has been teaching graduate-level creative writing classes on a non-tenured basis for 38 years, expressed to me a tension between her love and commitment to writing and the struggle to sustain a professional life by doing so. She cited her job responsibilities as a major obstacle that is rooted in a deeper societal issue:

> For the last 20 years I feel I've been engaged in academic piece-work. I get paid by the course, or by the student I work with. And there is a limit to how much I can physically take on, how much I can read and respond to, how many institutions I can drive to in a day.

Her experience is common among teachers of writing in higher education, who are often accomplished writers themselves, because full-time positions are scarce as compared with the number of qualified individuals. According to a 2020 report from the American Federation of Teachers (AFT), nearly 25 percent of adjunct faculty in the United States require public assistance and 40 percent struggle to meet essential household needs (AFT, 2020). The implications of this fact are far-reaching, because nearly half of faculty members at U.S. colleges and universities are employed part-time, and the majority hold contingent positions—more than 68 percent, according to 2023 numbers from the National Center for Education Statistics (Colby, 2023).

The struggle is real for teachers at all levels. For those of us in secondary schools who teach and want to write: how do we allow ourselves to block off time for writing when the demands of our paying jobs are ever-present and never-ending? How do we remind ourselves that our need and desire to write are not just valid but maybe even necessary to our own well-being and ability to care for others? Maybe even necessary to our ability to teach effectively?

Many teachers I know do love to write and wished they wrote more. For those of us who fall into this category, it's worth noticing and reflecting on this feeling of tension. Doing so might help us better understand and relate to the experiences of students who, overwhelmed with task completion and a plethora of responsibilities, struggle to devote the necessary time and effort to the encompassing task of writing.

## Embodying "For" and Embodying "A"

*Embodiment* is a term used in many ways, but I like to think of it as feeling at home in your body. Embodiment can aid in the writing process because it allows us to remain grounded in the present, which is where writing—as an act of creation—occurs. Difficulty accessing and truly sitting with the present moment makes writing of any kind more challenging because it impedes clarity.

Guiding students to access the "right" mental and emotional space for writing is challenging for teachers because doing so is challenging for anyone who is trying to write. Remembering this truth, while identifying the concrete and specific ways and reasons *why* it is difficult, can help us, as teachers, to mitigate these challenges—and maybe even help students learn how to do so for themselves.

This chapter has been focused primarily on embodying *for* a healing-centered approach to writing. Although embodiment can be a self-contained term, the word can also describe the concept of "taking on" a quality or idea. We say things like "She truly embodies the spirit of the organization" or "He is the embodiment of all I wish to be."

If we are not clear in *what* we are embodying, it makes us porous; what pours in is whatever dominates the water or air around us. So how can we embody the characteristics of a healing-centered approach to writing—one that is humanizing, affirming, empowering, liberatory, trauma-sensitive, restorative, and transformative?

First, we can prioritize our own psychic safety in addition to our students'; we can value positive experience over perfection and rigid conformity; we can foster belonging for ourselves and for our students; and we can believe in both them and us.

We can also extend ourselves "grace and space." We can build our own body awareness and remember why it matters. We can positively engage our multiple identities beyond our teacher selves. We can allow ourselves an arts-based approach of experimentation, engaging our creativity, imagination, and emotions. We can practice contemplative inquiry, giving ourselves space for silence and reflection. And we can foster communal experience, connecting with others and engaging with a larger sense of social purpose.

## References

AFT. (2020, August 10). *Report shows alarming poverty among adjunct faculty*. American Federation of Teachers. https://www.aft.org/news/report-shows-alarming-poverty-among-adjunct-faculty

Colby, G. (2023, March 16). *Data snapshot: Tenure and contingency in US higher education*. AAUP.

hooks, b. (1994). *Teaching to transgress*. Routledge.

Maté, G. (2022). *The myth of normal: Trauma, illness & healing in a toxic culture*. Avery.

Treleaven, D. A. (2018). *Trauma-sensitive mindfulness: Practices for safe and transformative healing*. W. W. Norton & Company.

# 11

# The Origins of a Healing-Centered Ethic

I believe that I have been teaching with a healing-centered ethos for a long time. By that I mean, my practice as a teacher has been shaped by the *intention* to establish a supportive space for people to heal through writing or healing their relationships with writing. I have aimed to create affirming spaces that are conducive to liberatory and transformative experience. Have I always succeeded? Of course not. Have I found myself being led astray by institutional standards and values unaligned with my own? By a desire to *appear* a certain way to my colleagues and supervisors? Yes, absolutely. Below that, though, has always been a deep commitment to the humanity, psychic safety, and possibilities of those beings with whose learning and growth I have been entrusted to participate and contribute. Where did this commitment come from? What informed the ways in which this commitment has grown and developed over the years? Certainly in large part from my own experiences as a writer and learner.

Yes, I was the child who wrote constantly in her notebooks. Yes, I was the student finding myself constrained by academic expectations of writing, only to find "my own voice" again later, but in pieces: the scholarly cut off from the imaginative and vice versa. Yes, I still grapple with navigating that spectrum easefully.

DOI: 10.4324/9781003752721-11

I have also been a person who has struggled with mental health: anxiety, depression, an eating disorder. A person who struggled with her social self: school avoidance, identity fragmentation, isolation, and confusion.

I still *am* that person—we never fully aren't—but I have also experienced immense transformations that have helped me to find freedom from many of the constraints and pains that coincide with these difficult experiences. That freedom has enabled me to help many others find a degree of freedom in their writing and lives as well. I learned not just to cope with but to *embrace* those more challenging parts of myself and my history, which formed an emotional well from which to draw empathy, compassion, and understanding for others.

That said, I do know the dangers of imposing our own worldview onto others and assuming that what is true and what works for us is the same as it is for someone else. I understand, too, that the imposition of our own worldviews can occur even when we do not intend for that to happen and actively try to avoid it. These gaps form the essence of bias.

As Topa and Narvaez (2022) write in *Restoring the Kinship Worldview*, "Caring, respect, generosity, empathy, and compassion must come first when we decide to offer advice or attempt to persuade anyone, as should respect for the person's autonomy" (pp. 242–243). Teaching is always, in a sense, an attempt to persuade, and so these guiding words are worth heeding: caring, respect, generosity, empathy, compassion, and respect for our students' autonomy *must come first*, before notions of what *we* think is best, especially when it's based mostly on our own narrow experience.

Yet, despite the dangers of presuming similarity, assuming our experience is starkly different from someone else's can also prevent us from seeing commonalities in our human experiences, which in turn can block access to empathy. And empathy is what makes compassion possible (Stevens & Taber, 2021).

Fear of bias, and the awareness of its very real harm, can sometimes lead people to aim toward being generic or neutral.

To be a non-person or to put their own personhood to the side in favor of so-called objectivity. But as Maté (2022) writes:

> The aim of healing work is not to shed the personality entirely but to free ourselves from its automatic programming, granting us access to what's underneath, to reconnect with what's essential about us.
>
> (p. 409)

Relating to others through and by making sense of our own identities and experiences can be a way to mitigate our biases and tap into genuine compassion—or what Maté calls "compassionate inquiry," an empathetic effort to genuinely see, know, and understand the self and other people, which demands "openness, patience, and generosity," both for self and for others (p. 412).

I think there is great opportunity for all of us as teachers in reflecting on the deeper, less conscious values, patterns, and priorities that influence our practices—the "automatic programming" Maté (2022) describes—and not just because our biases can skew our judgment but also because there can be so much wisdom in the things we do unconsciously every day, guided by intuitions that are honed through years of practice and commitment. By identifying this wisdom, we can replicate what works best and more effectively share strategies with others.

In this chapter, I share some of the inquiry work I have done to make sense of who I am and how my identities and experiences have shaped and continue to shape my approach to both teaching and writing. I do so in order to provide additional layers of context to the framework I outline in these pages. I also do so with an invitation for you to consider what factors have helped make you the teacher that you are. Which have been most prominent or apparent for you? Which might be less obvious?

## Professor Waitress

My career in education began with almost a decade of teaching college writing classes as an adjunct professor, paying the bills by also working as a freelance journalist and part-time waitress at my family's diner. After my first daughter was born, it became clear that I needed a full-time job—*one job*. Despite my grand visions of writing a book called *Professor Waitress*, I knew I wasn't selling those movie rights anytime soon.

During the interview for my first high school teaching job, I could feel the administrator's skepticism as he sat across the table from me, eyebrows raised, and asked how I would handle "classroom management." My comfort zone was working with college students, who were—at least to some degree—quite different from the 14-year-olds I might encounter in my classes. On top of that, he likely pegged me to be the "nice" teacher—the one who smiles too much and gets bulldozed by her students during the first week of school.

My reply may have surprised him, and I know it surprised me, when I referred to my skills as a diner waitress.[1]

I come from a diner family. My parents met when my father, newly immigrated from Greece, was working as a short order cook at his cousin's establishment, where my mother was a waitress and where *her* mother was a waitress, too. Though my mom was a decade younger than my father, she was wise beyond her years from helping her single mother raise my uncle. Despite the gaps between their languages and ages, and the many other differences they would discover in their 50 years of marriage, they fell in love and got married and had my older sister when my mother was still 19 years old. Shortly after, along with two of my father's cousins, they opened their own "Greek diner." By then an established concept within the tri-state area of New Jersey, New York, and Connecticut, the Greek diner was known for what the *New York Times* (Lewine, 1996) described as their "novel-length menus, mirrors, murals, tiles, bright lighting and revolving cases of gargantuan desserts."

While my father's circle of newly immigrated Greeks and Greek American relatives may not have believed that their marriage could work, my parents were determined to prove the doubters wrong. They devoted themselves to their family.

My mother learned the Greek language and essentially adopted the Greek culture as her own, as she became the one who brought my two sisters and me to spend our summers on the island of Andros while my father stayed behind to work in the restaurant. Though neither of my parents attended college, they encouraged my two sisters and me to pursue any dreams that we wanted. Certainly they urged us along some practical paths, but they never set limits on what they believed we could achieve. They created a loving, devoted family with big personalities and with complex, often unwieldy emotions and communication styles—fueled, to be sure, by cultural clashes so nuanced that they didn't quite register as the source of conflict.

Within this family, I was sometimes seen as "the quiet one." The ruminative one. The one lost in her own imagination and thoughts. From a young age, writing, for me—in the form of journaling, poetry, and fiction—was a source of escape, of reprieve, of enjoyment. It allowed me to process the rampant miscommunications that surrounded me. It helped me to slow down my thoughts and emotions, so that I could make sense of them. It helped me to feel understood—most of all, by myself. It gave me a space in which to imagine alternative worlds and ideas. Later, it became a space for me to articulate and validate my very real critiques of social culture that became increasingly clear to me as I grew older.

Outside the home, our family was fully immersed in the Greek American community of the Bridgeport, Connecticut area. We spent our holidays and birthdays together, we vacationed together—we became each other's extended families, a phenomenon that sociologist Evangelia Tastsoglou (2009) describes as the "reconstruction of the village clans" of rural Greece that became especially prominent among the waves of Greek immigrants who came to the New York metropolitan area in the 1960s and 1970s (p. 71).

In school, being Greek American meant everyone turning to look at me every time the name Plato was mentioned. It meant being asked to translate Ancient Greek words, which I couldn't do, because I spoke only modern Greek, and a simple conversational version at that. In classes, I felt uncomfortable with the room turning toward me to represent Homer and Aeschylus, and not just because it reminded me of my relative otherness in an extremely homogenous, White, monolingual, middle-class community. It was also because my own Greekness—the part I truly felt in my spirit—had nothing to do with those classical representations: the White marble statues and men in togas. It meant, if I could capture it in an image: my grandmother, my yiayia, cooking with vegetables from her garden in an outdoor kitchen surrounded by fields of brush or baking a storehouse of sweets for any neighboring villagers who might drop by in the coolness of the evening for laughter and music and drinks. It meant an agrarian island culture my father's side of the family had persisted in for countless generations.

But despite my discomfort, I also appreciated this recognition, however blurry, because in truth, I *did* feel different. I didn't watch the same movies as other kids. I didn't do playdates with friends from school, because I was at church almost every afternoon—at Greek school, Greek dancing class, or church volleyball. Avoidance of *dropí*—shame—loomed over us and created a strictness that restricted me from feeling fully integrated into the social world of my peers. Adherence to tradition, and a fierce commitment toward it, was intended in part to keep us insulated from mainstream American culture. We were expected to blend in with American society—enough, in the words of Isabel Wilkerson (2023), "to gain admittance to the powerful dominant majority" and benefit from it but not *become* it (p. 49).

But part of me already *was* it. So when a Greek American friend of mine remarked, when I was around six or seven years old, that I was "only half"—"half Greek, because your mom's not Greek," I felt it as a blow. At that time, my Greek American heritage and identity were so encompassing, so consuming, so deeply instilled as the thing to be proud of—the thing that made me and my family and our community who we *are*—that I could not receive this comment to mean anything other than: *half a person*. "But didn't you *become* Greek when you married Baba?" I asked my mother later. "No," she told me, "you can't just *become* Greek." To me, though, it seemed that she had. Finding home in the culture of Greekness had brought her joy and community, but from that point on, I also began to see and sense the erasure that coincided with this choice as well.

## Grappling with Hybrid Identity

I came from both sides of the Greek diner world—one that helped a generation of immigrants secure a "superior" position in society above the other. Indeed, the diner eventually afforded my family enough social standing that my sisters and I could access resources and opportunities that my Irish American grandmother had never come near. Yet the diner was a diner, and a Greek American one at that—kept in its place within the dominant strands of American culture. As the *New York Times* (Lewine, 1996) article referenced above describes:

> Diner experts do not even consider these newer luxe diners legitimate heirs to the tradition. They prefer the pre-fabricated, free-standing structures usually found along busy streets and highways like Queens Boulevard or 11th Avenue in Manhattan. And they see many modern Greek diners in New York as little more than coffee shops. "The effort to class up diners is always a kind of laughable thing," said Michael Stern who with his wife, Jane, wrote a book about diners, "Road Food," (1992, Harper Perennial). "They are never truly classy -- which is what's good about them."

"A laughable thing," those efforts to "class up." The *New York Times* article ends with this passage as its mic drop. To me, the subtext is clear: class access is not granted *that* easily.

I share this story, and ruminate so extensively on my relationship with my family's diner, because it is part of the inquiry work that I do, and have done, to sustain myself as a healing-centered educator. I've asked myself: what drew me to teaching? What made me the teacher that I am? What experiences and aspects of my background continue to shape my perspectives, my values, my relationships? What continues to shape my identity—both who I choose to be and how others see me? These are all questions you may ask yourself as well—all worth revisiting on an ongoing basis.

For me, the diner is one way for me to conceptualize my own hybridity—between social classes, between ethnicities, and between communities—which is important as I consider the ways in which I have experienced feelings of unbelonging or otherness and try to use that understanding as a means to imagine how people much more marginalized than myself may experience severe degrees of unbelonging and othering every day. Consider: when have *you* felt a sense of unbelonging? What was that like for you? How long did it last? What was the effect? What might have been the cause? What, if anything, could or did you do about it?

The *New York Times* quote above is a reminder of why, when I went to college and met my first Black female friends, I started to understand that I was both more White and less White than I thought I was. By this I mean, I began to understand the privileges and freedom from discrimination I experienced, while recognizing that my ethnicity was one whose racialization as White was relatively recent and conditional upon adherence to the dominant values and norms of Whiteness (Wilkerson, 2023). As Reesma Menakem (2017) writes in *My Grandmother's Hands*, "Italians, Irish, eastern European Jews, and other European immigrant groups were initially regarded as stupid, barbaric, and dangerous" until they were "socialized, colonized, and accepted by other Americans by being inducted into the false community of Whiteness" (p. 71). Collectively, people in these groups often chose assimilation over oppression because, with their relatively lighter skin tones and in a White dominant society, they had that choice to make.

These college friends of mine who happened to be Black young women kindly pointed out small instances where I was being essentialized based on my ethnicity ("How can you be Greek *and* vegetarian?") and tolerated my ignorance and slow learning when I questioned their experience ("The bartender didn't ignore you because you're Black, he just didn't see you!"). They helped me to see how, like Anna Carastathis (2017), author of *Intersectionality: Origins, Contestations, Horizons*, growing up with strong multiethnic ties in a very White-dominant community imbued me with the "ambivalent, ambiguous racialization" of a "very Greek identified" status (p. x) that "renders [someone] an outsider to both hegemonic and minoritized racial groups" (p. xiv). The in-betweenness can be confusing and uncomfortable.

But it was a shard off the sharp-edged broken glass of racism. Like Carastathis (2017),

> The idiosyncrasies of my experience hardly seem to matter in the grand scheme of a global system of White supremacy, in which my skin color and [in my case, U.S.] citizenship garner undeniable institutional privileges, and protect me from state violence and premature death. (p. xiv)

In my practice, the idiosyncrasies matter to the degree that they affect or contribute to my ability to *serve*—as an educator, researcher, and human being—toward the causes I care most about, including equity, justice, healing, and belonging for all.

While the diner helps me understand the nuances of my identity, it is also a way for me to make sense of my work ethic. And I don't just mean the stereotypical hardworking-child-of-immigrant narrative that I absolutely embody. I mean the ethic of the work itself: the care that has gone into my serving of the public.

## An Ethic of Service

Though I worked in the diner from a young age, doing mostly small jobs and eventually busing tables, my relationship with the social world transformed once I finally agreed to begin waiting tables. I'd been too shy and resistant until near the end of high school, preferring less interactive roles. Despite my hesitations, I fell in love with the job, and for me, it truly became an art. Over time, I developed and refined—as many servers do—a standard operating procedure that I could tailor to each group of customers as needed. My goal was to listen deeply to what was said and unsaid in order to discern what each person wanted and needed from me and to measure those wants and needs against what was possible (i.e., potatoes could not be substituted for bacon) and within my dignity (i.e., no need to smile because someone told me to).

Power, too, came into play within each interaction. Though I recognized the many ways in which I was in the disempowered role as *server*, I took my *service* role seriously because I sensed the vulnerability in each moment when a person told me what they wanted, each time they made a special request apologetically, embarrassed by their own tastes and hungers. This vulnerability equipped me with a type of power I felt compelled and obliged to handle with care.

My stance was to remain neutral and ready. My aim was to be non-judgmental, making no assumptions and reacting minimally, so as not to misread a serious claim as a joke. (You want whipped cream on your omelet? Sure! Who am I to judge? You want me to set your toast on fire? Not a problem.) In my work as a waitress, I learned to truly *enjoy* the people I served, and my affect grew increasingly warm and friendly. The practice of active kindness began to feel *natural*, embedded as habit and not at all forced. It allowed me to act upon a deep sense of connection I had always felt—even in my exceptionally reserved and introverted state—with other human beings.

That acute sense of connection had previously led me to retreat from the social world, because I grew too frustrated and angered by the ways in which people ignored or abused their connectedness. I felt acutely bothered by little acts of meanness I witnessed but deeply disturbed by subtle and overt expressions of bigotry that were taken for granted in my relatively homogenous Catholic high school and within the insularity of my Greek American community. I found myself a target, too, of comments about my dark, unruly hair and eyebrows, and the size of my nose. Even a teacher continuously pretended to misread my last name as "Feta." By late in my junior year, I had developed an eating disorder, and by senior year, I would leave school in the middle of every day to drive around in my car or do my work at a Burger King in a nearby town, where I could remain anonymous and fill my Diet Coke as many times as I wanted. Waitressing, in contrast, brought me back into connection with others, but with a sense of purpose: to *serve*.

In a sense, waitressing helped shape me as a teacher of writing just as much as my practice of writing did. It taught me how to listen deeply, anticipate needs, respond interactively, remain flexible, suspend judgment, communicate clearly, set and maintain boundaries, and offer paramount respect to every person in my care, no matter their race, gender, age, sexuality, class, appearance, or any other marker of identity. It taught me to serve from the heart but also with the criticality that comes from a lifetime of observation through the eyes of both a critical and creative writer, someone who (to paraphrase Freire & Macedo, 1987) reads the world in order to rewrite it.

In a healing-centered view such as my own, writing starts well before a single word is typed on a page. It involves so much more than sentences, paragraphs, headings, and citations. A healing-centered writing process involves the whole self, its history, experiences, and all of its relations. That is the case for our students, and that is the case for ourselves.

## Note

1 While the non-gendered term "server" is preferable in most cases, I retain the word "waitress" here, as it is the term by which I referred to myself while employed in this role, just as it was for my mother and grandmother.

## References


Carastathis, A. (2017). *Intersectionality: Origins, contestations, horizons*. University of Nebraska Press.

Freire, P., & Macedo, D. (1987). *Literacy: Reading the word and the world*. Routledge. Retrieved from http://www.ebrary.com

Lewine, E. (1996, April 14). The Kaffenion connection: How the Greek diner evolved. *The New York Times*. https://www.nytimes.com/1996/04/14/nyregion/the-kaffenion-connection-how-the-greek-diner-evolved.html

Maté, G. (2022). *The myth of normal: Trauma, illness & healing in a toxic culture*. Avery.

Menakem, R. (2017). *My grandmother's hands: Racialized trauma and the pathway to mending our hearts and bodies*. Central Recovery Press.

Stern, M., & Stern, J. (1992). *Roadfood*. Harper Perennial.

Stevens, F., & Taber, K. (2021). The neuroscience of empathy and compassion in pro-social behavior. *Neuropsychologia, 159*, 107925.

Tastsoglou, E. (2009). *Women gender and diasporic lives: Labor, community, and identity in Greek migrations*. Lexington Books.

Topa, W., & Narvaez, D. (2022). *Restoring the kinship worldview: Indigenous voices introduce 28 precepts for rebalancing life on planet Earth*. North Atlantic Books.

Wilkerson, I. (2023). *Caste: The origins of our discontents*. Random House.

# 12

# The Emergence of a Healing-Centered Research Project

What makes writing come more easily to some people than others? Why do some people hate and dread writing, while others love and seem to *need* it?

What makes certain types of writing feel more facile and enjoyable, while other types feel strenuous, taxing, or inaccessible?

Why does writing flow naturally for us on some days while feeling like a total exertion on others?

These are some of the questions that I have dwelt on as a writer and teacher for more than 20 years. While I have long held my own suspicions and senses, I embarked on a doctoral research journey in order to find answers that were more comprehensive. Although I read widely, interviewed participants, and analyzed data, I also closely examined my own experiences through autoethnography because it felt like the most honest way to approach and present my research.

So much of who I am and how I work as a teacher, writer, thinker, and human is intuitive. And yet it is important to acknowledge that my intuition is shaped and informed by my studies and experiences and, perhaps most of all, by my practices.

DOI: 10.4324/9781003752721-12

So I asked myself: what are the practices that have enabled me to experience writing in ways that are transformative, liberatory, and ultimately healing? How have those practices shaped who I am as a teacher of writing, for better and for worse? How can I refine the practices that shape my intuition with responsible scholarship and a broadened perspective?

I know I am not alone in this being guided by intuition, and I think there is great opportunity for all of us in reflecting on the deeper, less conscious values, patterns, and priorities that influence our practices—the "automatic programming" Gabor Maté (2022) describes. We may not always have the time or inclination to ask ourselves, on a deep level, *why* we do things in the way that we do, *why* we believe what we believe, and even *how* what we do and believe may be different from what we are *expected* to do and believe by our institutions. But doing so allowed me to gain clarity, on a more personal and embodied level, and set me on a path toward critical questions that could extend my inquiry well beyond my own experience.

In this chapter, I tell the story of one body's journey with writing as an illustrative example, representing some of the answers I found to the questions listed above.

## The Writing Pendulum Swings

For the first half of the summer before I started my doctoral program, I had been immersively writing a novel. While my children were in camp, I churned out pages with ease, in my favorite spot: full sunshine, on a coffee shop patio. Fellow patrons marveled at my endurance for the blazing heat. I smiled at them like a marathon runner in a 5K road race: *I could do this forever*.

And then, the day after my first doctoral program residency ended, my father had heart surgery. First a planned one and then an emergency one the next day, which resulted in his cardiac arrest, followed by days and weeks of not knowing if he would survive.

That day of the second surgery, as my sisters and mom and I waited for news in the waiting room we'd had to finagle our way into in those post-Covid days, my body felt like it might burst apart at any moment. I was trying to stay strong and positive and ultimately trying to keep it—my body—together. As the physical effects of fear and uncertainty overtook my efforts to tamp them down, I could feel the cortisol rocketing through my bloodstream like fireworks through a tube, and my skin buzzed with the aftershocks. I practiced deep breathing, chanted silent mantras, and drank cup after cup of hot water, until my father finally reached a point of fragile stability. That's when my body finally felt like it could hold itself together, but tenuously.

For days following, I couldn't eat. Couldn't read or watch television. I could barely sleep, and I could not get warm. My body could not return to homeostasis. My sympathetic nervous system had clicked into overdrive, on constant alert for another terrifying phone call or text message. The novel I had been writing so intensively since the start of the summer no longer seemed real at all.

In the days after the crisis, my mother, husband, daughters, sisters, uncle, nephews, and I camped outside the hospital for hours at a time each day, waiting for our turn to rotate into the intensive care unit. When my father's condition maintained a tepid stability for a few consecutive days after the surgery, my ability to eat returned with a few bites of tomato soup I was able to swallow as I sat on a patch of grass in the 90-degree humidity, wearing cotton leggings and a sweatshirt because I still could not get warm. Once I was able to eat again—and here is where I return to my "point"—I was able to start reading again, too, and I was able to write. Obsessively, in fact. In the early mornings and late nights when we couldn't be at the hospital, reading and writing were all I found myself wanting to do.

Just not creatively. I still had no mental, emotional, and therefore physical access to the novel.

I compiled a spreadsheet with hundreds of academic articles, tabulated by topic and focus. I read each article and wrote analyses, completing almost a semester's worth of coursework in two weeks and flying well beyond those benchmarks to "get ahead" with the early stages of my literature reviews. This space felt safe to me; it kept me grounded and helped me to essentially disassociate from the feeling of anticipating a crushing phone call at any moment. I was running on adrenaline, riding my sympathetic nervous system to its breaking point. In my view, I'd moved from the paralysis of a "freeze" response to the hyperactivation of "fight."

## The Body–Writing Connection

The fact that I was researching students' challenges with writing while observing and contending with my own was not just very "meta" but also highly useful to my inquiry. It helped me think more deeply, critically, creatively, and expansively about the relationship between writing and the body, and it launched an inquiry that resulted in the framework, theory, and thinking you see presented in the pages of this book.

What we think of as "writer's block" shows up in lots of different ways and arguably affects all writers at some point, no matter their interests, experiences, or skill levels. But what makes writer's block tricky is that how, when, and why it shows up are not so clear-cut or consistent. I've taught many students over the years who love to write, who sign up enthusiastically for a creative writing elective, only to find themselves halfway through the semester unable to write at all. I've taught other students who have no trouble writing poetry or in their journals but find it nearly impossible to work on a thesis-driven essay for their English or Social Studies class. I'd never consciously considered the *physical* and *somatic* challenges that contribute to and take the form of these selective blockages and stoppages with writing.

My experience with this extreme paradox between my inability to write creatively and my overwhelming compulsion to write analytically made me think more deeply, and become more curious, about the relationship between writing and the body—specifically the nervous system.

Analytical writing is a way of bringing *control* and *order* to a topic; it tames an unwieldy subject and process of inquiry into a relatively predetermined structure, and even though there are ways in which a person can creatively deviate from or extend the boundaries of that structure, the structure is *there* for anyone who has learned it. The material, no matter how complex, can be funneled and crammed—with lots of care and deliberation—into a logical form.

What we call "creative" writing, though, demands a certain relinquishing of control to the imagination. It calls on the capacity to sit with uncertainty for a sustained period of time, to trust the mind enough to let it wander and conjure alternatives to what it thinks it knows, alternatives to what comes next and what goes where.

In the midst of the stressful situation of my father's medical crisis, my ability to call upon the meandering mind was prohibited by the fact that I could not settle my body. My body had still not recovered from the acute onset of this potent dysregulation. My autonomic nervous system was struggling to do its job of modulating the flow of energy between the sympathetic side, which would alert me to danger, and the parasympathetic side, which would allow me to slow down and relax. I could no longer toggle freely back and forth between the analytical side of my brain, which wants to write in an orderly and logical fashion, and the imaginative side, which wants unfettered exploration and mental wandering.

Imaginative writing requires a degree of restful alertness—like yin yoga, which a yoga teacher once unscientifically described to me as requiring a state of 30 percent effort, no more, no less, an active state of *being* rather than *doing*. After weeks of operating at a metaphorical 100, my chiropractor warned me that my body was more likely to crash into a state of exhaustion at zero, with the parasympathetic side taking over completely, than achieve that ideal 30 percent.

In this sense, my challenges with writing helped me to better understand the challenges I was facing with my body, and vice versa. This understanding made me think about how writing can foster an experience of embodiment: of tuning into the body, to what it feels and knows, and attending to the somatic dimension. It made me think about how finding ease with writing can itself be a healing experience in terms of the nervous system. And how that very capacity for healing can be impeded by a disconnection from the body or by acute or chronic dysregulation within it.

Think of a time when you found it difficult to write. What did it feel like in your body? What was happening in your life at the time? How might these physical challenges show up for students while they're writing?

## Writing, Untamed

My nervous system's reaction to my father's health emergency magnified the effects of stress on my body and writing enough for me to perceive them, but it was not the first time or only way such difficulty had shown up in my life. In college, I was a skillful academic writer, able to write well-written and researched papers in one focused night of study. But like many young people, I felt unable to write creatively. I no longer journaled, as I did when I was younger, and I certainly wasn't writing fiction or poetry.

The floodgates of expressive writing opened back up for me in desperation when I was a junior in college, still riddled with anxiety, still school-avoidant, and now grappling with many of the struggles I fictionalized, years later, in my novel, *Waking Slow*. In the novel, the main character, Irinie, is sexually assaulted and then punishes her body by allowing her self-flagellating mind free reign as it aims to execute its project: the perfection of the soul. As if this impossible attainment could protect her from further harm.

But before that story became a novel, it began in small urgently written pieces for a memoir workshop class that I was ultimately encouraged by the teacher to drop because of absences and tardies. Which was painful and ironic to me because it was the only class I attended with any regularity at the time. Perhaps the teacher's policy was indeed that strict, but I've often wondered if the intensity of my approach—how badly I needed to write, how this writing had become the only thing that mattered to me at all at the time—struck her as unhealthy, *too much*.

Perhaps she recognized how I was coming apart and suspected that a break from this writing might be best. Perhaps she felt unequipped to guide me through the process. I'll leave my speculations there.

But for me, as a teacher, this memory raises so many questions: what do we, as teachers, do when expressive writing yields erratic behavior or emotional instability? Why does this happen in the first place? Do we encourage the student to keep writing, or do we try to shut it down?

## The Subordinated Role of Creativity in the Classroom

I work in a school where creative, reflective, and expressive writing activities are infused into almost every subject area, but it wasn't always like this, and it isn't always like that everywhere. Creative writing is often seen as a non-essential skill, unfair to teach and grade because, as I've heard many people say, "not all students are creative." Some, if not many, people think that creative expression cannot be taught, that it's innate or not.

In actuality, creativity is an essential part of being human. "How have we convinced millions of people that creativity is a skill only accessible to a select few," writes poet rupi kaur (2022), in *Healing Through Words*, "when the truth is that human beings are imaginative by nature, and it is our imaginations that helped us survive hundreds of thousands of years?" (p. ix). We teach things that are hard for students all the time; we consider it essential to do so. Why is it different with imaginative writing? Likely because it is seen as a peripheral skill, one involving emotion, which is typically held lower on the hierarchy of valued human attributes in schooling. It also involves uncertainty, which makes people uncomfortable.

Even when creative writing appears in the curriculum, analytical writing is still largely favored and taken most seriously. When we "successfully" teach students to use standard analytical writing structures and modes of expression, we pass on the relative peace that comes with order and a semblance of certainty. These structures and modes do not at least overtly require, or actively invite, the knowings of intuition—the kind that lives in the body. Often, they are relatively hostile toward them (a digression or unanswered question might get you "dinged" on an analytical rubric) because these alternative knowings *disrupt*. They disrupt clear arguments and well-organized structures and are not easily gradable using the typical assessment criteria and quantified point systems.

What would it take, and what would it mean, to help students move fluidly and easefully between the imaginative and the analytical? Between the parts of our selves—our minds, bodies, souls—that tend to dwell most comfortably within each terrain? And what would it mean to be able to write from both at once? Could it also help a writer find ease and equilibrium in the relationship between their parasympathetic and sympathetic nervous systems? Might that itself be healing? How can teachers of writing create stabler bridges and clearer, if guard-railed pathways between the domains of analytical and imaginative writing?

Writers need safe entry into the sacred space of creative or imaginative writing. But how can we as teachers help provide this? It has taken me a long time to figure out how to ground and slow myself down enough to access vulnerable writing, and I am constantly forgetting and then remembering again. Even still, even after all these years of experience and mindful practice, what works for me will change from day to day, moment to moment, project to project.

In a classroom filled with students—brimming with the magnitude of their promise and identities, along with their personal and collective challenges and traumas—the complexities are limitless. It seems impossible to imagine a paradigm that could work for all students and for all teachers. One that could work for *any* might be more realistic than one for *all*.

Still, when in the boundlessness of that very early stage in my doctoral studies, I wanted to try. I wanted to start by gaining a deeper understanding of what makes writing so hard, so painful, and even so oppressive for some people.

This query is where my doctoral research began, and the framework presented within these pages is where it led.

## The Recurrence of a Pain Crisis

A year into my research into healing-centered writing, studying the relationship between writing and the body, I did not anticipate that I would find myself in the midst of a "pain crisis" that left me bedridden and out of work for two weeks in late September of 2023. At that point, I decided to keep a "pain journal," documenting my own process of healing while reflecting on my work, identity, and life as a teacher, writer, researcher/scholar, and mom.

Simultaneously, for my coursework in arts-based research, I was analyzing a series of collage poems I created starting in March of 2020, during the Covid-19 pandemic, as part of autoethnographic inquiry. What took me longer to realize—what I had forgotten but then remembered, through the process of journaling—was that my collaging practice actually began, in part, after an earlier pain crisis, in September of 2019.

It wasn't my first pain crisis—I've dealt with chronic back and muscle pain since I was a teenager, and I walked with a cane in school while pregnant with my second daughter—but the reason I remember the exact time frame of the one in 2019 is that I felt unusually edgy and irritable at school, and I recalled snapping at a group of senior boys who had disappeared during a fire drill. They were laughing when they returned to class. "It's not funny!" I spat with a sharpness of tone that rose out of me in a frustration and impatience that caught me off guard. "I didn't know where you were! This is *serious*. It is my job to keep you safe!"

The enormity of that responsibility—for keeping kids safe—is never lost on me and was certainly not lost on me as rhetoric and questions of whether or not to arm teachers in the classroom circulated prominently in the news cycle that fall (Litvinov, 2019). Two of the boys who knew me from their sophomore year looked as surprised as I was by the edge in my voice. We shared a moment of mutual confusion and curiosity—*what* was *that?*—before I found my sense of self again and said with a sigh, "Just sit down." Months later, those same faces would be hiding behind black squares during online learning and would be waving from their cars as I wished them goodbye and good luck upon graduation.

Because I refused to take any significant time off during Fall 2019, when I could barely walk without excruciating pain, I limped around the school for months, drawing looks of concern—probably for my mental as well as my physical well-being—while I ever-so-slowly began to heal or, more accurately, patch myself up enough to function.

Fall 2019 was a difficult season for many people. By December, many of us—including my students—were exhausted by the political turmoil and uncertainty that built toward the January 6 insurrection at the start of 2021. I remember one student asking me, "Is it *always* like this? My dad says every generation thinks they're living through the worst times, but this seems pretty bad." And the shutdown hadn't even happened yet.

Before Covid, and while still healing from this pain crisis, I signed up for a Community Education art class. It was an attempt to get out of the house and do something good for my mental health, and it worked; the art class brought me back to life and infused new energy into my teaching.

In school, I found myself moved to do more than just "freewrite" along with my students in Creative Writing class; I wanted something more visual and physical, something that would get me back into my body but at the same time still involved words and poetry. I brought in magazines, scissors, and glue sticks and began making collages, modeling the type of exploratory experience I encouraged my students to have as well.

The collages I created were chaotic and incohesive but exciting for me. A few months later, when the shutdown occurred, I recalled this experience and turned to collaging as a way to find ballast while teaching in my dining room; while trying to help my first-grade daughter navigate online schooling without completely ignoring my three-year-old; while frantically reading the news for signs of hope, new guidance on whether or not to Lysol my groceries, and new facts to be frightened by. Also while beginning to imagine what returning to school could look like, now that we had glimpsed behind the veil of normalcy; now that a long-overdue racial consciousness was simultaneously emerging in vast numbers of White people who had never awoken to the realities of their own privilege and the presence of deeply embedded systemic injustices. In between sending links to articles and blog posts and lesson plans and new potential course texts to my fellow teachers in order to seize on the unique opportunity of the moment, I created dozens of collage poems before returning to the physical classroom in the fall.

These collages were notably different from the incohesive and chaotic ones I made before the shutdown. Some of them were aesthetically pleasing, and many of them contained an urgency and clarity that took me by surprise while crafting them. This difference, to me, represents some of the healing that occurred for me in the "pause"—in being *home* and making so much *art*.

The collages center around concepts of identity, community, society, and art. In many of them, I incorporated natural elements such as dried leaves and tiny pine cones which suggested to me, as I analyzed them years later, a longing to reconnect with the natural world.

So many of the collages expressed a craving for both solitude and community, for meaningful connections beyond the inundations of the social world, along with space for reflection and rest. One simply reads: "A community/that saw me/was important to me." Another, more of a poem, reads:

> Your spirit
> Finds its place in the
> Spaces
> that
> Light your path
> Toward
> A place to rest
> To be home
> to
> BE
> In the heart
> With questions
> of
> Art
> and
> Loss
> Where
> the
> Tender, fragile
> Extravagance
> of
> Inner work
> Makes room
> For answers
> and for
> Learning to love
> the Grayer realities.
> To feel the majestic
> in
> the
> Shallows
> as well as the deep.

This collage reflects an active desire to reconnect with lost aspects of self and provides a pathway toward doing so—a pathway I discovered through being home, reconnecting with an art practice, processing grief, and engaging with tough questions.

Many of the collages expressed political anger and frustration, toward myself and toward society. I began snipping words that were oddly trademarked and incorporated those into my poems as well. The text of one reads:

> Shrink and disappear
> Within
> Your
> downright delightful
> SimpliSafe™
> WhiteWalls®
> Believe
> It's a privilege to serve you.
> Imagine
> It's because you're worth it.™
> Say
> We're all so lucky to be here.
> Here™
> or
> Prepare for departure
> and
> Earn your merit badge in U.S. cultural history.

In this collage poem, I discovered anger and frustration with myself for feeling politically and socially neutralized in the classroom. By following my intuition, I began to find my political voice again. I hadn't even realized that I'd missed it.

I also began to *enjoy* writing again, coming to a deeper awareness of the nature of process versus product. Some of the collages are much less aesthetic, with a purpose of helping me realize something buried in my subconscious. Along those lines, the collaging helped me honor my intuition again by noticing my impulses and making mindful choices about whether or not to follow them. When words or images stood out to me, I would simply cut them out without thinking much at all about why. Gradually, I would start moving the pieces around, recognizing glimmers of joy or insight with certain juxtapositions until some sort of cohesion might form.

In short, it was a healing experience. And the healing was not always pretty. Healing is what Fariha Róisín (2022) in her book *Who Is Wellness For?* calls a "messy business" (p. 1). In this case, it involved a deep excavation of my own complicity in the very systems that were depleting, oppressing, and harming us all, but especially Black and all people of color, along with people marginalized by poverty, class, ability, gender, sexuality, religion, and neurodivergence. Nonetheless, or perhaps because of that direct confrontation, the collaging fostered healing not just from the effects of that current moment of global crisis—the fears, the losses, the uncertainties, the challenges—but from years of operating without enough such moments of pause.

Leigh Patel (2015), author of *Decolonizing Research*, writes about the importance of "pausing" as a "productive interruption to these competitive ways of being, doing, and knowing" that dominate our society. She argues that this pausing and stillness are not about "doing nothing" but instead are opportunities for reflective and careful processing and action. The goal is "to sit still long enough to see clearly what we need to reach beyond" (p. 88).

The forced "pause" that occurred on a global scale—with felt impacts at every level, from individual to relational to societal and throughout all of the natural world—illuminated the presence of a number of untreated, exposed, or calcified wounds, along with sources of ongoing hurt and harm. For those of us fortunate not to have suffered the worst effects, it was a collective movement *toward* wholeness, with many setbacks that required a constant re-positioning in the direction of healing. Many people found themselves looking around and seeing, as if for the first time, the water we had been swimming in. New, or at least different, ways of seeing and being and doing emerged, in part out of necessity and in part because of emerging awarenesses that made people *want* to change. Personally, I learned a lot, grew a lot, and changed a lot. One might say that all of us did.

But *how?* What did we learn and why? What have we retained? What did we abandon in the race back toward "normalcy"?

## The Healing Capacities of Art

As I lay on my couch four years after my pre-Covid pain crisis, with a heating pad on my back and my legs propped onto a pillow, allowing my body to heal before forcing myself back to my job, I realized that I had learned a great deal. Four years earlier, in 2019, I had been unwilling to *pause*, to take myself out of the workplace in order to give my body the rest that it needed. In doing so, I had prolonged the pain for months more than it might have endured otherwise.

I began to ask myself: what did I learn in the pause of 2020 that enabled me to give my body this time and space for healing in 2023? And how?

When we returned to school in Fall 2020—albeit hybridly, teaching half of our students online—I could not go back to the way things were before. I could not be who I was then, siloed and fragmented. Collaging for months in the same dining room where I taught my high school classes online *and* ate dinner with my family was an extreme experience of melding the various facets of my selfhood into one, and it was an opportunity to experience what such cohesion could feel like as well. I had, by necessity, found more ease in moving fluidly among the roles of teacher, writer, artist, and mother, in staying connected to and nurturing each one. I could and would not let that go as I entered the doors to my school building.

In an effort to remain on this healing path, I joined *Breathe for Change*, a yoga teacher and social-emotional learning facilitator program for people who work in schools. The program, based on founder Ilana Nankin's (2016) doctoral research, was designed to address the fundamental link between educator and student well-being, within a social justice and social-emotional learning context. Completing this training throughout the school year allowed me to re-enter the "new normal" with more clarity, self-awareness, and grounding.

I also became a lot more intentional and overt about the ways I speak up about topics that matter to me—the macro and micro ways in which systemic harm shows up in classrooms, curricula, policies, and practices, for example. I outed myself more explicitly as someone committed to social justice, small and large scale, at the expense of niceness.

I learned, too, to integrate my practice as an artist more fully into my daily life. I learned to be a little softer on myself and to honor my own needs. I granted myself the grace to be less beholden to the dominant values surrounding me, a shift that sometimes made me feel less connected to others but ultimately made me feel more whole and more connected to my sense of purpose as a teacher and human. More than anything, I loosened the reins of perfectionism, of my allegiance to false notions of "rigor" and "excellence" that were embedded into almost every facet of my life as a teacher.

Yet still, after all this learning, I lay bedridden four years later, immersed in graduate research, trying to understand how to honor the full humanities of teachers and students in the classroom. How to care for our minds, bodies, and souls in sustainable ways. How to create and maintain community and belonging for all.

I began to scoop up new questions. How do we attend to the artistic dimension in schools? How might a lack of attention to artful ways of knowing impact the bodies of students and teachers alike? How might feelings of unbelonging impede access to creativity and expression? How might an arts-based approach facilitate healing from the fragmentation that lives inside our bodies? A fragmentation perpetuated by dehumanizing systems and structures that surround us and at times feel like they are consuming us.

Luckily, that year I had the good fortune of being a LiberatED Fellow, which kickstarted with an educators' retreat in September. Founded by scholar Dena Simmons, the program grounds social and emotional learning in the values of "radical love, healing, and justice." Inspired by the words of Fannie Lou Hamer, "When I liberate myself, I liberate others," the program's justice-driven mention is to intentionally tend to the educators' role and needs in the care of students (LiberatED, n.d.). The program not only centers and forefronts the voices of Black, Indigenous, and all people of color while honoring all communities but also, genuinely, centers *joy*. That became clear to me from the first hour of the retreat, when the fire alarm unexpectedly went off in the conference center and we all gathered on the sidewalk outside the hotel, laughing amid the confusion. Someone in our group had brought a jump rope, and an extended, spontaneous session of double-Dutch ensued.

The LiberatED retreat, coinciding with my collage research and the reprisal of an acute pain crisis, helped me clarify my interests in the connections between writing and the body, writing and identity, writing and art, and how all of these concepts relate to healing. Together, these experiences illuminated the many questions I still needed to explore, which eventually resulted in the healing-centered framework and model I outline in the chapters of this book.

## References

kaur, r. (2022). *Healing through words*. Andrews McMeel.

*LiberatED | Origin Story*. (n.d.). LiberatED. https://www.liberatedsel.com/origin

Litvinov, A. (2019, April 25). *Lawmakers in these 6 states are pushing to arm teachers*. NEA. https://www.nea.org/advocating-for-change/new-from-nea/lawmakers-in-6-states-push-to-arm-teachers

Maté, G. (2022). *The myth of normal: Trauma, illness & healing in a toxic culture*. Avery.

Nankin, I. (2016). *Breathe for change: Changing the world, one teacher at a time* [Doctoral dissertation, University of Wisconsin-Madison]. ProQuest Dissertations & Theses Global.

Patel, L. (2015). *Decolonizing educational research: From ownership to answerability* (1st ed.). Routledge.

Róisín, F. (2022). *Who is wellness for?: An examination of wellness culture and who it leaves behind*. Harper Wave.

# 13

# The "Pivot Point" of AI

Before I shifted my emphasis to healing-centered approaches, I began my doctoral research with a focus on humanizing pedagogies. At that point, in July 2022, I was not anticipating how artificial intelligence (AI) would completely disrupt and potentially upend the entire landscape—above and below the dirt—of writing and writing instruction. I had not quite considered how *literally* the word "humanizing" would need to be taken.

When OpenAI officially launched ChatGPT four months later in November 2022, my initial reaction was not of panic; I immediately thought, *Well if that's not evidence of the need for a humanizing writing pedagogy—one that invites, and even necessitates, that students and teachers bring their own humanities and identities into the process and product of writing—I don't know what is!* I thought, maybe now we will *have* to revolutionize our methods.

That response was a so-called survival mechanism, or an astute instinct, not yet tempered by the reality of how hard it would be to steer our collective cultural ship in the direction of humanization against a tide that already pushes against our humanness, all the more forcefully now that the literal "robots" are truly poised to take over so much of what we do, on our own and together as humans.

With a swiftness that somewhat surprised me, the educational community leapt mostly from how to police AI's use,

DOI: 10.4324/9781003752721-13

soaring completely over "whether" to embrace it, to land on "how" it will be utilized and integrated. To me, it felt as if there had not been a moment's pause to consider what it means to incorporate AI into a system that has not yet figured out how to honor and preserve our multiplicity of intelligences as human beings in the first place. Every threat response was activated, but mostly: flight, freeze, and collapse. "Fight" felt too exhausting and self-defeating.

So I felt compelled, as an eternal optimist, to settle my nervous system and identify the *opportunity* in the moment. My criticality also prompted me to recognize the *imperative* of doing so.

Because the issue is not just about AI and how it stands to change everything. It is about the fact that our educational systems are still—and have for a long time been—in need of humanization for both students and teachers alike. With AI pervading more and more arenas with increasing normalization, we are at what Shawn Ginwright (2022)—who coined the term "healing-centered engagement"—might call a "pivot point." From here, we can clearly see the imminent danger of losing touch with our humanity and will need to *choose* to claim, preserve, and nurture the most important aspects of what it means to be human if we are to avoid further surrendering them.

## Why Writing (Still) Matters in the Age of AI

Personally, I choose not to use AI tools where and when I can avoid doing so. I understand that AI is embedded into my navigation use, online shopping, and search engines, to name just the fewest applications. But I will generally not seek the assistance of programs like Chat-GPT, Gemini, or DALL-E in the same way I took almost a decade to start using social media, because slow and mindful steps work best for me. (I'm usually the last person in the water at a pool party, too.) I am wary of the trust that inevitably comes with sustained use and normalization. I understand how rapidly and radically tools like these can change the ways we think and live. I know how quickly and easily we can begin to over-rely on these tools as we grow more familiar. Personally, I prefer to let the test cases run outside of my own experience before I choose how to partake. I do not—and do not *want* to—trust them, yet.

Professionally, though, I know that I have an obligation to familiarize myself with AI tools and experiment with their implementation in the classroom, not because I believe that the good of integrating AI will outweigh the harm and certainly not because I believe we are anywhere near grasping the potential consequences of doing so. As Ethan Mollick (2024), author of *Co-Intelligence: Living and Working with AI*, has written, "There is nobody who has the complete picture of what AI means, and even the people making and using these systems do not understand their full implications" (p. xix). What does that mean for those of us teachers who feel less technologically inclined?

The reason I know, professionally, that I must educate myself about large language models and their uses is that I teach, practice, and study critical literacy. Students will be expected to use these applications in the classroom and, eventually, in their professional lives. Part of literacy is learning to use a variety of tools to read the world and communicate our understanding. Just as with any other tool we expect them to use, our students will need practical experience in order to grasp the potential and limitations of using generative AI and develop the necessary skills for doing so effectively.

Furthermore, programs like Gemini, Claude, and ChatGPT generate *content*. Evaluating the soundness, integrity, and usefulness of the content they produce, then, is also a literacy matter.

The reliability issue goes well beyond the hallucinations that received a lot of attention early on; we now know that errors can be embedded so smoothly that they appear as fact. We also know that AI chatbots aim to please and will skew the information they provide us—and the tone with which they provide it—to our commands.

Worse yet, they reproduce our biases—current and historical. The inevitability of this bias is something that both staunch advocates and prognosticators of doom will agree on. "And because those biases come from a machine, rather than being attributed to any individual or organization," writes Mollick (2024), "they can both seem more objective and allow AI companies to evade responsibility for the content" (p. 36). In a landscape like this, critical literacy skills become more vital than ever.

Large language models are trained on generations of content produced by, in many cases, flawed and short-sighted individuals and societies. They operate on pattern recognition and so they inherently call upon the most dominant voices and perspectives, which are not always the most nuanced and are by definition not adequately representing the marginalized. Because these models are largely trained on material written in standardized American English, they also further normalize a white-washed, monocultural parlance. With the increasing use of AI for editing, research, and content generation, an already over-homogenized benchmark for writerly voice and expressed identity stands to worsen.

## "Human in the Loop"

While effective prompt writing seemed to dominate the early conversations about using AI in the classroom, it is clear that the responsiveness of AI systems will continue to improve to the point where the isolated skill of good prompt writing will matter less and less. Much talk is now centered on teaching students to be the "human in the loop"—a concept I can somewhat align toward. Many teachers are already doing this well: they require students to use AI tools for feedback on their writing and then carefully evaluate the AI's effectiveness in doing so; they allow students to generate topic ideas with AI and then make the case for why or why not to choose each one. In instances like these, AI becomes not just a resource but also a tool for teaching critical literacy.

Yet, taken wholesale, "human in the loop" also threatens to normalize a devaluing of human impetus. I like the way Australian literacy scholar Lucinda McKnight (Enriquez et al., 2024) puts it when she calls for us to "stand up and say, 'Hang on a moment, "human in the loop" with writing is a massive demotion of where humans sit in that process'" (p. 16).

A healing-centered approach to writing might educate students about what *can* be done with AI tools but, most importantly, what can *not* be done. AI cannot (at least yet and arguably may never) understand the information that it processes or produces. It cannot feel anything, even when producing pieces of "art" or music. It cannot be human. A healing-centered approach maintains and sustains our humanity. It retains the spiritual legacy of writing as a mode of expression that gives voice to our individual and collective voices, experiences, and histories. By repeatedly unfettering AI use in any part of such a process, we stand to lose too much.

Certainly, many of us are requiring handwritten essays more than we ever have in our careers for this very reason. Sometimes, it's a way of ensuring that a student's work is truly their own, but the benefits of handwriting transcend any punitive or controlling motivations. Studies have shown how writing by hand can promote learning and aid in memory retention, as it engages more neural circuits in the brain as compared with typing. Combined with this additional cognitive activation, the slowness of the process fosters both creativity, critical thinking, and reflection. Handwriting is also conducive to emotional processing and has been used in therapeutic settings for people who have suffered from brain injuries, strokes, or mood disorders (Marano et al., 2025).

I have found that, despite many initial complaints and grumblings, many students actually enjoy the process of writing by hand. After years of almost exclusively typing their essays, students seemed surprised to feel proud of what they produced when I started asking them to handwrite. Some would later *ask* to handwrite when offered the chance to type. Handwriting, for many students, is a much more methodical activity than typing; it requires more mindfulness and is less enabling of distraction. As a result, the words student writers choose to put on the page may be more vetted, more well considered, more processed.

When we do allow students to use digital technology, we teachers are also being deliberate about when and why—which itself is a positive outcome. Research suggests that this type of intentionality is crucial as we consider the long-term effects of typing's dominance as a writing modality (Van der Weel & Van der Meer, 2024). And we understand that, when technology is involved, it is nearly impossible to know for sure if AI was involved. Eventually, it may be nearly impossible to avoid using it, and maybe it already is, as AI-generated search results and suggestions appear for us whether we actively seek them or not.

When it's made so easy and accessible, the temptation to eschew the harder path can be too strong. Mollick (2024)—an advocate of human/AI "co-intelligence"—concedes that, "when faced with the tyranny of the blank page, people are going to push The Button." Though he requires his own students to use AI, he writes:

> The implications of having AI write our first drafts (even if we do the work ourselves, which is not a given) are huge. One consequence is that we lose our creativity and originality. When we use AI to generate our first drafts, we tend to anchor on the first idea that the machine produces, which influences our future work. Even if we rewrite the drafts completely, they will still be tainted by the AI's influence.
>
> (p. 116)

In other words, it will become nearly impossible to tell where the human ends and the robot begins, and vice versa. While there is something interesting and even opportune in such a melding, the potential ubiquity of this boundary erasure is what concerns me most.

The consequences of this phenomenon transcend the individual. The collective effect of our practices as educators is something we need to contemplate seriously. We as teachers are churning out writers, influencing their habits and attitudes, at volume. While inviting students to use AI to generate ideas might be a helpful way to isolate skills like editing and alleviate the crushing pressure some students feel when they see that cursor blinking against an all-white screen, doing so repeatedly and ubiquitously gives young people *less* practice with one of the absolute hardest parts of writing. And not just the hardest part of *writing* but the hardest part of *thinking*: where to start. Automated content gives us too much to go on, and it indelibly shapes the path we take. The collective consequences of this for humanity are vast.

## Applying a Critical Lens

By fostering opportunities for embodied experiences of writing that are healing-centered—by which I mean, humanizing, affirming, empowering, trauma-sensitive, liberatory, restorative, and transformative—I argue in this text that writers can experience firsthand what is missed through reliance on nonhuman content and idea generation.

A healing-centered approach might also explicitly educate students about the ethics of AI use, including the many risks of harm. These risks include the potential impacts not only on our minds and our humanity but also on the earth and our natural resources. A healing-centered approach also asks us to consider: who is profiting from their degradation?

And then there's the privacy issue. Even the most AI-literate users may not fully understand how their privacy is being compromised, how their data is or is not being used to train future models. Many students may never have thought about data privacy before and may not understand why it matters. Many of them *do* know that the environmental impact is staggering, as AI data farms rely on vast amounts of electricity and water, consuming fossil fuels and emitting greenhouse gases at an alarming rate.

And on top of all this is the impact on labor: what will happen to people laid off from companies choosing profit margins over their human resources? What sorts of jobs will our students have access to? How about those entering the workforce now, thoroughly prepared for a vanishing world?

Even AI companies trying to act ethically find themselves compromised. Mollick (2024) writes:

> Low-paid workers around the world are recruited to read and rate AI replies, but, in doing so, are exposed to exactly the sort of content that AI companies don't want the world to see. Working under difficult deadlines, some workers have discussed how they were traumatized by a steady stream of graphic and violent outputs that they had to read and rate. In trying to get AIs to act ethically, these companies pushed the ethical boundaries with their own contract workers.
>
> (p. 15)

In effect, conditioning ourselves to become reliant on AI is making us all complicit in the exploitations and harms we will likely work to undo later. Just as we are now, in many of our schools, requiring students to lock up their phones at the start of the school day—those same phones we teachers were encouraged to have students pull out and use in the classroom not too long ago, to scan a QR code or create an Instagram page for a class project—I believe we will someday strive to return to a state of non-AI interaction, a state we will no longer be able to fully reach.

I'll leave the discussion about AI, largely, here, where I am skimming the surface, by agreeing with what so many of us know: teachers need time, support, and resources to effectively learn and explore this terrain, in order to teach with and about AI tools in an informed and critical manner. We are being asked to contend with enormous changes, to innovate to a degree beyond belief, while maintaining all of the same standards we have always been asked to uphold. It is impossible. It is indeed the "paradox of limits and potential" that Angel Acosta (n.d.), founder of the Acosta Institute, says we need to hold in order to approach AI in an ethical and healing-centered way.

More and more, I believe that teaching in the age of generative AI will require that we prioritize safeguarding: against the erosion of our privacy, ethical integrity, and ultimately our human capacity. Some of this safeguarding will come through explicitly teaching students (and educating ourselves) about the dynamics and dangers of this technology, but more of it will need to come through the way we design our assignments, assessments, and rubrics, and the way we frame our objectives and values.

It will also require us to maintain criticality and apply our own values to everything that the AI companies—no matter how educationally aligned they seem to be—want to sell us. It may seem harmlessly engaging to offer students a chance to "chat with Frederick Douglass" or even the virtual version of a living person such as Malala Yousafzai in the form of an AI bot, but what happened to the critical, nuanced conversations about cooptation of voice that at one point were becoming nearly ubiquitous and increasingly, if insufficiently, nuanced? After the video of George Floyd's murder shook millions of people awake to the enduring horrors of racial injustice, good and important conversations about topics like appropriation emerged in educational spaces like never before, at least in *my* career. How far backwards have we catapulted ourselves if we are not just normalizing but buying into the marketing of such features?

Some people will continue to tell those of us who want to pause or slow the alacritous and accelerating adoption of AI that we are overreacting. They will draw comparisons to earlier technologies that seemed like the end of the world as we know it and point out how humanity has adapted and even thrived as a result. The point is valid. The comparison most frequently used to essentially tell English teachers to "calm down" is the calculator, and it makes sense; I'll let math teachers have their moment to say, *See how that feels?*

Indeed, just like some math tests allow students to use calculators and some do not, yes, we will sometimes ask students to write by hand, or on locked-down browsers, whereas at other times, students will have access to AI tools that we cannot control. Yet, as Mollick (2024) highlights, calculator technology was prohibitively expensive when it emerged, giving educators more than a decade to acclimate. He writes, "The AI revolution is happening much faster and more broadly" (p. 166), and we as teachers of writing are expected to somehow keep pace with our, and our students', integrities intact.

This book suggests a paradigm capacious enough to hold the broad spectrum of AI dispositions, from the critical and resistant to the enthusiastic and adoptive, because its focus is on intentionality. A healing-centered approach to writing in a world of AI *is* possible but only when we are clear on the whats, whys, and hows of our practices.

## References

Acosta, A. (n.d.). *Masterclass on artificial intelligence: A healing-centered approach to AI*. Acosta Institute. https://www.acostainstitute.com/masterclass-on-artificial-intelligence

Enriquez, G., Gill, V., Campano, G., Flores, T. T., Jones, S., Leander, K. M., McKnight, L., & Price-Dennis, D. (2024). Generative AI and composing: an intergenerational conversation among literacy scholars. *English Teaching: Practice & Critique (Emerald Group Publishing Limited)*, *23*(1), 6–22. https://doi.org/10.1108/ETPC-08-2023-0104

Ginwright, S. (2022). *The four pivots: Reimagining justice, reimagining ourselves*. North Atlantic.

Marano, G., Kotzalidis, G. D., Lisci, F. M., Anesini, M. B., Rossi, S., Barbonetti, S., Cangini, A., Ronsisvalle, A., Artuso, L., Falsini, C., Caso, R., Mandracchia, G., Brisi, C., Traversi, G., Mazza, O., Pola, R., Sani, G., Mercuri, E. M., Gaetani, E., & Mazza, M. (2025). The neuroscience behind writing: Handwriting vs. typing-who wins the battle? *Life (Basel, Switzerland)*, *15*(3), 345. https://doi.org/10.3390/life15030345

Mollick, E. (2024). *Co-intelligence: Living and working with AI*. Portfolio/Penguin.

Van der Weel, F. R. R., & Van der Meer, A. L. H. (2024). Handwriting but not typewriting leads to widespread brain connectivity: A high-density EEG study with implications for the classroom. *Frontiers in Psychology*, *14*, 1219945. https://doi.org/10.3389/fpsyg.2023.1219945

# 14

# Write the Way

## A Healing-Centered Model

My vision for what I call "Write the Way" has been swirling around nebulously in my consciousness for almost two decades after formally committing myself to a writing life—a life of writing and teaching writing. I imagined it vaguely as a capacious way of attending to and honoring all that writing is and can do, from the most pragmatic—*write the way to college*—to the most holistic—*write the way toward healing*.

As a doctoral researcher, I aimed not just to better understand what this kernel of inspiration was and could be but to actualize it in a way that aligns with critical consciousness and best practices. Developing each tenet of Write the Way became a process of infusing intuition fostered through deep experience with my own research and learnings from the wisdom and genius of scholars past and present.

DOI: 10.4324/9781003752721-14

## What Is "Write the Way"?

Write the Way, as I see it, is a network of pathways toward healing ourselves and our relationships—with writing, with ourselves, and with each other—as we move together in the direction of a healing world. It works with a broad definition of writing that includes both traditional uses of the written word *and* the idea of "writing the word and the world," a comparison to Paolo Freire and Donaldo Macedo's (1987) notion of "reading the word and the world." That means writing as a means of channeling imagination into action. Writing as a way of forging through confusion toward clarity. Writing as a way of connecting with others through thoughtfully constructed amalgamations of our thoughts, ideas, feelings, and knowledge. Writing as a way of hearing and articulating the latent missives of our minds, bodies, and spirits. Writing as a way of moving through the world with intention and understanding.

As a theoretical model, Write the Way is intended to help writers manifest answers to the following question: *What do I have to say, and how am I going to say it?* But also: *Where do I/we need to go, and how will I/we get there?*

The model is predicated upon a rhetorical paradigm, meant to help writers make *choices* through a process of reflective contemplation and critical and creative inquiry, with questions that break it down further:

- Authorship: *Who is the author of this journey?*
- Audience: *Who is on the receiving end of it?*
- Subject/argument: *What is it about, and what key idea or understanding sits at its core?*
- Form and style: *What shape will it take?*
- Purpose: *What is its point or meaning?*

Write the Way seeks not to reduce these questions to simple answers but to anticipate, address, and identify a healing way forward through the complexities, blockages, stoppages, and harmful experiences that can happen within each of these categories. In doing so, it seeks to help writers (and teachers of writing) become more critically conscious of socially situated barriers to easeful and liberatory expression. Even more so, it gives us—writers and teachers—a means by which to embody a process of healing-centered experience. Most of all, Write the Way is an invitation into a collaborative exploration of what it means to write and what it means to heal.

## The Tenets of "Write the Way"

The aim of a healing-centered approach to writing is not perfection or attainment but rather *movement* in the direction of healing. Such movement enables liberatory and transformative experience that transcends the bounds of a written product, and maybe even the bounds of individual experience, in order to contribute to a wider communal healing of the self in society and in the natural world.

The tenets of Write the Way are grounded in various facets, challenges, or opportunities for such healing and are thereby designed to foster and cultivate the type of awareness and observation that can promote mindful reflexivity. Each one reflects a strand or pathway of the larger approach to healing-centered writing outlined in this book. They are: *Who Is "I,"* involving identity and authorship; *The Body of Writing*, involving embodiment and form; *Forgot, but Then Remembered*, involving memory and reclamation; *Found Joy in Pieces*, involving fragmentation and collage; and *Stones to the Pile*, involving civic engagement and purpose. The tenets are deliberately ordered not to be linear or mutually exclusive but to grow from the self outward without losing the interrelatedness of each element involved (Figure 14.1).

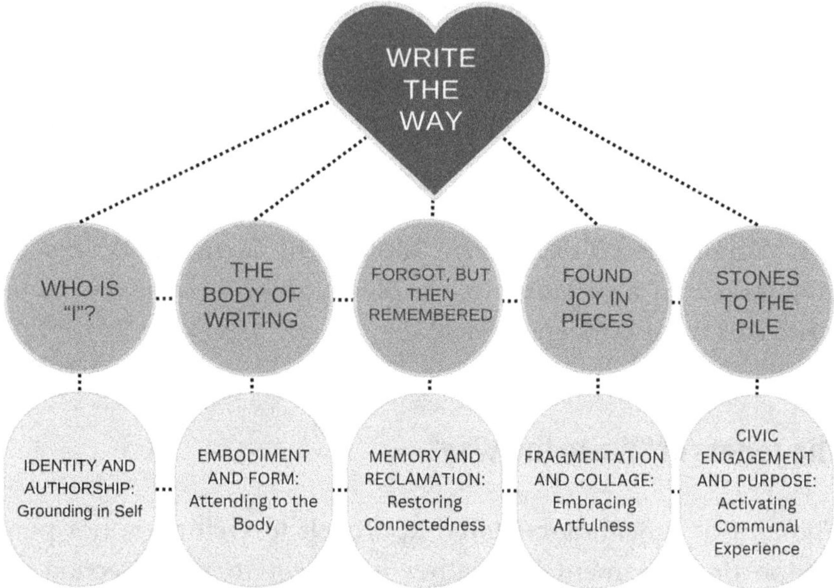


**FIGURE 14.1** Outline of Write the Way and its tenets.

## Who Is "I": Grounding in Self—Identity and Authorship

*Who Is "I"?* refers to a practice of seeing ourselves in context; it is about honoring and understanding the impacts of our identities on ourselves and others while recognizing and making space for the self that defies or transcends categorization. As a concept, "Who Is 'I'?" aims to provide a way of reflecting on, and sometimes deliberately crafting, our own representation to others. It can be a way of choosing to share our self in whole or in parts to an audience, depending on to whom we are speaking and why.

### Relevant Practices

- Identity inquiry
- Rhetorical analysis development (author, audience, argument, purpose, style)

### Reflection Questions

- Which aspects of myself do I bring to bear in my teaching? (Consider identities, interests, positionalities, experiences, memories, feelings, and thoughts.)
- Which aspects of myself do I forefront in my teaching?
- Which aspects of myself are not being explicitly invited into my teaching, and why?
- Which aspects of myself might I invite more fully and bring to bear within my teaching?
- Which aspects of self (identities, interests, positionalities, experiences, memories, feelings, and thoughts) do I encourage students to bring into their writing process?
- Which aspects of my students' lives and selves are not being explicitly invited into the writing process, and why?
- Where am I making space for students to make choices about the aspects of their lives and selves that they can choose to bring into the writing process?

## The Body of Writing

The Body of Writing is about fostering awareness around the act of creation: how it creates a body of work and how that work comes from and impacts the body. Does the writing deplete the body or replenish it? Does the body feel driven to write or driven *away* from writing? Does the body feel supported or abandoned while writing? It also attends to the body of the writing itself—what sort of shape is its body? How does it move? What does it sound like, look like, and feel like?

### Relevant Practices

- Mindful movement exercises
- Experimentation with forms of writing and expression

**Reflection Questions**

- What physical conditions have historically enabled me to write with ease or joy?
- What are the typical physical conditions for me when I need or want to write something?
- What degree of control do I have over those physical conditions?
- What does writing feel like in my body at various points in the process?
- Where do I feel tension in my body when I write?
- Where do I feel tension in my body when teaching or when reading student writing?
- What do my students' postures, facial expressions, and other affective behaviors potentially suggest about how they are experiencing the writing process?
- How can I create options within the learning space for students to find more physical comfort or ease while writing?
- How can I guide students to make mindful choices about how to position their bodies while they write?
- How might I offer reminders for students to ease the tension in their bodies while writing—to take a breath or stretch in order to release tension that builds, especially when writing complex or emotionally challenging material?
- What alternative forms or "bodies" of writing can I offer to my students for them to share and express their knowledge, ideas, or emotions?

## Forgot, but Then Remembered

"Forgot, but Then Remembered" is devoted to recovering what has been lost, healing from what has been hurt, or tapping into our inner knowing—those awarenesses we come to perceive or understand and then lose sight of or neglect. It acknowledges how remembrance is cyclical and sometimes the result of losing touch with, or forgetting, our connectedness. Focused on memory and reclamation, it aims toward restoring the writer's connectivity with themselves, with the subjects of their writing (which may include memory, family, experiences, and society), with the concept and actuality of audience, and with writing as a process and practice.

A process of remembering can happen gently, as in forgetting how much we love a place until we travel there again. It can also happen harshly. When we as human beings collectively "forget" our connectedness to the Earth, for example, we not only degrade the environment but also hurt ourselves through the effects of climate change and depletion of natural resources. Racism is another example. By forgetting our connectedness and passively accepting the construct of race, we have created inherently racist systems that most severely impact Black, Indigenous, and all people of color but ultimately harm everyone through White supremacy and isolation.

On a personal level, forgetting who we are and what we love may hurt us and make us feel devoid of purpose and energy, but it also deprives the people in our lives, our families, and our communities of all we have to offer in expressing our authentic selves.

**Relevant Practices**

- Reflecting on past experiences and memories (with writing and otherwise)
- Writing collaboratively
- Writing to connect/communicate with specific audiences or people

**Reflection Questions**

- What are some of the most powerful, meaningful, or enjoyable experiences I have had with writing?
- When have I felt particularly heard by someone else as a writer?

- Who might I want to connect with through my writing?
- What does my audience most need from me in order to understand or receive what I have to say?
- What are some of the most powerful, meaningful, or enjoyable experiences with writing that I have witnessed in my classroom?
- What am I curious about with regard to my students' knowledge, interests, experiences, and thoughts?
- How receptive am I, as their teacher, toward what my students have to say?
- How might I aid my students in recalling a love for or enjoyment in writing?
- Who (what individuals or groups) might my students choose to speak to, remember, or connect with in their writing?
- How might I create opportunities for students to share their writing with others?
- What might stand in the way of their knowledge, ideas, thoughts, or feelings being fully understood by their audience?
- How might I support students in serving as a receptive audience for one another?

## Found Joy in Pieces

"Found Joy in Pieces" is about recognizing the individual and collective fragmentations we experience as human beings and not denying, ignoring, or trying to force ourselves into a semblance of coherency but instead giving space to each of the pieces. It is about allowing those pieces to find their own connectivity through a process of intuition, experimentation, and discovery.

The idea for this concept derived, in large part, from my personal experiences of writing collage poetry during the Covid-19 pandemic, starting in March of 2020 (described in Chapter 12). It began with cutting words that appealed to me out of a magazines and moving them around into pleasing structures and forms that eventually became poems. The collage experience, for me, was in this sense a joyful one, because it gave me a chance to release an admission of how fragmented I felt. This release felt restful and playful and therefore joyful—the type of joy described in *The Book of Joy* by Dalai Lama, Archbishop Desmond Tutu, and Douglas Abrams (2016): "a more empathic, more empowered, even more spiritual state of mind that is totally engaged with the world" (p. 63). Many of the poems I composed emerged organically as meditations on art, writing, and teaching. They also took shape as a reckoning for me on subjects of identity, belonging, and civic responsibility.

Found Joy in Pieces is about embracing artfulness. Founded on the concepts of fragmentation and collage, it is also about embracing what feels good to the mind, body, and soul; it is about inviting experimentation and non-linearity, engaging intuition, and finding rest and restoration in joyful, artistic experience.

**Relevant Practices**

- Collaging with images and words
- Mixed media and arts-based engagement

**Reflection Questions**

- How open am I to uncertainty and experimentation—in my own writing, in students' writing, or in my teaching practice?
- What challenges might my students face when taking risks and experimenting in their writing, and why?
- Where might I find opportunities to practice, incorporate, or model uncertainty and experimentation, on my own or with my students?
- How might I bring elements beyond words into my teaching practice?
- How might I encourage students to bring elements beyond words into their writing process or product?

- How might I make space for my students to write experimentally or take risks with language and ideas?
- How might I suspend some of the constraints and loosen or release the need for certainty and knowing in my writing practice?
- Where do I see opportunities for students to experiment or take creative risks within their processes or practices?
- How might I bring elements beyond words more fully into the classroom experience/writing process for my students?

## Stones to the Pile

Stones to the Pile is about activating communal experience. Most notably focused on civic engagement and purpose, it encourages the writer to consider their social self—to see themselves in context and as potential agents of positive action and change. It offers the writer a paradigm for tapping into a greater sense of *purpose*; for writing their way toward a better world for themselves and others.

The phrase "Stones to the Pile" comes from the introduction to Alice Walker's (1997) book titled *Anything We Love Can Be Saved* and reads: "We can do nothing substantial toward changing our course on the planet, a destructive one, without rousing ourselves, individual by individual, and bringing our small, imperfect stones to the pile" (p. 4). In this book, Walker essays the connection between her writing and her activism and reflects on how, despite having "been an activist all of [her] adult life," she has "sometimes felt embarrassed to call [herself] one," out of the "common feeling" that civic-minded folks often experience fearing that their "own small stone of activism" is a "paltry offering" that pales in comparison with "the rugged boulders of heroism" they admire in others (pp. 3–5). Yet, as a civic-minded human being deeply in touch with the social and political contexts surrounding her, Walker gives space throughout her work for her conscientious self to shine through, and for her activist voice to step forward.

In the spirit of Walker's words, "Stones to the Pile" invites the social self to become more consciously expansive; it welcomes and even nudges the writer to discover, explore, and embrace the complex dimensions of their positionalities not just for the sake of making art, completing an assignment, or accomplishing a writing task but for the sake of a greater civic good. The tenet aims toward facilitating community-mindedness; toward considering how our own unique worldviews, experiences, ideas, questions, knowledge, research, or stories can serve a higher purpose, can serve others.

**Relevant Practices**

- Inquiry into the social dimension of self
- Reflecting and inquiring into sociopolitical and historical topics
- Writing for action and activism

**Reflection Questions**

- Why does writing matter?
- Why does the writing that my students do matter?
- Where do I see opportunities for more meaningful writing experiences in my classroom, teaching practice, or life?
- How can writing be used as a vehicle for social change?
- What matters to my students, and how can I find out?
- How can I provide students with additional choice and space to discover or write about what matters to them and their communities?
- How can writing be used in my class to help students make connections between what they are learning and what matters to them, to society, and to the larger world around them?

## References

Dalai, D., Tutu, D., & Abrams D. (2016). *The book of joy: Lasting happiness in a changing world*. Avery.

Freire, P., & Macedo, D. (1987). *Literacy: Reading the word and the world*. Routledge. Retrieved from http://www.ebrary.com

Walker, A. (1997). Introduction. *Anything we love can be saved*. Random House.

# Appendix

## Applying the Framework Reflexively

As many educators will attest, our required and prescribed professional learning too often bypasses what we are already doing and what we already know. My colleagues and I have spent many a professional learning session wondering why we need an "expert," sometimes flown in from across the country, to provide us with strategies we are already trying or to tell us what we already understand: things need to change. Maybe even *we* need to change: our approaches, our mindsets, our curricula, our policies, our practices. Certainly, these outside facilitators may offer some interesting answers as to the why and how. Yet we also know that—individually but *especially* as a collective community—we hold many of the needed answers ourselves. After all, we know our community, our students, our barriers, *ourselves*, and each other—admittedly, maybe too well; maybe to the point where it is hard to imagine change. But too often, this very real knowledge is under-utilized, under-appreciated, and under-examined.

While we may have many of the answers within us, what we don't always have are the time, space, and, quite frankly, the energy, momentum, and support to devote to a truly collaborative process of uncovering these answers through deep inquiry. We sometimes feel compelled to leap to the decision-making step without any real intention-setting or consensus-building, which could allow us to make conscious commitments and actions toward shared goals. Trying to make decisions from a place of mutual understanding, agreement, and value alignment is exhausting, messy, and at times seemingly impossible. We also frequently lack a structure for it.

The following two resources are intended to provide a kind of structure to support reflexive experiences, wherein educators can use the healing-centered framework outlined in this book to (1) assess the current state of their practice, classroom conditions, or institutional culture and (2) identify desired shifts. I refer to these experiences as "reflexive" because they are designed to impact our choices, not just once but recursively; to shape our actions into a practice that aligns with what we want it to be, do, and create.

The resources consist of questions broken into three categories: (1) *individual*, which focuses on your own relationship with writing; (2) *classroom*, which emphasizes your own individual pedagogy and practices; and (3) *collective/curricular*, which can be applied to the collective relationship with writing in your department, curricular team, school, or district.

The reflexive experiences these questions aim to foster can be self-directed, conducted in groups, or guided by a facilitator. Figure A.1 can be used to help direct the inquiry process.

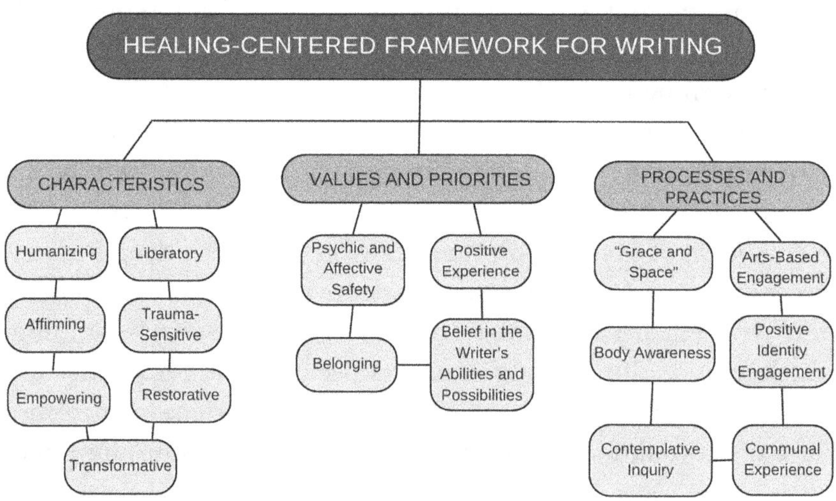


**FIGURE A.1** Healing-centered framework for writing.

## Questions for Reflecting on Current Conditions and Practice

| *Individual* | *Classroom* | *Collective/Curricular* |
|---|---|---|
| ◆ Which characteristics describe my current relationship with writing?<br>◆ What do I value and prioritize in my writing practice?<br>◆ What processes and practices enable (or have enabled) me to write with ease or joy? | ◆ Which characteristics describe how I believe writing is experienced in my classroom?<br>◆ What do I value and prioritize with relation to writing in my classroom?<br>◆ What might my students value and prioritize with relation to writing in my classroom?<br>◆ What processes and practices are integrated into or central to my classroom? | ◆ Which characteristics describe how writing is experienced in our lives, organization, learning spaces, or curricula?<br>◆ What do we value and prioritize with relation to writing in our lives, organization, learning spaces, or curricula?<br>◆ What processes and practices with relation to writing are integrated into or central to our lives, organization, learning spaces, or curricula? |

## Questions for Reflecting on Desired Shifts

| *Individual* | *Classroom* | *Collective/Curricular* |
|---|---|---|
| ◆ Which of the healing-centered characteristics most align with how I want my writing practice to feel?<br>◆ Which values and priorities matter most to me?<br>◆ Which processes and practices in the framework do I want to incorporate most in order to achieve these aims? Which are the most challenging for me? Which am I already practicing?<br>◆ What is missing for me, as a writer, in the framework? What else do I want or need? | ◆ Which of the healing-centered characteristics most align with how I want my students to experience writing?<br>◆ Which values and priorities do I need or want to bring more centrally into my daily practice?<br>◆ Which processes and practices would be most helpful to incorporate into my classroom in order to achieve these aims?<br>◆ Which processes and practices are the most challenging for me and my students?<br>◆ What is missing for me, as an educator, in the framework? What else might my students want or need? | ◆ Which of the healing-centered characteristics most align with how we want writing to be experienced in our lives, organization, learning spaces, or curricula?<br>◆ Which values and priorities do we need or want to bring more centrally into our lives, organization, learning spaces, or curricula?<br>◆ What processes and practices would be most helpful to incorporate into our lives, organization, learning spaces, or curricula?<br>◆ Which processes and practices are the most challenging for us to incorporate?<br>◆ What is missing in the framework? What else do we want or need? |